CAMBRIDGE STUDIES IN MEDIEVAL LITERATURE 3

Troubadours and Irony

From Petrarch and Dante to Pound and Eliot, the influence of the troubadours on European poetry has been profound. They have rightly stimulated a vast amount of critical writing, but the majority of modern critics see the troubadour tradition as a corpus of earnestly serious and confessional love poetry, with little or no humour. *Troubadours and Irony* re-examines the work of five early troubadours, namely Marcabru, Bernart Marti, Peire d'Alvernha, Raimbaut d'Aurenga and Giraut de Borneil, to argue that the courtly poetry of Southern France in the twelfth century was permeated with irony and that many troubadour songs were playful, laced with humorous sexual innuendo and far from serious; attention is also drawn to the large corpus of texts that are not love poems, but comic or satirical songs. New interpretations of many problematic troubadour poems are offered; in some cases the received view of a troubadour's work is questioned. New perspectives on the tradition as a whole are suggested, and consequently on courtly culture in general. The author addresses the philological problems, by no means negligible, posed by the texts in question, and several poems are re-edited from the manuscripts.

CAMBRIDGE STUDIES IN MEDIEVAL LITERATURE

General Editor: Professor Alastair Minnis, Professor of Medieval
Literature, University of York

Editorial Board
Professor Piero Boitani (Professor of English, Rome)
Professor Patrick Boyde (Serena Professor of Italian, Cambridge)
Professor John Burrow, FBA (Winterstoke Professor of English, Bristol)
Peter Dronke, FBA (Reader in Medieval Latin Literature, Cambridge)
Professor John Freccero (Rosina Pierotti Professor of Italian, Stanford)
Tony Hunt (Reader in French, St Andrews)
Dr Nigel Palmer (Lecturer in Medieval German, Oxford)
Professor Winthrop Wetherbee (Professor of English, Cornell)

This new series of critical books seeks to cover the whole area of literature
written in the major medieval languages – the main European vernaculars,
and Medieval Latin and Greek – during the period *c.* 1100–*c.* 1500. Its chief
aim is to publish and stimulate fresh scholarship and criticism on medieval
literature, special emphasis being placed on understanding major works of
poetry, prose and drama in relation to the contemporary cultures and
learning which fostered them. It will accommodate studies which bring a
special expertise or neglected body of knowledge to bear on the interpreta-
tive problems of important texts. Texts, genres and literary conventions
which, while significant in their own times and places and of considerable
value to the medievalist, have been undervalued or misrepresented in modern
times, fall within its range; and it will give space to innovative critical
approaches to medieval texts of all types.

Titles published
Dante's Inferno: *Difficulty and Dead Poetry*, by Robin Kirkpatrick
Dante and Difference: Writing in the Commedia, by Jeremy Tambling
Troubadours and Irony, by Simon Gaunt
Piers Plowman *and the New Anticlericalism*, by Wendy Scase
The Medieval Greek Romance, by Roderick Beaton

Other titles in preparation
The Genesis of Piers Plowman, by Charlotte Brewer
The Cantar de mio Cid: *Poetic Creation in its Economic and
Social Contexts*, by Joseph J. Duggan
Literary Theory in the German Middle Ages, by Walter Haug
(translated from the German)
Reformist Apocalypticism and Piers Plowman, by Kathryn Kerby-Fulton
The Divine Comedy *and the Medieval Other World*, by Alison Morgan

Troubadours and Irony

SIMON GAUNT

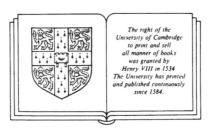

The right of the
University of Cambridge
to print and sell
all manner of books
was granted by
Henry VIII in 1534
The University has printed
and published continuously
since 1584.

CAMBRIDGE UNIVERSITY PRESS

Cambridge

New York   New Rochelle   Melbourne   Sydney

CAMBRIDGE UNIVERSITY PRESS
Cambridge, New York, Melbourne, Madrid, Cape Town, Singapore, São Paulo

Cambridge University Press
The Edinburgh Building, Cambridge CB2 8RU, UK

Published in the United States of America by Cambridge University Press, New York

www.cambridge.org
Information on this title: www.cambridge.org/9780521354394

First published 1989
This digitally printed version 2008

A catalogue record for this publication is available from the British Library

Library of Congress Cataloguing in Publication data
Gaunt, Simon.
Troubadours and irony.
(Cambridge studies in medieval literature; 3)
Bibliography.
Includes index.
1. Provençal poetry – History and criticism.
2. Irony in literature. 3. Troubadours. 4. Sex in
literature. 5. Courtly love literature. I. Title.
II. Series.
PC3304.G38 1989 849'.12'091 88–25827

ISBN 978-0-521-35439-4 hardback
ISBN 978-0-521-05848-3 paperback

And eek men shal nat maken ernest of game
Chaucer

Contents

Acknowledgements

This book began its life as a Ph.D thesis for the University of Warwick and assumed its present form at Downing College, Cambridge. I should like to express my gratitude to Professor Donald Charlton and to the members of staff of the French Department at Warwick for the six happy years I spent among them, both as an undergraduate and as a postgraduate student, and for the many acts of kindness they have shown me. Similarly, the Master and Fellows of Downing College provided me with a warm and scholarly environment in which to work as a Research Fellow.

Texts from A. Del Monte's edition of Peire d'Alvernha and W. T. Pattison's edition of Raimbaut d'Aurenga are reproduced by kind permission of Loescher Editore S.p.A. and the University of Minnesota Press. I am grateful to Professor Aurelio Roncaglia for permission to reproduce his re-editions of poems by Marcabru.

Ruth Sharman greatly facilitated the writing of chapter 6 by lending me a copy of her edition of Giraut de Borneil before it went to press; I should also like to thank her for her careful and efficient subediting. I have been lucky, during the preparation of this book, to benefit from the comments and guidance of John Marshall, one of my thesis examiners, and Tony Hunt, my editor; though Professor Marshall and Tony are in no way responsible for the shortcomings of my work, they have helped me to avoid more than the occasional blunder.

Many friends and colleagues have given me help and support over the years but Ruth Harvey, Sarah Kay, Dafydd Evans, Richard Goddard, Philippa Levy, Betty Talks, Helen and David Constantine, Ritchie Robertson, James Graham-Campbell, Sylvie Plantin and Leslie Hill deserve special mention. Above all, however, I should like to thank two friends: Mark Treharne for his support, advice and companionship and Linda Paterson, my research supervisor, whose teaching can only be described as illuminating.

Abbreviations

Du Cange	C. du Cange, *Glossarium manuale ad scriptores mediae et infimae latinitatis*, 10 vols. (Halle, 1772–84)
FEW	W. von Wartburg, *Französisches etymologisches Wörterbuch*, 25 vols. (Tübingen, 1922–)
Godefroy	F. Godefroy, *Dictionnaire de l'ancienne langue française*, 10 vols. (Paris, 1880–1902)
LR	M. Raynouard, *Lexique roman*, 6 vols. (Paris, 1836–44)
PC	A. Pillet and H. Carstens, *Bibliographie der Troubadours* (Halle, 1933)
PD	E. Levy, *Petit dictionnaire provençal–français*, fifth edition (Heidelberg, 1973)
PL	J. P. Migne, *Patrologiae cursus completus. Series Latina*, 225 vols. (Paris, 1844–64)
PSW	E. Levy, *Provenzalisches Supplement-Wörterbuch*, 8 vols. (Leipzig, 1894–1924)
REW	W. Meyer-Lübke, *Romanisches etymologisches Wörterbuch* (Heidelberg, 1935)
TL	A. Tobler and E. Lommatzsch, *Altfranzösisches Wörterbuch*, 10 vols. (Berlin, 1925–)

Note on the texts

Our knowledge of the troubadours' language is far from complete and the sense of many texts remains problematic on linguistic, as well as literary, grounds. The Occitan texts I quote will thus always be translated. As specialists will want to know on what basis I have arrived at a translation, I give philological notes where necessary, but in order not to clutter the text unduly for the general reader, I have placed them in an Appendix. In some cases I have altered texts as established by editors, usually to restore a manuscript reading: this will be indicated at the end of the line in question by an asterisk, and the alteration will be justified in the Appendix. Similarly, when I have re-edited a text from the manuscripts, the critical apparatus and variants are to be found in the Appendix. The editions of all texts used are those cited in the bibliography unless otherwise indicated in the Appendix or the notes; where more than one edition of a poet or work is cited, the edition usually used will be indicated in the bibliography and in the Appendix where appropriate.

Introduction

It has become fashionable to discuss irony in medieval literature, but this is not simply a reflection of modern preoccupations. The word *eironeia* is first used in Plato's *Republic*; throughout the Middle Ages we find *ironia* discussed in rhetorical manuals; Erasmus wrote that he disliked extravagant praise because it was akin to *ironia*; and Balzac warns his readers against misunderstanding *quelque ironie* in his work.[1] Irony, it would appear, rears its head throughout the entire tradition of European literature and thought.

If irony in medieval literature has proved a particularly popular subject in recent years, this is perhaps because critics in the past have tended to assume that medieval authors were unlikely to be ironic.[2] Such a unilateral approach to medieval literature led scholars such as Peter Haidu and Dennis Green to devote studies to irony in the medieval romance and Green concluded 'courtly literature, and with it the romance, shows a predisposition towards the critical, and therefore towards irony and parody from the beginning'.[3] The view that courtly romance is often permeated with irony, though still controversial, is now widely held and it is thus all the more surprising that irony in the medieval lyric should have attracted so little attention.

Indeed, although he allows for the possibility of irony in the lyric, Green suggests that irony is less likely in lyric poetry than in narrative texts, and in this he reflects the view of D. C. Muecke, that on the whole lyric poetry is not a form of writing that lends itself to irony.[4] Are they right to see the lyric as a genre which is generally not ironic, or should we perhaps reconsider such texts?

Green talks of the 'introspective, self-contained poetic realm' of the lyric poet and suggests that the presentation in the lyric of 'the experience of love from the partial point of view of one of the partners' is a factor that makes irony less likely in the lyric than in romance; but is not the notion of the hallowed ingenuousness of the lyric poet a somewhat Romantic anachronism?[5] Is there no room for humour or critical distance in lyric poetry? Whilst it is true that lyric poetry can be devoted to the expression of intense feelings, such as love, which the poet has no wish to undermine or ridicule, a poet need not address himself to problems of the heart and in any case he can be as aware of paradox, of the instability of surface meanings or of the oscillation between different types of feelings, as other writers. Moreover, as the lyric is the type of literary discourse in which most attention is demanded for details of style

I

and the particular placing of an individual word, in some instances it may be a better vehicle for irony than prose.

Even a cursory glance at the corpus of the troubadour lyric shows that it is not concerned exclusively with intense feeling or with love. The troubadours discussed moral, political, even religious issues in their poetry, often critically or satirically; there is also a sizeable corpus of comic poetry. In these texts they are likely to be as predisposed towards irony as the authors of romances. Furthermore, even in their love poetry the troubadours might have a predisposition towards irony, for the troubadour love lyric often draws on a set of conventions, on a predefined notion of *fin'amor*, which not all troubadours accept. Questioning the conventions of *fin'amor* within the framework of a courtly love poem is obviously an ideal recipe for irony, for the poet is simultaneously confirming and denying his adherence to the tradition.

The conventions of the troubadour lyric extend, however, beyond any conventional notion of *fin'amor*. For scholars who subscribe to the 'formalist' view of medieval poetry, a medieval poet composed his text drawing on an ever-growing cluster of *topoi* and the aesthetic of the medieval lyric lay in variations in the combination of clichés, figures, music and rhythm. If such a view were adopted, subjectivity in the medieval lyric would be unlikely, for the theme would be merely a pretext and therefore unimportant;[6] by the same token, irony would be virtually impossible, for to posit irony one generally, though not always, has to assume that the import of language extends beyond form, that an external and concrete referent exists, even if its precise nature is unclear.

The 'formalist' approach to medieval lyric poetry has been challenged in recent years by scholars such as Linda Paterson, Sarah Kay and Jörn Gruber. Paterson concentrates on the troubadours' different approaches towards the art of composition and Kay argues that a strong sense of self emerges from many troubadour lyrics. Gruber, in his seminal work *Die Dialektik des Trobar*, radically reinterprets the patent conventionality of the troubadour and trouvère lyric which led to the 'formalist' approach.[7]

In Gruber's view the entire corpus of troubadour poetry can be seen as one 'dialectic', each troubadour reacting not only to the work of his contemporaries, but also to those of past generations (pp. 256–7). Quite apart from semantic intertextual references, a troubadour might borrow rhyme sounds, rhyme words, formulae, key words or rhyme schemes from another troubadour in order to indicate that some kind of intertextual play is taking place (pp. 98, 183–4). Gruber argues that each troubadour attempted to outdo his predecessors and contemporaries. Drawing on the notion of Hegelian dialectic he suggests an awareness of what he calls *das Prinzip der intertextuellen Aufhebung* ('the principle of intertextual sublation'), which involves the simultaneous affirmation, negation and surpassing of another text or texts, is essential if a troubadour poem is to be appreciated properly (pp. 98–101, 254).[8]

Clearly, if Gruber is correct that intertextuality plays such a key rôle in the poetics of the troubadours, irony will be crucial to the 'dialectic'. If a poet is to take up themes, rhyme schemes, sound patterns and key words from another poet and yet differentiate his own work through sublation, he is faced with one of two alternatives: he can indicate his debt to the other poet and differentiate his own poem explicitly, or he can communicate this implicitly. The second alternative will often lead to irony, for irony depends upon the implicit rather than the explicit, and it is especially frequent when some form of criticism is intended. Superficially, a poem might appear to redeploy hackneyed conventions, but if they are undermined through irony, it might be open to an entirely different interpretation.[9]

In theory then, one might expect irony to occur in the troubadour lyric in satirical and moralizing poetry, in comic texts, and in some love lyrics: it is particularly likely when intertextual play takes place. If it goes undetected, the meaning attributed to the text may be the opposite of that intended by its author. I hope that an awareness of irony in troubadour poetry may lead to a fruitful re-examination of some texts and consequently that humour may be perceived where it was intended. In some cases I believe that an analysis of the way a troubadour uses irony may reveal something about his *eloquentia*, consequently about his place in the troubadour tradition and, by extension, about the tradition itself, with all the ramifications this may have for courtly culture in general. Indeed, on a broader scale, it is interesting to see how the poets who founded modern European vernacular poetry treat a figure of speech which is apparently common to all European literature.

The problems posed by discussing a literary device such as irony, the perception of which depends on the discernment of implicit meanings and on the reconstruction of an author's unstated intentions, are manifold. Not least of these problems is the meaning of the word irony itself, for it is often used loosely, or given epithets such as 'Socratic', 'Romantic', or 'dramatic'. I shall consequently devote the first chapter of this book to a description and discussion of different types of irony, both medieval and modern, and attempt therein not only to define my own frame of reference, but also to posit the theory of irony the troubadours themselves may have known and by which they may have been influenced. This chapter will serve as a starting point for the study of irony in selected early troubadours.

The scope of this book has been defined chronologically. I take as my corpus the first three generations of troubadours, up to and including those mentioned in Peire d'Alvernha's satire *Cantarai d'aqestz trobadors*. There are two reasons for this. First, the first three generations of troubadours provide a rich variety of texts with ample material for a study of this kind. Secondly, beyond that period there is such a plethora of troubadours that it becomes impossible to justify deciding to discuss, for example, the poems of Arnaut Daniel and not those of Bertran de Born. I thought it preferable to undertake a thorough survey of a short period, rather than a selective survey of a longer period, which might lead to undesirable omissions. This is not to say that discussion of irony in later texts would not be worthwhile: on the contrary, I

3

Introduction

believe that the type of analysis undertaken in this book could profitably be applied to troubadours like Guilhem de Berguedà, Arnaut Daniel, Guilhem Ademar, Raimbaut de Vaqueiras, Peire Vidal, Bertran de Born and Peire Cardenal – to name some obvious candidates – and I would hope that my comments on the irony of the early poets might provide a basis for the re-examination of the later part of the tradition as well.

I have accepted Rita Lejeune's dating of Peire's satire (1161–2) and of the third generation of troubadours. I include in my corpus only those mentioned in this poem.[10] Although this is to a certain extent arbitrary, it does provide a convenient line which can be drawn between earlier and later troubadours. Of course, not all the troubadours in my corpus are ironic, and none is ironic all the time. A chapter is devoted to each of the troubadours I intend to concentrate on: Marcabru, Bernart Marti, Peire d'Alvernha, Raimbaut d'Aurenga and Giraut de Borneil. These troubadours were selected either because irony appears to be an important element in their *eloquentia*, or because an awareness of irony in their poems might lead to a re-interpretation of some texts. The glaring omission in this 'rogues' gallery' is, needless to say, Guilhem IX, but I felt that his poems have been inspected so closely, by so many eminent critics, that any analysis I might offer would contribute little to furthering our understanding of them. I shall consequently only use his poems to illustrate points and demonstrate types of irony in my opening chapter, which will also look briefly at the work of a poet who is rarely ironical, Bernart de Ventadorn, perhaps the greatest love poet of the courtly tradition, with a view to providing a perspective on the analysis of irony in the tradition as a whole.

I do not claim to isolate or study every instance of irony in the early troubadour lyric or even in the work of the troubadours discussed. Such a humourless approach would seem inappropriate to the subject. In any case, irony often depends upon the existence of an initiated and an uninitiated audience. Would it not be arrogant to assume that we must always belong to the initiated audience when we are looking at poetry from a different culture, composed eight hundred years ago?

Laura Kendrick's fascinating book *The Game of Love: Troubadour Wordplay* (Berkeley, 1988) appeared after this book had gone to press. She offers many interesting insights into the humour of some of the poets I study.

I

Irony: medieval and modern

The purpose of this chapter is to examine a working definition of irony which is suitable for the interpretation of ironic texts, with particular reference to medieval literature. My starting point is the work of Dennis Green on irony in the medieval romance, but I will also draw upon the theoretical work of Vladimir Jankélévitch and D. C. Muecke. Green defines irony in *Irony in the Medieval Romance*:

> irony is a statement, or presentation of an action or situation, in which the real or intended meaning conveyed to the initiated intentionally diverges from, and is incongruous with, the apparent or pretended meaning presented to the uninitiated. (p. 9)

I found this definition to be the most satisfactory of those used by scholars to examine irony in medieval literature; the reasons for this will emerge during the course of this chapter.

As the meaning of the English word 'irony' is not the same as that of the classical and medieval Latin word *ironia*, I shall begin with a brief survey of the medieval theory of *ironia* and related figures and tropes, with a view to showing the theory of irony a troubadour might have known. The broader modern view of irony will then be examined and this will be followed by a discussion of the particular problems posed by positing the presence of irony in medieval literature and particularly in the troubadour lyric.

THE MEDIEVAL THEORY OF IRONY

There are no examples of the word irony in Old French or Occitan treatises on literary composition before the fourteenth century.[1] However, Latin rhetorical manuals suggest that some medieval writers were acquainted with a trope called *ironia* and other figures and tropes we might consider ironic today. My aim is not to suggest that the troubadours imitated, in a servile manner, models set by figures and tropes in the manuals, but rhetoric was studied widely in schools as part of the basic curriculum and models set for a student writing in one language must have filtered through in some form when the same student wrote in another language. The influence of rhetoric on vernacular writers is now generally accepted, and although opinions as to the nature and scope of this influence vary, recent research on the troubadours shows that some at least were steeped in Latin culture and may even have been educated as clerks. When approaching texts by troubadours like Marcabru, Peire d'Alvernha, or Giraut de Borneil, rhetoric is clearly a useful critical tool.[2]

There is a plethora of rhetorical manuals from classical times onwards and the study of the influence and diffusion of any particular manual or of any one rhetorical device is necessarily complex. My own comments will be brief, my aim being an overview.[3] My sources for this study are: from the classical period, Quintilian, Cicero and the unknown author of the *Rhetorica ad Herennium*; from the late-classical and early-medieval periods, Donatus, Bede, Cassiodorus, Pompeius, Martianus Capella, Julian of Toledo and Isidore of Seville; and from the twelfth and thirteenth centuries, Geoffrey of Vinsauf, Hugh of St Victor, Matthew of Vendôme, Gervase of Melkley and Boncompagno of Signa.[4] This list is by no means exhaustive, but it is representative of authors who were well known in the Middle Ages and of medieval theorists who discussed irony.

The influence of classical rhetoricians on education and on rhetorical writing in the Middle Ages is well documented, but as with the authors of later manuals, they were not all addressing the same public. Some manuals were written as elementary textbooks and others for more advanced students and scholars. From the outset there appear to have been two traditions in the presentation of figures and tropes: one deriving from Quintilian, who provides a detailed discussion of *ironia*, the other from the more widely diffused *ad Herennium*, which does not, although glosses do identify as such the first type of *allegoria* it describes. There can be little doubt that Quintilian's work is more sophisticated than the *ad Herennium*, that it was written for intellectuals and that this was realized in the Middle Ages. Although Quintilian was not widely read, his influence was immense, both because of his reputation, and because of the importance of later writers for whose work the *Institutio oratoria* is clearly a source, either directly or indirectly, for example Donatus, Bede, Isidore, Julian, Gervase and Hugh. The fact that an explicit discussion of *ironia* only occurs in this tradition is not in itself surprising: the authors of basic textbooks like the *auctor ad Herennium* and his followers Martianus Cappella, Cassiodorus, Matthew and Geoffrey were perhaps not prepared to discuss such a complicated and difficult trope as *ironia*, even though they show an awareness of it, much as a French teacher will allude to the subjunctive long before actually introducing it into the classroom.[5]

My main sources for the discussion of *ironia* are therefore Quintilian, Donatus, Bede, Isidore, Julian, Hugh and Gervase. Amongst these writers, the treatment of *ironia* is relatively consistent. It is a trope and a species of *allegoria*:[6] 'allegoria est tropus quo aliud significatur quam dicitur . . . Huius

6

species multae sunt, ex quibus eminent septum: ironia, antiphrasis, aenigma, charientismos, paroemia, sarcasmos, astismos' (Donatus, *Ars maior* III.6: 'allegory is a trope in which the meaning is other than what is said. There are many types of this trope, of which seven are prominent: irony, antiphrasis, enigma, charientismos, paroemia, sarcasm and asteism'). Isidore, Bede and Julian echo Donatus. Gervase excludes two of these tropes from his discussion of *allegoria*, but analyses them elsewhere. Quintilian, Donatus' source, does not specifically divide *allegoria* into seven main tropes; the division is nevertheless implicit in his discussion because he mentions five species explicitly and describes the other two in detail without naming them, but saying they are kinds of *allegoria*. Only Hugh does not make these tropes species of *allegoria*, but he does discuss them together and in the same order as his source.[7]

Definitions of *allegoria* are always very general: it presents one thing in words and another in meaning. It is both a trope in its own right and a generic heading for other tropes. As a trope in its own right it is closely related to what we understand by the word allegory today and the notion of an allegorical level of meaning was common in the Middle Ages. However, allegory did not, in the Middle Ages, have the more precise meaning it sometimes has today when we use terms such as 'an allegorical figure': this may have been thought of as a type of the figure *conformatio* (personification, see *ad Herennium* IV.53.66) or as a type of metonymy.[8] If, as a generic heading, *allegoria* includes many devices which allow one thing to be said when another is meant, what distinguishes *ironia*?

Ironia is always the first trope to be discussed under the heading of *allegoria*: 'ironia est tropus per contrarium quod conatur ostendens' (Donatus, *Ars maior* III.6: 'irony is a trope by means of which one thing is said whilst its exact opposite is meant'). In his discussion of *ironia* Green makes much of the fact that Pompeius, a fifth-century commentator on Donatus, gives a definition of *ironia* which is different from the standard definition used by all other rhetoricians. Pompeius substitutes for *per contrarium* the word *aliud*: 'ironia est quotienscumque re vera aliud loquimur et aliud significamus in verbis' (*Commentum artis Donati*, p. 310: 'irony occurs whenever the true thing is other than what we say and other than what we mean by the words'). Green argues that the use of the word *aliud* shows that Pompeius was aware of the inadequacy of *per contrarium* as key words in a definition of irony: 'alternative definitions of rhetorical irony take account of such doubts by avoiding any extreme statement involving the term *per contrarium*, common to Donatus and Isidore, and by suggesting that the real meaning merely diverges from the apparent meaning. Pompeius therefore substitutes *aliud* for *contrarium*.'[9] He further argues that Isidore makes the same distinction by implication when he classes *ironia* as a species of *allegoria*, which he calls *alieniloquium* ('a way of saying something else'), and he thus tries to prove that some medieval rhetoricians had moved away from a simple definition of *ironia* (the expression of meaning by language of opposites) towards the more complex and infinitely more satisfying definition of irony which he proposes, in which the stress is on the fact that the intended meaning of what is said merely diverges from the literal meaning. In other words, he is trying to show that some people in the Middle Ages had a 'modern' view of irony, and saw it as more than standard *ironia*, as defined in the manuals.

However, this is to misrepresent the possible meanings of the word *ironia* in the Middle Ages. Green gives no other examples of a medieval rhetorician, besides Pompeius and Isidore, giving the definition he is looking for.[10] Moreover, he quotes Pompeius out of context, for although he says that Pompeius is forced to distinguish between *allegoria* and *ironia*, he does not continue his quotation beyond the initial definition: 'ironia est quotienscumque re vera aliud loquimur et aliud significamus in verbis; non ita ut diximus de allegoria, quando aliud dicimus et aliud significamus, non, sed isdem verbis potes et negare et confirmare; sola autem pronuntiatione discernitur' ('irony occurs whenever the true thing is other than what we say and other than what we mean by the words; not as we said of allegory, when we say one thing and mean another, no, but when you can both deny and affirm in the same words; it can only be discerned through delivery'). Green thus omits the most important part of the discussion, and he does not explain how Pompeius makes the distinction between *ironia* and *allegoria*. Pompeius' point is that the former can both confirm and deny the literal meaning of the statement; in other words, *ironia* occurs when the intended meaning of a statement is the opposite of the literal meaning and not when the meanings simply diverge as in allegory and as in Green's definition of irony. It is also important to note that Pompeius' work is not a rhetorical manual, but a commentary on Donatus, and that he does not seek to dispute Donatus' definition, but to elucidate it for students.[11] Isidore does indeed call *allegoria alieniloquium* (*Etymologiae* 1.37.22), but he also makes it clear that *ironia* is the type of *alieniloquium* which functions *per contrarium* and there is no question of the distinction between opposition and divergence Green argues for: 'ironia est sententia per pronuntiationem contrarium habens intellectum' (*Etymologiae* 1.37.23: 'irony is present when the delivery of a statement makes the meaning the opposite of what is said'). There seems to be no justification for arguing that medieval rhetoricians ever considered *ironia* to be anything other than a trope which functioned by language of opposites. *Ironia* therefore signifies that the true meaning of a statement which uses this trope is the opposite of its literal or pretended meaning.[12]

Medieval rhetoricians and scholars either misunderstood or were unaware of the notion of Socratic irony. It is only mentioned in passing, though not named, in the *ad Herennium* (III.2.3) and it is referred to in the less well-known texts of Cicero (*De officiis* 1.30.108 and *De oratore* II.269–70). Quintilian gives Socratic irony a much more detailed treatment by distinguishing between irony, the trope, and irony, the figure of thought, the latter being the type of irony 'by which a man's whole life may be coloured, as was the case with Socrates' (*Institutio* IX.2.46). However, none of the later rhetoricians analyse Socratic irony and it is obvious from passing references that they did not understand the term as used by Aristotle, Quintilian and Cicero, for the term is consistently glossed as modest self-depreciation rather than feigned self-depreciation in order to mock or deride.[13]

One striking feature of *ironia* is that it is often linked to the practice of praising someone when criticism is intended. As Green points out, Isidore of Seville and Boncompagno of Signa both see *ironia* as feigned praise, but the notion may be more commonplace than he suggests.[14]

All medieval rhetorical manuals are united in the importance they attribute to panegyric. The *ad Herennium* divides rhetoric into three categories, the epideictic, the deliberative and the judicial, the epideictic being 'devoted to the praise or censure of some person' (1.2.2). Quintilian stresses the importance of panegyric even further, dividing all rhetorical speeches into those intended to praise, *laudatio*, and those intended to blame, *vituperatio* (*Institutio* III.7). Many of the models students would have had to study in the Middle Ages would have been examples of classical panegyric, and manuals often say, when discussing a figure or trope, how appropriate it is to praise or censure (for example *ad Herennium* IV.31.42, IV.34.45, IV.49.62). Hyperbole was thought to be particularly appropriate to panegyric (*Institutio* VIII.6.76), which might go some way towards explaining the excesses of medieval eulogy. Medieval audiences were not unusually credulous; they recognized hyperbole as a standard device used in panegyric.

Ironia is almost consistently described as suitable to *vituperatio*: 'ironia est cum per simulationem diversum quam dicit intellegi cupit. Fit autem aut cum laudamus eum quem vituperare volumus' (Isidore, *Etymologiae* II.21.41: 'it is irony when, through pretence, it is desired that something different from what is said be understood. This is the case when we praise what we want to vituperate'). Isidore, always aware of subtleties, goes on to say that the *ironia* may also work the other way round, in other words pretending to criticize someone one in fact intends to praise, but the majority of rhetoricians stick to the 'false praise' formula.[15]

The idea first occurs in Quintilian and he gives by far the most detailed discussion:

on the other hand, that class of allegory in which the meaning is contrary to that suggested by the words involves an element of irony, or as the rhetoricians call it *illusio*. This is made evident to the understanding, either by the delivery, the character of the speaker or the nature of the subject. For if any of these three is out of keeping with the words, it at once becomes clear that the intention of the speaker is other than what he actually says. In the majority of tropes it is, however, important to bear in mind not merely what is said, but about whom it is said, since what is said may in another context be literally true. It is permissible to censure with counterfeit praise and praise under a pretence of blame. The following will serve as an example of the first: 'since Gaius Verres, the urban praetor, being a man of energy and blameless character, had no record in his register of the substitution of this man for another on the panel ...'
(*Institutio* VIII.6.54–5)

9

Quintilian's example is taken from Cicero's speech *Pro Cluentio* (XXXIII.91), Gaius Verres being the object of Cicero's indictment three years before this speech was made, for the misgovernment of Sicily.

It is worth making the distinction here between flattery and 'false praise'. Whether or not flattery is sincere, the flatterer wishes to curry favour. The intentions of 'false praise' are quite different. Praising someone for qualities he or she manifestly does not possess draws attention to his or her inadequacies. What short person enjoys being called 'Lofty'? Of course, a knowledge of the speaker's intentions is desirable for the correct understanding of such a jibe and it is impossible to reconstruct precisely a medieval author's intentions, but it may be possible to do so to a certain extent by looking closely at the context of the passage in question. In all events it is obviously crucial to distinguish between praise, sycophantic flattery and biting satire.

Evidence that the notion of ironic 'false praise' survives right through the Middle Ages can be found in the work of the thirteenth-century rhetorician Boncompagno of Signa:[16]

irony is the unadorned and gentle use of words to convey disdain and ridicule. If he who expresses irony may be seen, the intention of the speaker may be understood through his gestures. In the absence of the speaker, manifest evil and impure belief indict their subject . . . Hardly anyone can be found who is so foolish that he does not understand if he is praised for what he is not. For if you should praise the Ethiopian for his whiteness, the thief for his guardianship, the lecher for his chastity, the lame for his agility, the blind for his sight, the pauper for his riches, and the slave for his liberty, they would be struck dumb with inexpressible grief to have been praised, but really vituperated, for it is nothing but vituperation to commend the evil deeds of someone through their opposite.

Consider also these lines from Geoffrey of Vinsauf's *Poetria nova*:[17]

> Contra ridiculos si vis insurgere plene,
> Surge sub hac specie: lauda, sed ridiculose;
> Argue, sed lepide gere te, sed in omnibus apte;
> Sermo tuus dentes habeat, mordaciter illos
> Tange, sed irrisor gestus plus mordeat ore. (431–5)

If you wish to bestir yourself against ridiculous men, begin in this manner: praise, but with ridicule; discourse, but bear yourself facetiously – although always appropriately. Let your discourse have teeth; speak of the ridiculous bitingly, but let your mocking bite more than your words.

What conclusions can be drawn from all this? First, as Green suggests, followed by Knox, there is strong evidence that the traditional view of irony in the Middle Ages saw the trope as criticism through feigned praise: it is therefore possible to talk about a 'false praise *topos*'. Secondly, given that all literate people were trained in rhetoric, it is not unreasonable to assume that most educated people would have been aware of the *topos*. Thirdly, given that the point of studying rhetoric was to put it into practice, we should expect to find examples of the 'false praise *topos*', both in literature and in other types of writing. If these conclusions are correct, the medieval view of panegyric may be more complex than it appears at first glance and we, as readers of medieval texts, should perhaps proceed with caution whenever we come across unwarranted praise or praise that seems exaggerated.

Have we any evidence that medieval writers consciously used this type of *ironia*? Knox has amassed considerable evidence from Latin literature to show that some writers were aware of this use of *ironia* and its implications.[18] This is the case, for example, in an exchange of poems between Peter of Pisa and Paul the Deacon, important figures at Charlemagne's court. In the first poem Peter showers resounding praise on Paul, but Paul's reply makes it clear that he, at least, understands this praise to be ironic:[19]

> Totum hoc in meam cerno prolatum miseriam,
> totum hoc in meum caput dictum per hyroniam.
> Heu, laudibus deridor et cacinnis obprimor.

I can see that all this is turned towards my ridicule, all this is said about my person ironically. Alas, I am derided by praise and oppressed by jeering.

This exchange, although it may express genuine rivalry, is nevertheless friendly and the tone lacks the bite of sarcasm.[20] However, our view of Peter's poem is radically modified by Paul's reply, and without it we might misinterpret Peter's praise.

Perhaps the most appealing example of 'false praise' from the Middle Ages comes in a panegyric of Henry of Kirchberg, *Carmen satiricum*, composed by Nicholas of Bibera between 1280 and 1282. At the beginning of his poem Nicholas claims:

> Sim quod yperbolicus, homo forte putabit iniquus,
> Vel quod ob invidiam mea scripta ferant yroniam,
> Aut est fortasse, qui me putat antifrasse
> E de pol in cura michi erit ulla figura,
> Sed rem sicut erit mea musa revolvere querit.   (5–9)

I quote Knox's translation:[21]

> There be men so diabolic
> to think my praise hyperbolic;
> or venture with an envious leer,
> I write these lines with *ironia*;
> or take my meaning amiss,
> and claim I use antiphrasis.
> But figures none here shall I use,
> the truth alone enjoins my muse.

Nicholas then launches into an extravagant panegyric some nine hundred lines long. At the end of the poem he declares that all the evil things written about Henry on the walls of his native Erfurt should be dismissed as groundless slander (lines 922–8). He chides the *pueros* responsible, but feels never-theless compelled to give an example of their calumny:

> Hic est Henricus, decreti doctor iniquus,
> Saccus avaricie, qui simea philosophie,
> Emulus est pacis, fons litis, iens sine bracis,
> Iuris perversor, ani cum pollice tersor,
> Suppressor veri, fur latro, peripsima cleri
> Et pater erroris maledictus in omnibus horis!   (929–34)

This is Henry, the crooked doctor of canon law, a bag of greed, the ape of philosophy, the rival of peace, the source of strife, he goes around trouserless, this perverter of the law, a wiper of his arse with his thumb, a suppressor of the truth, a burglar, a robber, the scourge of the clergy, the father of error, cursed in every hour.

The mention of this slander surely draws attention to it; actually repeating it makes quite sure it will stick in the hearer's or reader's mind. It would appear that Nicholas was using a common signal to irony at the opening of his poem. What better way to indicate to your public that you are being ironic than claiming a little too emphatically that you are sincere? Nicholas's praise of Henry has damned him far more effectively than any vituperation could have done, for the extended 'false praise' has highlighted, through contrast, his real character, in Nicholas's mind at least, as depicted by the slanderous graffiti.

Such an explicit textual signal to irony may not always be present, but scribes occasionally indicate, through glosses, that they considered some panegyric ironic. This is the case with a panegyric of the pope and Rome, composed by Henry of Würzburg between 1261 and 1265. Henry talks at some length about the lack of corruption and simony in Rome and this in itself is suspicious. Why mention it at all? Some manuscripts give no indication that the panegyric is to be understood ironically, but others make it clear they suspect irony, providing glosses such as 'yronice loquitur' and 'incipit ironia'.[22]

By far the strongest evidence that 'false praise' was widely recognized in the Middle Ages comes in glosses not to a medieval text, but to a classical one. Lucan's *De bello civili* opens with extravagant praise of Nero:[23]

when your watch on earth is over, and you seek the stars at last, the celestial palace will welcome you, and the sky will be glad. But to me you are already divine; and if my breast receives you to inspire my verse, I would not care to trouble the god who rules mysterious Delphi, or to summon Bacchus from Nysa; you alone are sufficient to give strength to a Roman bard.

Modern critics of Lucan are unanimous in their interpretation of this passage. They see him as a disgusting sycophant, shamelessly flattering Nero. How-ever, in the Middle Ages, as B. M. Marti has shown, Lucan's praise was consistently interpreted in glosses as ironic.[24] We shall, of course, never know which is the correct interpretation, but is this panegyric not somewhat double-edged in the light of Nero's deeds as described by Lucan further on in his work? Is it really a compliment to say one's verse has been inspired by the perpetrator of such atrocities?

Although there are no surviving examples of reflexes of *ironia* in romance vernaculars until the fourteenth century, there is some evidence to suggest that vernacular writers could also, in some circumstances, equate exaggerated praise with criticism. Before turning to specific examples of this, it is worth making a small, but significant, semantic point about the Occitan word *gabar* and its Old French cognate *gaber*. They usually mean 'to boast', 'to praise too much', 'to exaggerate', 'to joke', or 'to ridicule'.[25] The following is an example of Occitan *gabar* meaning 'to praise too much':[26]

> Ges hom de lui nom poc gabar
> Car li vertatz sobrava·l dih.

Indeed no man could praise him too much, for the truth went beyond what words could say.

Old French *gaber* may well have the same meaning in Fénice's lament in *Cligés*:

> Mesavenu? Voire par foi,
> Morte sui, quant celui ne voi
> Qui de mon cuer m'a desrobee,
> Tant m'a losengiee et *gabee*.
> Per sa lobe et par sa losenge
> Mes cuers de son ostel s'estrenge,
> Ne ne vialt o moi remenoir,
> Tant het et moi et mon menoir.   (4411–18)

Given the semantic range of the words *gabar* and *gaber*, it would seem likely that in some cases the word could incorporate an idea of 'false praise', which would make the two examples I have just quoted much clearer.

There is no shortage of examples of mistrust of excessive praise in troubadour poetry. In the first surviving *pastorela*, Marcabru depicts a clumsy and oafish knight attempting to win the favours of a quick-witted shepherdess. The knight's advances are full of praise, though hardly subtle:

> Toza, fi·m ieu, gentils fada,
> Vos adastret, quam fos nada,
> D'una beutat esmerada
> Sobre tot'autra vilana;
> E seria·us ben doblada,
> Si·m vezi'una vegada,
> Sobira e vos sotrana.   (xxx, 43–9)

Wench, said I, a noble fairy bestowed upon you a beauty superior to that of any other peasant girl; and it would be more than doubled, if I saw myself just once, with me on top and you underneath.

The reply rebuffs the knight in no uncertain terms:

Seigner, tan m'avetz lauzada,
Que tota·n sui enojada. (50-1)

My lord, you have praised me so much that I am very angry about this.

One can understand her anger at the knight's advances, but what she actually says is that she is angry because he has praised her too much, as if this in itself were reprehensible. The only reason this should be so is that exaggerated praise was recognized as criticism.

The same idea is expressed explicitly towards the end of the twelfth century by Peire Vidal:

E trop lauzars es mentida
Maintas vetz senes doptansa. (ii, 34-5)

And praising too much is, without a doubt, often a lie.

Peire, the eternal joker, goes on in the same poem to praise his lady:

Tant avetz bon pretz e fort,
Bona domna que valors
Vos lauza mais que lauzors,
Per qu'eu retrac ma chanso
Novela ab novel so. (51-5)

Good lady, your worth is so great and strong that your good qualities praise you more than praise itself, wherefore I recite my new song with its new tune.

The insistence on the words *lauza* and *lauzors* must have reminded Peire's listeners of his emphatic condemnation of excessive praise a few stanzas earlier and it is difficult not to suspect irony here.

Raimon de Miraval takes the idea a stage further, equating excessive praise with mockery:

Tuich cist trobador egal,
Segon qu'ill ant de saber,
Lauzon dompnas a plazer,
E non gardon cui ni cal;
E qui trop plus que non val
Lauza sidons, fai parer
Qu'escarns ditz e non ren al. (vi, 41-7)

All these troubadours, according to what knowledge they have, praise in the same manner ladies whenever they like, without considering who or which one it is; and the one who praises his lady more than she deserves makes it look as if he is mocking her, and nothing else.

This is probably an attack on flatterers, but the point Raimon is making is that praise can be interpreted as criticism and have an effect opposite to that of flattery. Raimon Vidal de Besalú, a thirteenth-century Catalan poet who wrote in Occitan, repeats this warning in his *Abrils issia*, quoting Raimon de Miraval on the subject:

Irony: medieval and modern

Ni trop lauzar, si tot li fatz
s'empeguisson, no vulhatz;
car, .i. dels sabers mens prezatz,
es atressi com trop blasmars.
E si·n voletz esser plus cars,
a·n Miraval venretz ades
que dis allunhat dels engres
que per entendre son cabal:
'En que trop mais que no val
lauz si dona, fay parer
qu'esquern diga e non y es al.'
Non lauzetz trop onrat capdelh.   (1722–33)

Nor do you want to praise too much, even if all the fools commit this fault; for, one of the least valued forms of knowledge, it is the same as criticizing too much. And if you want to be more worthy, you will refer at once to Sir Miraval, who said, averse as he was to impetuous people who are too agreeable at court: 'the one who praises his lady more than she deserves makes it look as if he is mocking her, and nothing else'. Do not praise an honoured patron too highly.

Raimon Vidal's advice was intended for *jongleurs*, for whom it would obviously have been important not to have their praise misinterpreted as *ironia*.

As already indicated, medieval *ironia* would appear to be a more specific device than modern irony. The words *per contrarium*, which occur in virtually all definitions, leave no room for the divergence from, or incongruity with, the literal meaning of a statement that characterizes the modern view of irony typified by Green's definition, quoted at the start of this chapter. This narrowness of the concept of *ironia* is an indication of the shortcomings of restricting oneself to medieval rhetorical terminology in the study of medieval texts and whilst it might be argued that it is inappropriate to apply modern critical tools and terms to such texts, as Green points out, our appreciation of our literary heritage would be greatly impoverished if we limited ourselves to the critical theories of the period we were studying.[27] Are there any other figures and tropes in the manuals that we might think of as ironic?

The obvious place to look for other ironic figures and tropes is amongst the tropes directly related to *ironia* as a species of *allegoria*. These tropes have been described in some detail by other scholars, so I shall limit myself here to cataloguing briefly definitions of those that lend themselves particularly well to irony: *antiphrasis, charientismos, sarcasmos* and *astismos*.[28]

Antiphrasis always follows *ironia* in the manuals and the two tropes are seen as closely related: 'antiphrasis est unius verbi ironia' (Donatus, *Ars maior* iii.6: 'antiphrasis is irony expressed in one word'). Isidore makes an additional comment which clarifies this definition: 'inter ironiam autem et antiphrasim hoc distat, quod ironi pronuntiatione sola indicat quod intellegi vult, sicut cum dicimus omnia agenti male: "Bonum est, quod facis"; antiphrasis vero non voce pronuntiantis significat contrarium, sed suis tantum verbis, quorum origo contraria est' (*Etymologiae* 1.37.25: 'there is this difference between irony and *antiphrasis*, that irony indicates the meaning it wants simply by expression, as for example when we say to someone who does everything badly "What you do is good"; *antiphrasis*, however, does not signify its opposite by the voice of the speaker, but only by the words he uses, whose origins are the direct opposite of their present meaning'). *Antiphrasis* occurs then when one word is intended to designate the opposite of its literal meaning. It differs from *ironia* only in that with *ironia* the whole statement is intended to mean the opposite of what it says, while the irony of *antiphrasis* depends upon the meaning of just one word.

Charientismos, the fourth trope classified under *allegoria*, is closely related to euphemism: 'charientismos est tropus, quo dura dictu gratius proferuntur' (Donatus, *Ars maior* III.6: 'charientismos is a trope which uses pleasanter terms to express harsh ideas'). Most medieval rhetoricians give the following example of *charientismos*: a person asks 'is anyone looking for me?' and receives the reply 'Good Fortune!', from which he understands nobody has been looking for him.[29] Quintilian's example is perhaps clearer: instead of telling the Athenians they must abandon their city, Themistocles urges them to 'commit her to the protection of heaven' (*Institutio* IX.2.92). This is clearly ironic: the contrast between the gentle expression and the reality of the situation underlines the harshness of what is being spoken of and those who are aware of the true meaning of the euphemism will laugh at those who are duped by it.

Rhetoricians agree that *sarcasmos* is an unpleasant trope: 'sarcasmos est plena odio atque hostilis inrisio' (Donatus, *Ars maior* III.6: 'sarcasm is hostile mockery and full of hatred'). It has been suggested that *sarcasmos* need not be ironic and that it can state its meaning unequivocally.[30] However, the literal meaning of a statement using *sarcasmos* must diverge from the intended meaning because the trope is a species of *allegoria*, in other words a type of what Isidore called *alieniloquium*. This is confirmed by the example of sarcasm given by Bede, that of the Roman soldiers mocking Christ on the Cross with the taunt 'Hail! King of the Jews!' (*De schematibus* II.2.12). Sarcasm is always ironic, even though the initiated audience usually only exists by implication because the true meaning is so thinly veiled.

The last of the seven tropes to be discussed under the heading of *allegoria* is *astismos*: 'astismos est tropus multiplex numerosaeque virtutis. Namque astismos putatur quisquid simplicate rustica caret et faceta satis urbanitate expolitum est' (Donatus, *Ars maior* III.6: 'asteism is a trope of many and varied virtues. For everything that is free of a simple rusticity and sufficiently polished with urbane wit is considered to be asteism'). Other definitions of asteism are equally vague. Isidore and Julian say it is the opposite of sarcasm (*Etymologiae* 1.37.30, and *De vitiis* 101–2), whilst others tend to transcribe Donatus word for word. I would suggest, along with Haidu, that asteism represents an attempt by the rhetoricians to systematize a quality which does not lend itself to categorization: ironic tone.[31]

Irony: medieval and modern

Looking beyond the immediate confines of *allegoria*, there are several other figures and tropes that may lead to irony, most of which are to be found in the manuals belonging to the tradition of the *ad Herennium* under the heading *significatio*. Although these figures also occur in Quintilian, they are not taken up by the rhetoricians influenced by his work.[32]

Significatio is a figure which leaves more to be suspected than has actually been asserted. It has five species: hyperbole, ambiguity, logical consequence, aposiopesis and analogy (*ad Herennium* IV.52.67). From the general definition alone *significatio* can be seen to have qualities that lend themselves to irony. By using the word 'suspected' (Latin *in suspicione*), the *auctor ad Herennium* implies that some members of an audience will fail to grasp the meaning of a statement using *significatio* and the audience is thus implicitly divided into the initiated and the uninitiated.

Hyperbole, the first subspecies of *significatio*, is also a trope in its own right, and as such it is usually dealt with separately along with the other tropes (for example, *Institutio* VIII.6.67). It is 'a manner of speech exaggerating the truth whether for the sake of magnifying or minifying [sic] something' (*ad Herennium* IV.33.44). Quintilian points out that hyperbole can be used to create humour:

it is enough to say that hyperbole lies, though without any intention to deceive. We must therefore be all the more careful to consider how far we may go in exaggerating the facts, which our audience may refuse to believe. Again hyperbole may often cause a laugh. If that was what the orator desired we may give him credit for his wit; otherwise we can only call him a fool.   (*Institutio* VIII.6.74)

Hyperbole can be used straightforwardly to express admiration or to emphasize, but it can also be used to ridicule when the qualities attributed to something or someone are patently beyond belief. This latter use of hyperbole clearly creates irony.

Significatio per ambiguum is nothing more than a pun: 'the emphasis is produced through ambiguity when a word can be taken in two or more senses, but yet is taken in that sense which the speaker intends' (*ad Herennium* IV.53.67). This is, of course, ironic because the speaker's words have one meaning whilst he actually intends another.

Significatio per consequentiam and *significatio per abscisionem* both work by implication. The former occurs when one states one thing which implies another by association, for example 'quiet you whose father used to wipe his nose with his forearm' (*ad Herennium* IV.54.67). This implies a personal insult though none is made explicit. The latter occurs when the speaker breaks off what he is saying and refuses to go on, though a further, unstated meaning is already clear by implication. Both these figures say one thing and mean another and therefore have ironic potential.

The last form of *significatio* is produced by analogy (*per similitudinem*): 'we cite some analogue and do not amplify it, but by its means intimate what we are thinking' (*ad Herennium* IV.54.67). If the analogy is obvious, then this figure is not ironic, but in the example given here, it clearly is: 'Do not, Saturnius, rely too much on the popular mob – unavenged lie the Gracchi.' Saturnius' power depended on his ability to manipulate the mob in Rome; the Gracchi were slain by the mob. The analogy is thus used to mock Saturnius and once this has been realized the statement has considerable ironic force.

Apart from the figures listed under *significatio, contentio* and *occultatio* also have ironic potential. *Contentio* occurs when a speaker's or writer's style is built on contraries (*ad Herennium* IV.15.21). This figure can, of course, be used non-ironically, but when opposites are brought together in an exaggerated manner irony will probably ensue and this is the case in the example given in the *ad Herennium*: 'flattery has pleasant beginnings, but also brings the bitterest endings'. *Occultatio*, or paraleipsis, is nearly always ironic; it occurs 'when we say that we are passing by, or do not know or refuse to say that which we are precisely now saying' (*ad Herennium* IV.27.37). The intended meaning of paraleipsis is so thinly veiled that in invective it is closely akin to sarcasm.

If these figures have ironic potential, others could easily lead to irony. The manuals abound with references to pretence and hidden meanings; Quintilian talks of making covert attacks and suggests that orators pretend to admit to a fault in order to create a good impression (*Institutio* VII.4.28 and VIII.2.24). The *auctor ad Herennium* encourages dissimulation (*dissimulatio*) in order to obtain the advantage in an argument and he explains how to make people laugh by assuming a facetious tone without changing one's gestures, or how to convey mockery through gesture without changing the tone of one's voice (*ad Herennium* XIV–XV.25–6). There can be no doubt that irony exists in theory, as well as in practice, in the Middle Ages, even though *ironia* did not mean what we understand by the word irony today. Although medieval theory does not allow for the divergence between literal and intended meanings that often characterizes modern views of irony, when reading the work of educated medieval writers, a knowledge of the figures and tropes described in this section, and rhetorical theory in general, can nevertheless help the modern critic to be receptive to irony.

Even so, rhetoric is of limited value to the modern critic discussing irony in medieval texts. Rhetoric is an attempt to impose logical patterns on the use of language, which is often illogical and resists systematization. Quintilian defines a trope as 'an artistic change of a word or phrase from its proper signification to another' (*Institutio* VIII.6.1), and the meaning of the word has changed little since then. All tropes, including irony, are therefore to some extent artificial categories, which is why distinctions between them are not always easy to make, but they all share one feature: one thing is said and another *specific* meaning is understood. Such rigidity is hardly surprising, for medieval scholars believed there was a close mimetic relationship between words and things. However, modern thinking on irony and modern critical theory in general allow for the slippery nature of language, for its untrustworthiness as a means of faithfully and reliably depicting the world, or representing a system of values, without sudden and unprecedented shifts in meaning. In a statement intended ironically there will not necessarily be a specific ironic meaning. In other words irony need not imply a specific alternative meaning; it may simply produce a distance from the text, undermine what is said, and create a vague *malaise* that things are not quite what they seem, without actually implying what may replace the surface meaning it destroys. Medieval theory does not appear to allow for this type of irony.[32]

MODERN IRONY

Green arrives at his definition of irony in his article '*Alieniloquium*' by building upon the simplest of dictionary definitions to reach, in seven stages, his more useful and comprehensive interpretation. In this section I will examine critically Green's definition, drawing on the songs of Guilhem IX to illustrate how irony functions and thus also showing that irony was present from the beginning of the troubadour tradition as it has survived in manuscript form.[33]

Dictionaries generally define irony in terms very similar to those used by the medieval rhetorical manuals and such a definition is Green's starting point: 'a figure of speech in which the intended meaning is the opposite of the words used' (*SOD*, I, 1113). This basic type of irony occurs frequently in everyday life: for example, a common remark on a rainy day might be 'What beautiful weather!'; an obviously intentional inversion of the literal meaning of a statement is not hard to understand.

There is irony depending on an opposition between real and intended meaning in the first of Guilhem IX's *companho* poems:

> Companho, farai un vers covinen,*
> et aura·i mais de foudatz no·i a de sen,
> et er totz mesclatz d'amor e de joi e de joven.   (I, 1–3)

Companions, I will compose a seemly verse, and there will be more folly in it than wisdom, and it will be all mixed up with love and joy and youth.

There is a lacuna of one syllable in the first line. As the text is preserved in the manuscripts, Guilhem claims that he will compose a 'seemly' poem. He goes on to ask his companions to help him choose between two horses:

> Dos cavals ai a ma sselha, ben e gen;
> bon son ez ardit per armas e valen;
> ma no·ls puesc tener amdos, que l'uns l'autre non consen.
> (7–9)

I have two horses to my saddle, beautiful and noble; they are good and bold in arms and worthy; but I cannot keep them both, for one will not tolerate the other.

In the penultimate stanza, however, it transpires that the two horses are in fact two women and that Guilhem has been comparing the qualities of the two mistresses as if they were horses:

Troubadours and irony

Cavalier, datz mi conseill d'un pensamen:
anc mais no fui eissarratz de cauzimen:
re no sai ab cal me tenha, de N'Agnes o de N'Arsen.   (22–4)

Knights, give me advice concerning a thought of mine: never before have I been so troubled by a choice: I do not know which one to stay with, Lady Agnes or Lady Arsen.

Guilhem's poem is obviously not 'seemly' at all.

Various interpolations have been suggested for the first line, but the simplest solution is to leave the manuscript reading as it stands even though it is hypometric.[34] In the manuscripts the line is clearly ironic: it so patently contradicts the facts that the real or intended meaning must be the opposite of the literal or pretended meaning. In other words *covinen* is intended to convey *descovinen*, just as 'beautiful' is intended to convey 'dreadful' in the comment about the rain. The humour of the poem depends on the poet's pretence, in this first line, that what he says will be seemly, and the audience's gradual realization that it is not. Once the subject of the poem is realized, many words become ambiguous sexual metaphors, for example *garnimen* 'equipment' (line 11), *encavalguatz* 'mounted' (line 12) and *corren* 'swift' (line 13). The names of the women themselves are probably either puns or irreverent references to real women, or both. The poem derives its appeal from constant ambiguity and through this ambiguity Guilhem succeeds in transgressing the limits of propriety. The irony of the first line intensifies the humour by leading the audience to expect something quite different, and yet at the same time it draws attention to the transgression.[35]

It is worth making the point that scholars are divided on the interpretation of this poem. Most detect irony, but some give a spiritual or mystical analysis.[36] If this poem is ironic, it shows that irony is always open to misunderstanding, that two interpretations are always possible.

Defining irony merely as a device which allows one to mean the opposite of what one says soon proves to be inadequate, however, for the real meaning of an ironic statement need not be the opposite of its apparent meaning: it might simply represent a divergence from it or a qualification of it. An admirable example of how the compass of irony may extend from the opposite of the literal meaning of a statement to a slight qualification of it is the French popular song *Tout va très, très bien Madame la Marquise*. Madame la Marquise telephones her servant to check that all is well at home. She is told that the meal has been burnt, but that otherwise 'tout va très, très bien', which is the last line of the refrain. In subsequent verses she learns that the meal was burnt because her house had burned down, all her loved ones are dead, all her priceless possessions destroyed, and so on. The first time the refrain is sung there is only a small disparity between the literal and real meaning. As it becomes clear that in fact 'tout va très, très mal', the disparity grows and the irony intensifies until the real meaning of the refrain is exactly the opposite of the literal or pretended meaning.[37]

Irony: medieval and modern

In the example just examined the compass of irony might be illustrated as extending along a straight line between two opposite poles. Wherever on this line the ironic meaning is deemed to be situated the referent remains the same. However, in an ironic statement in which the real or intended meaning merely diverges from the literal or pretended meaning, there need be no polarity of this kind. To illustrate this point Wayne C. Booth cites the example of the poster reading 'ignore the hungry and they'll go away'.[38] The reader recoils from the literal truth because it is morally unacceptable. In Booth's words, he or she must 'delve to a deeper meaning', and come to the conclusion that the statement means 'give to our fund or the hungry will die'. The irony of this statement does not depend on opposition between apparent and intended meaning; it depends on a disparity between real and pretended meanings and on a referent that is not mentioned.

Irony depending on a disparity between literal and intended meaning abounds in Guilhem's poetry. Few would hesitate to consider ironic the ambivalent sexual metaphors in *Companho, farai un vers* or the extended metaphor in the same poem by means of which Guilhem describes two mistresses as two horses: the literal meaning is rejected in favour of a 'better' meaning which is entirely different, involving a referent which is not mentioned until the end of the poem, but which some members of the audience may nevertheless discern beforehand.

Other examples of this type of irony in Guilhem's work occur in *Compaigno, non puosc mudar* (II) and in *Ben vueill* (VI):

> Si non pot aver caval, [ela] compra palafrei.　　　　　(II, 18)

If she cannot get a warhorse, she will buy a palfrey.

> E quan l'aic levat lo tauler
> espeis lo datz;
> e·l dui foron cairat valer,*
> e·l tertz plombatz.　　　　　(VI, 57–60)

And when I had raised the gaming table I cast the dice: and two of them were squared and of value, and the third weighted.

In the first example Guilhem is talking about women who are guarded and kept away from male society. The context leads to an immediate rejection of the literal meaning in favour of the intended meaning, that is that a woman will sleep with a servant, designated here by the inferior *palafrei*, when she cannot sleep with a knight, who rides a *caval*, generally a stallion. The verb used here to designate the sexual act, *comprar*, makes it clear that the lady's encounter with her servant is sordid and demeaning. In the second case Guilhem is ostensibly describing a game of dice; in fact the dice are a metaphor for the male organs, the gaming table represents the woman's dress or sexual organs. There can be little doubt about this interpretation, for earlier in the poem Guilhem referred to the game as a *joc grosser*, 'a lewd game' (line 45), and boasted 'qu'ieu sai jogar sobre coisi' ('and I know how to play on a cushion', line 25).

If it is accepted that irony is present in the examples I have just examined, it will not have escaped notice that the line between irony and metaphor or ambiguity is becoming somewhat blurred; it is also apparent that in these examples a sexual act is suggested without explicit obscenities. Two important points are raised by this.

First, irony is an ideal vehicle for sexual innuendo. In most cultures it is to a greater or lesser extent taboo to designate a sexual organ or act explicitly, depending on the context.[39] When social decorum is being observed, for whatever reason, and sexual acts or organs are designated implicitly, irony will probably ensue. This is because the allusion must retain its ambiguity if it is to be socially acceptable, communicating two different levels of meaning.

Secondly, a definition of irony which allows for a divergence between literal and intended meaning invites comparison with definitions of metaphor or allegory, both of which allow one thing to be said and quite another to be meant. The distinction between irony and other types of figurative speech lies not in formal differences, for metaphor, allegory, metonymy and synecdoche can all be used ironically, but in the ironist's intentions.

Since everyone has an equal opportunity to understand an ironist's intended meaning, he does not set out to mislead any one member of his audience. However, as the intended meaning must be inferred, in some cases some people will fail to grasp it. In all the examples of irony from Guilhem's poems discussed thus far, it is possible to imagine a listener or reader taking him literally and being duped by the pretended meaning: both meanings, pretended and real, remain possible. The ironist is implicitly dividing his audience into two groups: the initiated and the uninitiated. In Muecke's words: 'a sense of irony depends for its material upon a lack of sense of irony in others, much as scepticism depends upon credulity'.[40]

The existence of the uninitiated may be hypothetical. It is hard, for example, to imagine anyone not grasping the ironic import of a statement which is patently opposed to the facts of a situation, such as Guilhem's claim that *Companho, farai un vers* will be *covinen*. However, the effect of an ironic statement depends upon the possibility that someone will misunderstand and take it literally. Even the sharpest of minds will need a few seconds to realize that a statement is contrary to, or at odds with, the facts; there is always a moment of doubt during which everyone, except the ironist, belongs to the uninitiated audience.

Irony is élitist. Although it is difficult to determine whether this is a cause or an effect of irony, the creation of an élite is certainly desirable to the ironist. He wants to show that his intended meaning is better than the apparent meaning of the statement; he points to the stupidity of the uninitiated in his audience and of the unsuspecting victim of his irony. The initiated in his audience are de facto promoted to the same rank as the ironist; they have understood the subtlety and complexity of the situation. This élite immediately feels smug about its new-found status, and so is more receptive to the ironist's message. The fear of being thought stupid will often lead people to agree with an ironist, thus providing him with a further psychological weapon.

Jankélévitch argues that irony has inherent moral qualities, that it is always *une bonne conscience*; this is also the position of Booth.[41] Irony may indeed correct stupidity and point to a more subtle truth, but there is often an element of cruelty involved. Even when there is no direct victim of the irony the uninitiated audience is being patronized and treated condescendingly: irony can be savage as well as moral.

It is the creation of the initiated and uninitiated audiences and the constant possibility that the ironist may be criticizing or denigrating that distinguishes irony from other figurative modes of speech. Metaphor or allegory are used to embellish, to further the understanding of every listener or reader. There is no deliberate attempt to create an élite: some may not understand, but obscure metaphors or allegories have never been considered a virtue. Moreover, whilst several layers of meaning may remain possible in metaphor, allegory, irony or other figurative modes of speech, in all except irony the various levels of meaning remain, each one complementing the others; with irony, as soon as the ironic meaning has been deduced, the literal meaning is undermined and, in part at least, discarded. Those who accept it are automatically considered inferior, part of the uninitiated audience. Thus, when a metaphor is used to create an initiated and an uninitiated audience, as in *Companho, farai un vers* and *Ben vueill*, it is being used ironically.

The existence of an initiated and an uninitiated audience is implicit in much troubadour poetry. The famous *tenso* between Raimbaut d'Aurenga and Giraut de Borneil about the *trobar clus* and the *trobar leu* could, for example, be interpreted as a controversy about whether one should compose poetry that is understandable to all or whether one should compose for a group of initiates.[42] The seeds of this desire to please only the discerning few can be traced back to the poetry of Guilhem IX:

> E tenhatz lo per vilan, qui no l'enten,
> qu'ins en son cor volontiers [res] non l'apren. (1, 4–5)

And consider the man who does not understand it [the poem] or learn it willingly in his heart to be a rustic.

Guilhem, like all ironists, is mocking those who do not understand his irony, in this case all those who really believe his poem will be *covinen* and who will take the metaphor of the two horses literally.

Similarly, Guilhem divides his audience into initiated and uninitiated in *Ben vueill*:

> Ben vueill que sapchon li pluzor
> d'un vers, si es de bona color
> Qu'ieu ai trat de bon obrador;

23

qu'ieu port d'aicel mester la flor,
et es vertatz,
e puesc ne trair lo vers auctor,
quant er lasatz.   (VI, 1-7)

I would like most people to know whether a verse, which I brought forth from a good workshop, is of good colour; for I bear the flower in this craft, and this is the truth, and I can call the verse as a witness to this when it is bound up.

As Leslie Topsfield points out, Guilhem is leading his audience to expect a song about poetry and to a certain extent this illusion is maintained in the following stanza:[43]

Eu conosc ben sen e folor,
e conosc anta et honor,
et ai ardiment e paor,
e si·m partetz un joc d'amor,
    no soi tan fatz
no sapcha triar lo meillor
d'entre·ls malvatz.   (8-14)

I can indeed discern wisdom and folly, and I can discern shame and honou_ and I am bold and afraid and if you share a game of love with me, I am not so stupid that I cannot tell the best from the pitiful.

Why should Guilhem talk here of 'telling the best from the pitiful'? For Topsfield, *'partir un juec d'amor* means to have a courtly debate about love and merely hints at the levels of gaming and sexuality which will soon appear',[44] but the expression is more overtly ambiguous than this. Guilhem is warning his audience that the poem is really about sexual prowess, although this will only become clear at the end of the poem, with the sexual metaphors of the dice and gaming table. Those who realize this are the *meillor*, those who do not are the *malvatz*. When Guilhem reveals that he is boasting of his erotic skills as well as his skill as a poet, those who missed his signal to irony will also realize that he called them *malvatz*, and implicitly placed them in the unin-itiated audience. As Stephen Nichols suggests, *li pluzor* in the first line of this poem is a term which excludes as well as includes and he may well be correct to translate it (albeit rather freely) as 'the Happy Few'.[45]

If the ironist is misleading a section of his audience, what is the difference between irony and lying? Jankélévitch makes a distinction between *la bonne conscience ironique* and *la mauvaise conscience menteuse*. Whilst I cannot agree with him that irony is always a sign of a *bonne conscience*, his distinction here between irony and lying is useful. A lie is essentially self-interested and designed to be believed; irony, though it may be believed by some, is designed to be understood.[46]

A key word in Green's definition of irony is 'intentionally'. It is, of course, possible to be ironic unintentionally. One only has to think of the Christian fundamentalist broadsheet during the Vietnam war reading 'Kill a commie for

Christ.'[47] However, like Green I shall limit myself to intentional irony, for otherwise the temptation to hunt for irony everywhere in medieval literature would be too strong. In Muecke's words, 'since the failure to detect irony is regarded by some as reflecting upon one's intelligence, those of us who have a horror of being thought unintelligent tend to overcompensate and claim to see ironies in what was not meant to be ironical at all'.[48] If the spirit of the texts to be studied is to be respected, any interpretation involving irony must limit itself to 'the irony of an ironist being ironical'.[49] But how can we tell when irony is intentional?

If an ironic statement is uttered in the presence of the person or people who are intended to understand the ironic meaning, ironic intentions may be indicated through tone of voice or gesture. As troubadour poems were intended for oral delivery, troubadours and *jongleurs* presumably did indicate irony in this way. However, this is obviously of little help to us, for we can only guess at how the texts may have been performed.[50] There may sometimes be textual signals to irony, but an examination of the text alone may not always be sufficient to discern irony.

The only way to be sure that a statement was intended ironically is to have a detailed knowledge of the personal, linguistic, literary, cultural and social references of the speaker *and* his audience. For example, in the case of the poster reading 'ignore the hungry and they'll go away', a knowledge of the frame of reference is crucial to the detection and understanding of its irony. Unless we know that the statement is intended to be received by people who believe it is morally unacceptable to allow their fellow men and women to die of starvation, we cannot assume it to be ironic. To quote Muecke, 'we must assume that sometimes at least, we cannot tell whether an expression is or is not ironic unless we know how it is related to its context in reality'.[51]

I am aware that I am touching here on one of the thorniest problems in modern critical theory. If structuralists stressed the importance of context in any interpretation of a literary text, deconstruction implicitly denies the need to have a knowledge of the text's frame of reference. In other words critics need go no further than the text itself; they can divorce it from its cultural context. The focus of interest is the reaction of the modern reader to the text, not any meaning its author may have intended.[52] In the context of his work on irony Muecke has reacted strongly against such an approach to literature.[53] He stresses, rightly in my view, that some texts, whether they are ironic or not, may only be fully appreciated with knowledge of their cultural context.

To turn specifically to medieval literature, it is absurd to claim a text can be divorced from its cultural context. Putting aside problems of comprehension, which are by no means negligible, a modern reader might derive some pleasure, benefit or insight from reading a medieval text abstracted from its context, but how can its full import be realized without a knowledge of the society, literary tradition and mentality that helped to produce it? We speak a different language and are removed in time from medieval writers by eight hundred years.

A knowledge of the context, and, for that matter, the intertext, is crucial to the interpretation of some medieval poems. Our knowledge may not be as complete as we would like, but we should always use it as a frame of reference. The literary criticism undertaken in this book starts from the premise that its aim is to attempt to increase our knowledge of the text, in however modest a fashion and however incompletely, as it was conceived by its author and as it might have been perceived by its initial public. The response of the modern reader, whilst by no means considered unimportant, is of secondary interest. It is, of course, impossible to scrutinize the past discarding our modern cultural references and prejudices, and every critic writes from his or her personal standpoint, but I endeavour to distinguish at all times between modern and medieval reception. If at times the distinction seems unclear, *mea culpa*.[54]

In Guilhem IX's poetry, it is clear how crucial a knowledge of his social environment and his own cultural references is, not only to a reconstruction of his intentions and consequently to the perception of irony in certain poems, but also to the understanding of his poetry as a whole. At the most basic level, the force of the riding metaphors in *Companho, farai un vers* would be considerably weakened if we knew nothing of the aristocratic and chivalric society in which Guilhem lived.

The pitfalls of not attempting to take stock of a medieval author's possible intentions can be illustrated by the following lines from the *Chanson de Roland*:

> En la citét nen ad remés paien
> Ne seit ocis u devient chrestïen.　　　　　(101–2)

Of course, one cannot be sure that the poet is not being ironic here, but whereas a modern reader with little or no knowledge of medieval culture might consider the irony obvious, ironic intentions behind this statement are hardly likely. Indeed it invites comparison with the slogan 'Kill a commie for Christ'; the author does not consider killing in the name of Christ un-Christian.

Another key word in Green's definition is 'incongruous'. Whereas a divergence between real and pretended meaning is a fact which it might be possible to establish objectively if enough is known about the context of a statement, incongruity is a quality which depends for its detection upon a subjective reaction. Incongruity creates irony by modifying, sometimes only slightly, the meaning of a statement: it might derive from the use of two incongruous words within the same sentence, particularly when this involves oxymoron; it might also derive from the presence of two incongruous ideas, from an incompatibility between a word and its context, or from the use of a style which is inappropriate to the content.

A statement may have all the formal qualities of irony (that is grammatical and linguistic qualities of opposition or disparity), and yet still not be ironic, if it was not so intended and if there is no element of incongruity between real and intended meaning.[55] In *Molt jauzens*, for example, Guilhem extols the power of his lady's *joi*:

> Per son joi pot malaus sanar,
> e per sa ira sas morir,
> e savis hom enfolezir,
> e belhs hom sa beutat mudar,
> e·l plus cortes vilaneiar,
> e·l totz vilas encortezir. (IX, 25–30)

A sick man can be cured through her joy and through her anger a healthy man can be killed, and a wise man made foolish, and a handsome man have his beauty impaired, and the most courtly man become vile, and the most vile be made courtly.

Of course, the lady does not really have these powers and if the poem were humorous, bringing together opposites in this way might indicate irony. However, there are no grounds for suspecting irony here: opposites are brought together to illustrate the extent of the lady's power over Guilhem. Formal qualities that might elsewhere indicate irony are here an embellishment.

A poem which may be ironic and which revolves around a feeling of incongruity is Guilhem's *Farai un vers de dreit nien*. The poem has been interpreted variously as a burlesque poem, as a love poem containing elements of Augustinian thought, as a parody of the courtly love lyric, as an exposition of nihilistic philosophy, as verging on the metaphysical, as a rhetorical exercise, as an elaborate example of the trope *aenigma*, as a boasting poem, as an introspective analysis of a paradoxical psyche, as a development of the *vigilans dormire* theme, as a deliberately partly humorous and partly serious poem playing on debating techniques taught in schools, and as a poetic statement of psychological uncertainty.[56]

The poem is obviously open to more than one interpretation. Clearly, an examination of the poem's cultural context greatly enriches our view of the text, but this is also a poem in which irony may be detected by an examination of the text alone. From the start there is a feeling of incongruity between style and content:

> Farai un vers de dreit nien:
> non er de mi ni d'autra gen,
> non er d'amor ni de joven,
> ni de ren au,
> qu'enans fo trobatz en durmen
> sus un chivau (IV, 1–6)

I will compose a verse about nothing at all: it will not be about me nor about anyone else, nor will it be about love, nor about youth, nor about anything else, rather it was composed whilst I was sleeping on a horse.

The first line is ambiguous: it could mean 'I will compose a verse about nothing at all', or 'I will compose a verse on the theme of pure nothingness.' This could be taken, on the one hand, as an intentional joke: Guilhem's song is to be of little import, it has no serious theme. On the other hand, the poem may be a serious discussion of nothingness. The opening stanza, like the rest of the poem, is a string of doleful negative constructions (*nien/non/ni/non/ni/ ni*). This, together with the quasi-philosophical-sounding first line, makes the poem seem serious, but the tone is incongruous with the content, for the poem is not about anything at all (lines 1–4), it is composed whilst the author slumbers on horseback and it systematically negates every proposition it makes, because, as the poet admits, he does not care:

> Amigu'ai ieu, non sai qui s'es:
> c'anc no la vi, si m'aiut fes;
> ni·m fes que·m plassa ni que·m pes
> ni no m'en cau.   (25–8)

I have a friend, I do not know who she is, for I never saw her, believe me; nor did she ever do what might please me or displease me, nor do I care.

Guilhem's intentions are patently comic, for how can the poem be serious if the poet is so indifferent to his apparently serious theme?

    Two important points emerge from this discussion of irony in *Farai un vers de dreit nien*. First, incongruity between style and content may lead to parody. Parody occurs whenever an author adopts a style or a persona which appears on one level to be serious, but which he or she then goes on to undermine and often to ridicule; usually the style or persona is recognizably not the writer's own, but one can, or course, parody one's own style. Scholars are probably correct to argue that *Farai un vers de dreit nien* is a parody: whether Guilhem intended to mock philosophical debates on 'nothingness', or rhetorical techniques, or nihilistic despair, or courtly love, is hard to say. Perhaps he was intending to mock them all.

    Secondly, the type of irony used in *Farai un vers de dreit nien* differs from the irony discussed thus far. In all the other examples of irony, whether the intended meaning was opposed to or divergent from the pretended meaning, a specific intended meaning could be deduced once irony had been detected. In this poem Guilhem's irony undermines the literal meaning of what is said without suggesting an alternative. There is no absolute truth: there are only questions and uncertainty. Jankélévitch sees this type of irony as an extremely subtle mode of speech: 'l'ironie ne sert plus à connaître, ni à découvrir l'essentiel sous les belles paroles, elle ne sert qu'à survoler le monde et à mépriser les distinctions concrètes'. This type of irony can produce distance from a text, an uneasiness about apparent meanings, without actually implying what may stand in their place, or in Jankélévitch's words, 'l'ironie . . . charge l'absurde d'administrer lui-même la preuve de son impossibilité'.[57]

Irony: medieval and modern

Guilhem's *Farai un vers de dreit nien* may have been intended as more than a joke, but it would seem unlikely that in this poem he is making a positive statement about anything.

The poet or writer will sometimes, but not always, give a signal to the fact that he or she is being ironic. When irony is not immediately obvious, a signal may cast doubt upon the apparent meaning of a statement, lead the initiated audience to suspect irony and thus to search for the intended meaning.

We have lost oral and visual signals to irony in troubadour poetry, but there are various types of textual signals, such as contradictory statements, inappropriate style or register, or a particular formula that an author uses to indicate that he is being ironic. Examples of the first two types of signals have already been discussed. Guilhem's tone is inappropriate to the content of *Farai un vers de dreit nien*; in the same poem he systematically negates every proposition he makes. There may also be signals of this kind in *Companho, farai un vers*:

> Companho, farai un vers covinen*
> et aura·i mais de foudatz no·i a de sen,
> et er totz mesclatz d'amor e de joi e de joven. (I, I–3)

By admitting his poem is to have more *foudatz* than *sen* in line 2, Guilhem contradicts the claim that his poem is to be *covinen* and this alerts his audience to the possibility of irony. *Mesclatz* in line 3 may also be a signal. As Topsfield shows, it can mean 'adulterated' as well as 'mixed' and 'many coloured'.[58] The word is clearly incongruous with the pretended style and as such may be a signal to irony.

What of the third type of signal to irony? What kind of formulae or expressions could we expect troubadours to use to indicate irony? In medieval Latin and Italian texts, Knox finds that superfluous affirmations of sincerity or exaggerated professions of belief are often signals to irony. He lists words such as *sane*, 'surely', *ita sane*, 'yes surely', *scilicet*, 'of course', *vero*, 'truly', *videlicet*, 'clearly', *nempe*, 'assuredly', *profecto*, 'indeed', *invero*, 'indeed', *certamente*, 'certainly', and *veramente*, 'truly', as such possible signals.[59] Knox also finds that *credo*, 'I believe', may often introduce an ironic statement and this reinforces Green's conclusion that *cuidier* may often be a signal to irony in the Old French romance.[60]

These words and expressions provide a superfluous reinforcement to the proposition they qualify. Since they are unnecessary the listener or reader wonders why they have been included and concludes either that they are sincere, but the mark of a flawed style, or that they are deliberately included to undermine the proposition by exaggerating its veracity. A modern analogy might be *Private Eye* apologizing 'most sincerely' after a libel case. In the case of *cuidier*, the verb draws attention to the fact that the proposition is a statement of opinion and consequently indicates that it may not be true. Any irony derived from the use of *cuidier*, or its Occitan cognate *cuidar*, may in

29

certain cases be intensified because both verbs can also imply 'to think erroneously'.[61]

However, the accomplished ironist might not give any signals to irony in order to demand a greater intellectual effort from his audience. This paring down of signals to irony so that there is nothing but a de facto divergence between real and intended meaning is called 'the principle of economy' by Muecke.[62] The more economical the ironist, the greater the subtlety of his irony is likely to be.

The only element of Green's definition of irony that remains to be discussed is how the presentation of an action or situation can be ironic. This introduces two new concepts: dramatic and situational irony. Dramatic irony occurs when a character in a play or a narrative is unaware of the reality of a situation whilst the audience or the reader, and possibly other characters in the play or narrative, are aware of the situation and of the character's ignorance.[63] Situational irony, sometimes called the irony of fate, occurs when events do not turn out as they were expected to, as, for example, when a pickpocket has his pocket picked.[64]

Although an ironic statement can clearly be referred to as 'verbal irony', in literature the distinction between verbal and situational irony or dramatic irony is not always particularly clear, for the irony of a situation must necessarily be presented verbally, and will consequently often be surrounded by a good deal of verbal irony as, for example, in the presentation of the ironic situation in Guilhem's *Farai un vers pos mi sonelh* (v), where the narrator pretends to be deaf and dumb in order to gain the sexual favours of two ladies. By dint of the word 'presentation', Green's definition includes dramatic and situational ironies which depend on verbal irony.

The advantage of this definition is that it includes ironies where the intended meaning is the opposite of the apparent meaning, ironies where the intended meaning merely diverges from the apparent meaning and ironies where no specific alternative meaning is suggested, but where the literal meaning is undermined; it also addresses the problem of intentions and shows that irony cannot easily be systematized. Finally, it is preferable to the simpler dictionary definition because it states clearly that there are two levels of meaning in any ironic statement, each directed at a different section of the audience.

The meaning of the word irony has evolved considerably since it was first used and for some critics it designates concepts that have little to do with the type of figurative speech just described. It is therefore perhaps as well to list explicitly here types of irony I do not intend to discuss, and to explain why. First, Romantic irony:[65] it would clearly be anachronistic to talk about Romantic irony in troubadour poetry. Secondly, world irony, a quasi-philosophical term meaning the belief that there is a fundamental irony of human existence if there is no life after death.[66] To look for world irony in the troubadours, or indeed in any literary tradition that has an absolute faith in God, would also be anachronistic. Thirdly, Cleanth Brooks and his followers, whose critical methods were known as 'the New Criticism', used the word 'irony' to designate the way in which 'the parts of a poem relate to each other'. As Brooks himself admitted, this is a patently imprecise use of the word.[67]

In recent years one school of academics, sometimes called Robertsonian after its founder D. W. Robertson Jr, has argued that *all* courtly literature is ironic because it does not correspond to reality and because it is at odds with Christian doctrine. What these scholars mean by irony is not altogether clear; the implication is that where literary convention seems to be at odds with the values of the society that produced it, it must imply an ironic (or allegorical) affirmation of the 'real' system of values behind it. Green counters such arguments admirably, demonstrating how Robertson fails to take account of the many different attitudes towards love and other themes that are to be found in courtly literature and of the complexity of many medieval texts. He adds, using *Aucassin et Nicolette* as a case in point, that a parody of a system of values which did not exist would seem very unlikely.[68] Furthermore, the Robertsonian view of medieval literature makes no allowance for one of the main pleasures to be derived from literary texts: the playing out of fantasies, feelings and ideas that are suppressed in real life.

However, the Robertsonian school's use of the word irony raises two important questions that highlight the problems of discussing irony in courtly literature. First, what are the motives of the courtly author who writes ironically? Secondly, if, as the lyrics of Guilhem IX, or indeed Chrétien de Troyes' romances, suggest, irony at the expense of courtly convention is endemic in courtly literature from its inception, and if, as Robertson rightly tells us, what modern critics call 'courtly love' does not appear to correspond to any real social practices, what exactly is the butt of this irony? In other words, how are we to locate a norm against which to measure critical distance produced through irony when the earliest examples of the two main courtly genres, lyric and romance, appear to be permeated with irony?

THE IRONIST'S MOTIVES AND THE 'COURTLY CONSENSUS'

No definition of irony, however comprehensive, can explain why someone should wish to be ironic, nor why a medieval poet in particular should be moved to express himself or herself ironically.

The main reason why a poet should wish to be ironic is aesthetic: irony allows for subtlety and flexibility. In any ironic statement there are two levels of meaning, even if one level of meaning is simply that the literal meaning of the text is being undermined without any alternative being suggested; for the initiated at least, one level of meaning will nearly always correct the other and appear to present a better way of thinking. Irony rejects simplistic generalizations; it shows that something is not as simple as it might at first appear. However slanted irony may be towards one point of view, it will always appear to be objective because it offers an alternative opinion. Irony suggests apparent neutrality. This feigned detachment is even more striking given that the ironist, by flattering the object of his irony, or appearing to do so, can usually make it seem as if the fool is revealing his own stupidity. Irony is the ideal vehicle for criticism. Moreover, the successful ironist has more power than the poet who expresses himself non-ironically: he can pander to the tastes and requirements of one section of his public whilst ridiculing its trite and commonplace ideas and use of language for another section of his audience. Irony is thus a formidable weapon. Furthermore, as it generally involves a careful and precise use of language, the ironist must weigh his words carefully. Irony is a sophisticated and aesthetically pleasing mode of speech.

One common effect of irony is humour. Henri Bergson demonstrates how ambiguity often leads to comedy: 'on obtient un effet comique quand on affecte d'entendre une expression au propre alors qu'elle était employée au figuré'. This is, of course, one of the reasons why irony is so often funny, but Bergson also shows the importance in humour of laughing *at* someone and there can be little doubt that the initiated audience will laugh *with* the ironist *at* the uninitiated audience.[69]

Many of the reasons why a medieval poet should wish to be ironic are similar to those a Roman, Renaissance, Romantic or modern poet might have: it would be erroneous to assume that a medieval poet did not wish to amuse or convince his audience, that he did not wish to criticize or satirize, or that he did not strive for the greatest possible degree of subtlety. There is, however, one reason why a medieval poet in particular might wish to be an ironist.

The constraints on a medieval poet were far greater than those on a modern one. He was often tied to a patron, often obliged by social and literary conventions to adhere to a set subject, and he worked in a poetic tradition based upon the use of *topoi*. Any poet who did not wish to compose conventional poetry, or who wanted to criticize the courtly ideal, would be likely to have recourse to irony. Moreover, if one accepts Gruber's contention that intertextuality is crucial to an appreciation of the medieval lyric, that a 'dialectic' runs throughout the tradition, irony must play an important part in what he calls 'the principle of intertextual sublation', for what other mode of speech allows for simultaneous affirmation and denial?

The poetry of Guilhem IX indicates that the dialectic of *trobar* and the irony this often involves are present in the troubadour tradition from the outset. In the ambiguous *Ben vueill*, Guilhem claims to be the acknowledged master (*maistre certa*, VI, 36) of poetry (or is it love?), which implies a desire to compare his work to that of other poets (or lovers?). Elsewhere, he compares his mastery of *paraulas* to the *estraing lati* of others, implying that whereas their talk of love is empty, his words signify fulfilment:

> Qu'eu non ai soing d'estraing lati
> que·m parta de mon Bon Vezi;
> qu'eu sai de paraulas com van,
> ab un breu sermon que s'espel:

que tal se van d'amor gaban,
nos n'avem la pessa e·l coutel.   (x, 25–30)

And I do not care about any strange language which might part me from my Bon Vezi;
for I know about words, and how a short speech can spread; for some go about
boasting of love, while we have the reality [literally 'the piece and the knife'].

Though no songs by contemporaries of Guilhem survive, he gives the impression that he is composing in a community of poets. Moreover, several of his songs imply that this community already has a 'courtly' code of practice that is to a certain extent fixed, in other words a 'courtly consensus' against which an individual poet can measure his own feelings, actions and writings.[70] Guilhem himself is the author of apparently serious love songs as well as the humorous and ironic texts I have studied, and he talks, for example, about the *aizimens*, 'rules', of love:

> D'amor no dei dire mas be.
> Quar no·n ai ni petit ni re?
> Quar ben leu plus no m'en cove!
>   Pero leumens
> dona gran joi qui be·n mante
>   los aizimens.   (VII, 7–12)

I should not say anything but good about love. Why do I have nothing from it? Because I indeed do not deserve any more! But it easily gives great joy to whoever keeps its rules.

In *Companho, farai un vers*, Guilhem ironizes at the expense of *amor*, *joi* and *joven* (I, 3), for the text turns out to have little to do with love, joy and youth, despite his claim that they are the subject of the poem; but the fact that these words are grouped together indicates that they are already part of a conventional courtly vocabulary which Guilhem is using ironically.

Guilhem has sometimes been credited with the invention of 'courtly love' (whatever one understands by the term) and a chronological development from the 'humorous' to the 'serious' texts has thus been supposed.[71] Alternatively, critics have suggested that the sophistication of his love lyrics indicates that he was working in an already well-established tradition and that his love lyrics are merely the first to have survived; according to this view his humorous texts are a throw-back to an earlier, less sophisticated type of poetry.[72] Speculation of this kind seems rather pointless, but it is nevertheless striking that his love poetry has all the elements, albeit in a somewhat embryonic form, of what was later in the twelfth century to become the conventional courtly *canso*. There is no need, however, to explain Guilhem's love lyrics by discarding or discrediting the humorous texts; it is more interesting to regard his songs as containing not just an affirmation of the courtly code, but also a denial, through humour and irony, of its validity as a monolithic system of values. If one considers his surviving work as a whole, Guilhem is neither a courtly poet nor a humorous poet, he is both; we have no

33

chronology for his poetic output, we cannot posit a progression from one type of poetry to another. Guilhem is engaged not just in a dialectic with other troubadours, but also in a dialectic with himself, constantly looking at two sides of a question, oscillating, as he himself suggests in *Companho, farai un vers* (I, 2), between two opposite poles, *sen* and *foudatz*, wisdom and folly.[73]

It is not necessary to suppose the existence of a string of serious courtly texts to understand why Guilhem should be ironic at the expense of a 'courtly consensus'. He clearly revels in proposing an idea, then negating and surpassing it. From the outset the courtly lyric questions its own assumptions and it is thus no coincidence that the image of playing should be so strong in Guilhem's *Ben vueill*:

> Eu conosc ben sen e folor,
> e conosc anta et honor,
> et ai ardiment e paor;
> e si·m partetz un joc d'amor,
>   no soi tan fatz
> no sapcha triar lo meillor
> d'entre·ls malvatz.   (VI, 8–14)

I can indeed discern wisdom and folly, and I can discern shame and honour and I am bold and afraid and if you share a game of love with me, I am not so stupid that I cannot tell the best from the pitiful.

This stanza could be read as built upon dialectic; opposites are brought together dramatically and implicit in Guilhem's argument is the division of his audience into the initiated and the uninitiated. But playfulness underpins the whole poem as Guilhem allows the metaphor of poetry for love, ubiquitous in the troubadour tradition, to retain its ambiguity throughout, leaving the audience unclear as to whether he is boasting of his skill as a poet or of his skill as a lover. The notion of a *joc d'amor* is obviously intended to anticipate the obscene gaming imagery of the last stanzas (*datz, tauler*), but it also neatly epitomizes his attitude to both poetry and love: Guilhem is playing a game which he will share with his audience.

Critics have tended to view Guilhem's playfulness, his apparent irreverence in the face of the 'courtly consensus', as exceptional; some go so far as to discuss his poetry in terms that suggest he had a split personality.[74] It will be the contention of this book that Guilhem's playful and questioning approach to composing poetry, though perhaps more pronounced than that of some other troubadours, is typical of the tradition rather than anomalous and that irony is the chief manifestation of this.[75]

This is not to say that a serious view of *fin'amor* never existed. Guilhem clearly presupposes that love is a serious matter for discussion as well as a subject that lends itself to irony and this is an assumption that underlies much troubadour poetry. However, critics have tended to allow the serious side of the troubadour lyric to blind their perception of its playfulness. It should not be forgotten that troubadour poetry was, as far as we know, a form of public entertainment and that troubadours, or the *jongleurs* performing their work, were entertainers as well as poets. Even in the work of troubadours who appear to devote themselves exclusively to serious love poetry, there are signs that they were aware they were participating in a literary game as well as writing first person poetry.

Bernart de Ventadorn, for example, is thought of as the courtly poet *par excellence*. All his surviving poems are about love and he is the first major poet apparently to accept totally the conventions of *fin'amor*.[76] His great gift was to adopt the persona of the archetypal courtly lover in an idealized courtly world just as the conventions of *fin'amor* were becoming really fashionable. One of the prerequisites of *fin'amor* is sincerity and Bernart's rhetoric makes him appear more sincere than any of his rivals:

> Chantars no pot gaire valer,
> si d'ins dal cor no mou lo chans;
> ni chans no pot dal cor mover
> si no i es fin'amors coraus.
> Per so es mos chantars cabaus
> qu'en joi d'amor ai et enten
> la boch'e·ls olhs e·l cor e·l sen.   (xv, 1–7)

Singing can be worth little if the song does not come from the heart, and a song cannot come from the heart, if there is no sincere, pure love there. Because of this my singing is perfect, for to the joy of love I devote my mouth, my eyes, my heart and my wisdom.

Bernart was giving his audience what they wanted: a sincere lover, totally committed to *fin'amor* and to the courtly illusion. When Bernart chooses to maintain this illusion,[77] irony has no part in his poetry. Irony dissimulates, questions, criticizes, mocks, undermines conventions and, above all, brings down to earth. Bernart's chosen rôle on the courtly stage leaves little room for questioning the values by which he purports to live his life and to a certain extent much of his work is therefore an ideal example of the 'courtly consensus' taking over and apparently ruling a person's poetic world.

However, even Bernart de Ventadorn can undermine the 'courtly consensus' and allow the playful side of courtly culture to predominate. I take as my example *Be m'an perdut* (xii):

> I   Be m'an perdut lai enves Ventadorn
> tuih mei amic, pois ma domna no m'ama;
> et es be dreihz que ja mais lai no torn,
> c'ades estai vas me salvatj'e grama.
> Ve·us per que·m fai semblan irat e morn: 5
> car en s'amor me deleih e·m sojorn!
> ni de ren als no·s rancura ni·s clama.
>
> II   Aissi co·l peis qui s'eslaiss'el cadorn
> e no·n sap mot, tro que s'es pres en l'ama,
> m'eslaissei eu vas trop amar un jorn,   10
> c'anc no·m gardei, tro fui en mei la flama,

35

que m'art plus fort, no·m feira focs de forn;
e ges per so no·m posc partir un dorn,
aissi·m te pres s'amors e m'aliama.

III No·m meravilh si s'amors me te pres,   15
que genser cors no crei qu'el mon se mire:
bels e blancs es, e frescs e gais e les
e totz aitals com eu volh e dezire.
No posc dir mal de leis, que non i es;
qu'e·l n'agra dih de joi, s'eu li saubes;   20
mas no li sai, per so m'en lais de dire.

IV Totz tems volrai sa onor e sos bes
e·lh serai om et amics e servire,
e l'amarai, be li plass'o be·lh pes,
c'om no pot cor destrenher ses aucire.   25
No sai domna, volgues o no volgues,
si·m volia, c'amar no la pogues.
Mas totas res pot om en mal escrire.

V A las autras sui . . . eschazutz;
la cals se vol me pot vas se atraire,   30
per tal cove que no·m sia vendutz
l'onors ni·l bes que m'a en cor a faire;
qu'enoyos es preyars, pos er perdutz;
per me·us o dic, que mals m'en es vengutz,
car traït m'a la bela de mal aire.   35

VI En Proensa tramet jois e salutz
e mais de bes c'om no lor sap retraire;
e fatz esfortz, miracles e vertutz,
car eu lor man de so don non ai gaire
qu'eu non ai joi, mas tan can m'en adutz   40
Mos Bels Vezers, e'n Fachura, mos drutz,
e'n Alvernhatz, lo senhor de Belcaire.

VII Mos Bels Vezers, per vos fai Deus vertutz
tals c'om no·us ve que no si'ereubutz
dels bels plazers que sabetz dir e faire.   45

I

All my friends over there towards Ventadorn have indeed lost me, since my lady does
not love me; and it is fitting that I should never return there for now she is harsh and
unkind to me. And this is why she is angry and hateful towards me: because in her love
I find delight and pleasure! She can complain of or reproach me with nothing else.

II

Just as the fish rushes the bait and knows nothing until it's caught on the hook, so I
rushed into excessive loving one day, for never was I careful until I was in the flame
which burns me more fiercely than would a fire in a furnace; and because of this I
cannot leave it at all, so does it keep me close and bound to love.

III

I am not surprised if love holds me thus prisoner, for I do not think a more gracious
body exists in the world: it is fair and white and fresh and gay and smooth and

36

everything I desire and wish for. I cannot talk ill of her for there is none in her; for I would have done if I knew of any, but I do not, wherefore I do not speak of it.

IV

Always will I want her honour and good, and I shall be her liege man, lover and servant, and I shall love her whether she likes it or not for one cannot capture a heart without killing it. I know of no lady, whether she likes it or not, whom I could not love if I wanted to. But everything can be badly interpreted.

V

And so it's the other ladies that get me; any one of them who wishes to can draw me to her, as long as the honour and the good she thinks of doing me are not too expensive; for it is unpleasant to court in vain; and I can tell you this through my own experience, for I have suffered from this since that beautiful, perfidious woman betrayed me.

VI

I send joy and greetings to Provence and more goodwill than one could describe; and I make an effort and work miracles for I send them what I do not possess, for I do not have joy, except for that which I get from my Bels Vezer, and sir Fachura, my friend and sir Auvergne, the lord of Beaucaire.

VII

My Bels Vezer, through you God works miracles so that one cannot see you without being delighted by the pleasant things you say and do.

The apparent confusion and contradictions in this poem have caused critics problems both in the Middle Ages and in more recent times, but perhaps the problems this text poses can be resolved if it is interpreted as being ironic.[78]

The opening line is ambiguous. It could mean 'they have lost me in Ventadorn', in other words 'I have gone forever', or alternatively 'the people of Ventadorn have harmed me irrevocably'. There is ironic ambiguity from the outset. How 'sincere' then is the love Bernart sings of? The burning images in stanza II evoke lust and in stanza v he makes it clear exactly what kind of reward in love he is after, for the financial metaphor evokes the idea of contractual exchange, suggesting that the ladies he is courting are little better than prostitutes. He further implies that he is no longer prepared to be subservient to pay court to ladies. He has had enough of being the fawning courtly lover; he knows what he wants and has decided that he can get it without the elaborate courting he has undertaken in the past (line 33). Bernart is obviously questioning the conventions of fin'amor.

Much of the confusion surrounding this poem stems from the fact that critics have assumed that it is all about one lady. In fact a close reading reveals that it is about two. Bernart has lost one lady 'towards Ventadorn', in the Limousin, and now he is courting Bels Vezer in Beaucaire. He claims still to consider his first lady worthy and to be totally devoted to her, but he does so in such an exaggerated fashion in stanzas I, III and IV that it is hard not to suspect irony, particularly since in stanza v the apparently secure prison in which love held him in stanza II suddenly releases him to court any lady who will have him. The sincerity of his courting of his second lady is consequently suspect, for if all his impassioned declarations to her predecessor are empty

37

rhetoric, how should she feel about his love for her? It is thus interesting to note that in line 41 there is a variant that radically alters the tone of the end of the poem. Manuscripts *ADGQS* read *mos drutz*, *IKMNRV* read *sos drutz* (*O son drutz*). If the reading *sos drutz* is adopted, Bernart is admitting publicly to courting a lady who already has another lover and the whole act of courting becomes a cynical game.

The tone of the whole poem is ironic and sardonic. In stanzas IV and V, Bernart says he will love ladies whether they like it or not. This can be read in two ways. Bernart could be saying that he has adopted the rôle of the courtly lover and he is consequently going to play it come what may, or he could be bragging that he could seduce any lady if he set his mind to it. The playfulness of this poem is more reminiscent of Guilhem IX than of the image of himself Bernart generally projects. The poem may or may not be about real people; in either case the idea of a poet who claims to be a practitioner of *fin'amor*, as Bernart does in this poem, changing from one lady to another undermines considerably the conventions he apparently follows.

Even Bernart de Ventadorn is not immune then to irony, but this song is not typical of his poetry. On the whole he consciously projects himself as the perfect lover and perfect poet:

> Non es meravelha s'eu chan
> melhs de nul autre chantador
> que plus me tra·l cors vas amor
> e melhs sui faihz a so coman. (XXXI, 1–4)

It is no wonder if I sing better than any other singer, for my heart draws me more towards love, and I am better fashioned to do its bidding.

The fact that Bernart so deliberately opts for the 'courtly consensus' in most of his poems makes him an ideal yardstick against which to measure the irony of other poets at the expense of courtly convention, and it is thus hardly surprising that when his contemporaries wish to mock the 'courtly consensus', his work is often the specific target.

2

Marcabru

Marcabru's poetry stands apart from that of all other early troubadours. The work of an inspired poet, it is devoted not to the anguished self-examination and laments of the courtly lover, but almost exclusively to satire, moralizing and polemic. Yet his influence both on his contemporaries and on later troubadours is so great that it is difficult to appreciate their work without a knowledge of his poetry: Marcabru occupies a crucial position in the troubadour tradition.

Irony is obviously an ideal weapon for the satirist and there is hardly a single poem where Marcabru is not ironic in some way. I believe an awareness of irony in Marcabru's work will, in many instances, enrich our view of the texts; in some cases it may help to explain hitherto obscure passages. Moreover, an examination of his use of irony may further our understanding of his *eloquentia* and help us to focus on his position not only as a moralist, but also as an entertainer: despite the ostensibly serious nature of his subject matter, Marcabru can be as playful as many of his contemporaries. I propose to examine first the possible influence of rhetoric on Marcabru's irony, secondly his ironic sexual metaphors, thirdly his use of signals to irony, fourthly his use of parody, and finally irony dependent on intertextuality.

MARCABRU AND THE RHETORIC OF IRONY

Marcabru's knowledge of rhetoric and his attitude to acquired eloquence have already been thoroughly examined by Linda Paterson: he was well versed in rhetorical techniques and his attacks on the abuse of eloquence form an integral part of his moral code.[1] The most obvious point of departure for a study of irony in Marcabru's songs is therefore his knowledge of the medieval theory of irony, for if he was acquainted with rhetorical theory it is also likely that he knew the trope *ironia* and other ironic figures and tropes which feature so prominently in Latin rhetorical manuals.

One approach to Marcabru's use of rhetorical irony might be to quantify his use of ironic figures and tropes. However, this would be of limited value or even misleading. An ironic statement depends on context and once isolated from its context, any irony may disappear: a list of examples of any given figure or trope would therefore be meaningless. Moreover, despite the confident definitions in the manuals, some figures and tropes are in practice difficult to tell apart and the process of classification can be highly subjective. The problems of classification are best illustrated by an example. In his edition of *A l'alena del vent doussa* (II), Peter Ricketts refers to line 24, 'gilos que·s fan baut guazalhan', as *ironique* (p. 113). The irony here depends upon the meaning of the word *guazalhan* and the use of the word *baut* in this context. *Guazalhan* means a man who looks after another man's flock of sheep for a share in the profits from the flock: the word is related to *gazalha*, 'profit', to *gazal*, 'prostitute', and to *gazalhar*, 'to bring together'. The context is that the jealous husbands entrust their wives to guardians to safeguard them from sexual encounters with other men, without realizing that the guardians themselves are sleeping with them:

> IV Si·ls gilos s'en van seguran
> e li guardador jauzion,
> ges egual no chant e respon,
> qu'ilh van a clardat e ses lum;
> quan vols, t'en pren ab eis lo broc. 20
>
> V D'aquestz sap Marcabrus qui son
> que ves luy no van cobertan
> li guandilh vil e revolum:
> gilos que·s fan baut guazalhan
> meton nostras molhers en joc. 25

IV
If the jealous husbands go away feeling safe, and the guardians are joyful, I do not sing the chant and response to the same tune, for they can go there in daylight or in the dark; when you want to, he beats you with the stick itself.

V
Marcabru knows who these people are, for they do not hide their vile, subtle subterfuges from him: jealous men, who happily become herdsmen, gamble with our women.

These stanzas are rich in allusions. *Jauzion* (line 17) may have sexual overtones, whilst the image of 'singing and replying' may be intended to evoke the liturgy, thus introducing an implicit contrast between the guardians' baseness and Marcabru's own virtue. This idea may well be picked up in the following line: the guardians go to the women either in daylight or 'without light', which could be taken literally, giving the sense 'in the dark', or metaphorically, giving the sense 'without moral illumination'.[2] Finally, the expression *metre en joc* could imply oblique criticism of Guilhem IX, who uses gambling metaphors to designate the sexual act.[3]

The word *guazalhan* is ironic here because it implies a reversal of the expected position of the husbands and the guardians. Marcabru may be implying that the husbands are taking a share in other men's 'profits' (in other words sleeping with other men's wives), or indulging in promiscuity, if

40

guazalhan is taken as the present participle of *gazalhar*, or even condoning prostitution, given that *guazalhan* is clearly etymologically connected to *gazal*. However, the husbands, who ought to be exploiters in this situation, are in fact portrayed as exploited, even though this is never explicitly stated. If the sheep/shepherd metaphor hinted at by the precise meaning of *guazalhan* is retained, the husbands, who are the real owners of the sheep (in other words their wives), are merely allowed a share in the profits from them (in other words their wives' sexual favours) by the men they pay to look after them, but who behave as their real owners. The use of the word *baut* heightens the irony because it draws attention to the husbands' stupidity and creates an opposition between the contentment they feel with the situation as they see it, and how they would feel if they knew what was really happening.

The line 'gilos que·s fan baut guazalhan' is clearly ironic, but how would it be classified as an example of an ironic figure or trope? It could be seen as an example of *ironia* because the intended meaning might be seen as the opposite of the literal meaning (the husbands happily become *guazalhan*/they are not happy about becoming *guazalhan*); it could also be seen as an example of *sarcasmos* if delivered with sufficient venom, or the words *guazalhan* and *baut* might be considered as examples of *antiphrasis* (individual words used ironically). Alternatively, *guazalhan* could be seen as an example of *significatio per consequentiam* (implying more than is said) or *astismos* (urbane wit). Some ironic statements are clearly easier to classify than this, but the majority could still be classified under more than one heading.

I do not propose, therefore, an exhaustive study of Marcabru's use of ironic figures and tropes, but a selective survey of the range he uses, in order to illustrate his dexterity in the use of rhetorical devices when being ironic and the possible influence of rhetorical theory on his use of irony.

The notion of *ironia* in the Middle Ages was much narrower than the modern concept of irony. Medieval rhetorical manuals indicate that *ironia* occurs when the intended meaning of a statement is the opposite of its literal or apparent meaning; they also say it is an ideal trope for vituperation and 'false praise'. In *Al prim comens* (IV) there is a perfect example of *ironia*:

> VI Moillerat, li meillor del mon
> Foratz, mas chascus vos faitz drutz,
> Que vos confon,
> E son acaminat li con
> Per qu'es Jovens *fora*banditz   35
> E vos en appel'om cornutz.

> VII Lo pretz del dan e del barat,
> De calque part sia vengutz,
> Ant moillerat;
> Et ieu ai lo lor autreiat,
> E Jois es entr'els esbauditz   40
> E Donars alqes mantengutz.

VI

Husbands, you would be the best men in the world, but each one of you becomes a lover, which destroys you; and the cunts are on the march, which is why youth is banished, and you are called cuckolds.

VII

The husbands have the value of the compensation and the trade from wherever it may come, and it is I who have granted it to them; and joy is happy among them and generosity is upheld a little.

Marcabru criticizes here husbands who become lovers. The alliteration in lines 31–2, the vulgar language (*con, cornutz*) and the pejorative, financial vocabulary (line 37) make the tone that of vituperation. Furthermore, Marcabru taunts the husbands in his audience: it is he who grants them whatever they have. In the light of this outspoken criticism the propositions in lines 41–2 that joy is happy among husbands and that generosity is maintained can only be ironic.[4] The fact that generosity is only upheld 'a little' (*alqes*) is probably a signal to the *ironia* of the whole statement. The effect of this *ironia* is to intensify the criticism of the husbands, to condemn them through 'false praise'.

If one common aim of *ironia* is criticism, one common result is humour. Consider, for example, this stanza from *Per savi·l tenc*:

> Fols pos tot cant au romanssa;
> Non sec razo, mas bozina,
> Car s'Amors viu de rapina,
> Autrei c'Amors s'amoreia
> E que Costans es costanssa
> E fals usatges dreitura. (XXXVII, 49–54)

Since the fool recounts everything he hears, he does not follow reason, but chatters mindlessly, for if love lives on rapine, I grant that love is infatuated, that Constant is constancy itself and evil ways are righteousness.

The humour stems from the ludicrous nature of the statements in lines 51–4 and is at the expense of the *fols* who is stupid enough to believe what is patently untrue. 'Amors viu de rapina' represents the opinion of the fool, but by comparing the line's veracity to that of statements that are clearly absurd Marcabru indicates *ironia*. The effect is intensified by word-play within the stanza. *Amoreiar* is related to *amors* etymologically despite the opposition in meaning, that is between love-sickness or infatuation, an impure state, and love, a pure state. Given the fascination with etymologies in the Middle Ages, the more cultivated members of the audience are likely to have noticed this. Similarly, Marcabru plays on the meaning of *costan*, 'constant'. If all the propositions in lines 51–4 are to be understood as *ironia*, then Costans, who ought to be reliable because of his name, is not. Marcabru uses the name Costans twice elsewhere: in *Al departir* (III, 26), where Constans is listed among a group of frivolous men, and in *Dirai vos en mon lati* (XVII, 11), where he is called 'dons Costans l'enganaire' ('sir Constant, the deceiver'). Either

Marcabru

Costans is an ironic *senhal* for a vacillating man which Marcabru's audience would have recognized as such, whether the man in question were real or imaginary, or he was a man known to be inconstant and Marcabru is punning on his name.[5]

Marcabru often uses courtly vocabulary ironically and this usually involves *antiphrasis*, for example:

> Cest vest la blancha camiza
> E fai son seinhor sufren
> E ten si dons a sa guiza. (XI, 62–4)

This man puts on the white shirt, cuckolds his lord, and holds his lady at his will.

As Ruth Harvey points out, the use of the expression *si dons* here ought to imply that the lover is in a subordinate position to the woman, whereas in fact it is she who is in the weaker position because he can do what he likes when he likes with her.[6] Moreover, there is a stylistic clash here because the word belongs to the courtly register, yet Marcabru's tone is far from courtly. The literal meaning of the term *si dons*, implying the woman's superiority, is thus inverted for the initiated audience, and the ensuing irony amounts to harsh criticism: despite appearances, this woman is certainly no lady in Marcabru's eyes. As the irony operates on the level of a single word, it must be considered *antiphrasis*.

Marcabru's use of *antiphrasis* is not, however, confined to courtly vocabulary. He often produces *antiphrasis* through oxymoron, for example:

> Car pot la coa mover,*
> Cest fai *la nuoich son jornau*,
> Don engenrra un bel fill,
> Per que sobreseignoreia. (XXXVIII, 32–5)

Because he knows how to move his tail, this man makes the night into his day's work and thus will he sire a fine son, through whom he lords it over everyone.

> 'Toza de gentil afaire,
> Cavaliers fon vostre paire
> Que·us engenret en la maire,
> Car fon *corteza vilana*.' (XXX, 29–32)

Oh, noble wench, your father, who begat you in your mother, was a knight, for she was a courtly peasant woman.

In each case the word intended as *antiphrasis* is juxtaposed to a word that implies its opposite. *Jornau* is ironic because the man's 'day's work' is pleasurable and because it is done at night. *Corteza*, in the second example, is ironic because in the strictest sense of the word, the *vilana* cannot be *corteza*, for the word is derived from *cort* and its primary meaning is thus 'of the court'.

Sarcasmos is a difficult trope to distinguish in practice because any ironic trope or figure can become sarcastic if the delivery is sufficiently venomous.

43

Troubadours and irony

Marcabru's tone often smacks of sarcasm, as in the following stanzas from *Al prim comens* (IV):

IV   Joves homes de bel semblan
        Vei per Malvestat deceubutz;   20
        Que van gaban
        'De so mil essais encogan*
        Farem qan lo temps er floritz',
        Mas lai reman lo gabs e·l brutz.

V   Cill ant l'usatge del gosso   25
        Que ditz qand sera a la lutz
        Fara maio,
        Puois qand es lai qui l'en somo,
        Non er escoutatz ni auzitz,
        Anc per lui non fo dolatz fustz.   30

IV
I see young, good-looking men deceived by evil, for they go about boasting: 'we shall test ourselves in this a thousand times before the year is out, once spring comes again'. But that is an end to the boasting and the noise.

V
These men behave just like a lap dog who says he will build a house when the evenings get lighter, for when that time comes, whoever urges him to do so will neither be listened to nor heard; never was a piece of wood planed by him.

The word *joven* is loaded with meaning for Marcabru.[7] Here he uses the adjective *joves*: it can have its literal meaning 'young', but it can also clearly imply all kinds of virtues related to *joven*. These young men, however, possess none of the qualities of *joven*, but are deceived by *Malvestat*. *Joves* must therefore be understood ironically, as must the words *de bel semblan*, which could mean 'handsome' or 'who appear to be good', but which imply 'but who are not good'. The vice of the *joves homes* is empty boasting and by the end of the stanza the vituperation is so intense that the tone is sarcastic. The theme of empty boasting and the attack on the *joves homes* is continued in the next stanza, as is the opposition between winter and summer. Marcabru now describes the young men as having 'the habits of a lap dog'. The source of this image is one of Aesop's fables:[8] it is unpleasant but appropriate. The lap dog makes a great deal of noise for a little creature, like the young men in the previous stanza, and it runs to whoever will throw it a morsel of food. The dog in Aesop's fable says it will build a house when the summer comes. When it is asked to do so it does not, and the man who exhorts it to fulfil its promises is not heeded. As in the fourth stanza, the vituperation in the fifth intensifies towards the last line, and once again the tone is sarcastic. If the intended meaning is so thinly disguised, this is in the nature of sarcasm.

    Charientismos, saying something unpleasant in an agreeable manner, can be as hard to distinguish from other tropes as sarcasm. It is particularly close to

44

Marcabru

euphemism or litotes. In *Quan l'aura doussana bufa* Marcabru would appear
to be using this trope:

> E·l jelos bada e musa
> E fai badiu badarel,
> Car qui l'autrui con capusa
> Lo sieu tramet al mazel,
> E qui l'estraing vol sentir,
> Lo sieu fai enleconir
> E·l met en la comunailla.
>
> Ges non viu de manna dreicha
> Cum fetz lo trips d'Israel. (XLII, 15–23)

And the jealous man gapes and waits in vain with his stupid, idle curiosity, for the man
who hews another man's cunt is sending his own to the slaughter, and he who wishes to
feel a strange one makes his own envied and puts it with the communal property.

He indeed does not live off real manna like the tribes of Israel did.

The tone of lines 15–21 is virulently vituperative. Some words are clearly
pejorative (*jelos, badarel, comunailla*), others have unpleasant connotations
(*capusa, mazel* and possibly *enleconir*); the word *con*, though more common
in the Middle Ages in Occitan and in Old French than its Modern French and
English cognates, is nevertheless vulgar, and consequently unflattering if not
to say insulting to the woman it designates. In this context the word *manna*,
with its connotations of spiritual and physical well-being, is startling. It
emphasizes the immorality of the *jelos* and implies a contrast between the
sensual pleasure he takes, manna of a kind, and true manna from heaven.
Literally all Marcabru says is that the *jelos* does not live on manna. The
intended meaning, however, is that he lives sinfully and as this is expressed
euphemistically these lines are an example of *charientismos*.

Examples of *significatio*, a figure which leaves more to be suspected than has
actually been asserted, abound in Marcabru's work. In *Al prim comens*, for
example, he seems to use *significatio per ambiguum* (punning):

> Lo pretz del dan e del barat,
> De calque part sia vengutz,
> Ant moillerat. (IV, 37–9)

Husbands have the value of the compensation and the trade from wherever it may
come.

Pretz can mean 'price', 'value', 'reputation', 'distinction', 'payment' and
'glory'; *dan* can mean 'damage', 'compensation', 'sin', or 'gift'; *barat* can
mean 'trade', 'ruse', or 'trickery'. The financial flavour to the vocabulary
Marcabru uses here is probably in itself indicative of denigration and mockery.[9] One way of translating these terms literally would thus be 'Husbands
have the value of the compensation and the trade from wherever it may come.'
This implies that the husbands are, as usual, getting the better deal, but the

45

financial metaphor hints at unflattering parallels between prostitution and the promiscuity Marcabru sees all around him. If read for an ironic meaning the lines could also be translated 'Husbands pay the price of the damage and the trickery, from wherever it may come', or 'Husbands have the reputation that comes from the damage and the trickery, from wherever it may come.' The ambiguity of *pretz*, *dan* and *barat* create heavy irony in these lines, for there is a divergence between the literal meaning conveyed to the uninitiated, and the several layers of intended meanings, conveyed to the initiated.

Significatio per consequentiam occurs when one states something which implies another by insinuation. This is what Marcabru does in *L'autrier jost'una sebissa* (xxx) through the voice of his *pastora*:

v   – 'Toza de gentil afaire,
Cavaliers fon vostre paire   30
Que·us engenret en la maire,
Car fon corteza vilana.
Con plus vos gart, m'etz belaire,
E per vostre joi m'esclaire,
Si·m fossetz un pauc humana!'   35

vi   – 'Don, tot mon ling e mon aire
Vei revertir e retraire
Al vezoig et a l'araire,
Seigner', so·m dis la vilana;
'Mas tals se fai cavalgaire   40
C'atrestal deuria faire
Los seis jorns de la setmana.'

v
'Oh, noble wench, your father, who begat you in your mother, was a knight, for she was a courtly peasant woman. The more I look at you, the more beautiful you are to me, and through your joy, I am happy, if only you were a little kinder to me.'

vi
'My lord, I can see all my lineage and family returning and going back to the sickle and the plough, sir,' thus said the peasant woman to me, 'but there is a person who pretends to be a knight who ought to do the same for six days of the week.'

There is a constant opposition between nobility and low birth in these stanzas. The knight attempts to compliment the *vilana* by suggesting that her father must have been a knight, not realizing that he thereby casts aspersions on her legitimacy. The peasant woman then mocks the knight by using the words *ling* and *aire*, both of which imply nobility, to describe her peasant family and this irony is then intensified by the implications of the rest of the stanza. As the knight is only *cavalgaire* in the vicinity, it is not unreasonable to assume that *tals* (line 40) refers to him. The shepherdess may simply mean that her suitor is lacking in knightly virtues when she says he ought to go to work like her peasant family. However, what she actually says is that he 'pretends' to be a knight, in other words, that he is not really a knight at all, and therefore, by

46

implication, that he is a peasant like herself. Given that the knight has just cast doubt on the virtue of the peasant woman's mother, it is possible that she is now returning the compliment, implying that the knight is one of the bastard children, born of noble women who sleep with their servants, whom Marcabru so despises and with whom he is so obsessed. It is as if the knight and the peasant women have undergone a complete rôle reversal: she is now noble and he a peasant.

Similarly, in *Dirai vos en mon lati* (xvii), Marcabru mocks, through *significatio per consequentiam*, men who bring up other men's children as their own:

> v   Eras naisson dui poilli   25
>   Beill, burden, ab saura cri
>   Que·is van volven de blanc vaire
>   E fan semblan aseni;
>   Jois e Jovens n'es trichaire
>   E malvestatz eis d'aqui.   30
>
> vi   Moillerat, ab sen cabri,
>   A tal paratz lo coissi*
>   Don lo cons esdeven laire;
>   Que tals ditz: 'Mos fills me ri'
>   Que anc ren no·i ac a faire: 35
>   Gardatz sen ben badoï.

v

Now two foals are born, beautiful, frisky and with golden manes which are turning from white to piebald, and they look like donkeys; Joy and Youth are traitors here and evil is born of this.

vi

Goat-witted husbands, you arrange the cushions for such a man, wherefore the cunt becomes a thief; for such a husband says to me: 'My son is laughing at me!', when he never had anything to do with it. You really have the intelligence of an idiot.

Once again the tone is vituperative. Goats in medieval bestiaries represent lechery and there may therefore be a pun on *sen*, 'wisdom', and *sen*, 'the senses'.[10] The words *cons, laire* and *badoï* are pejorative and Marcabru is once again attacking the nobility and what he considers their unacceptable promiscuity. In this context the statement that the cuckolded husband 'never had anything to do with it' invites closer inspection. On one level this line could mean that the man did nothing to provoke his son's laughter; on another it could imply that he had nothing to do with fathering the child.

In all these instances of irony the influence of Latin rhetorical manuals may be perceived. It is striking, apart from the fact that these instances of irony conform to definitions of figures and tropes, that Marcabru uses irony as the manuals suggest *ironia* should be used, to criticize and vituperate. Often, when he appears to praise, he is in fact criticizing, and it might therefore be concluded that the notion of 'false praise' was no stranger to him.

Indeed, in one poem Marcabru maintains his use of the 'false praise *topos*' throughout the whole text. *Emperaire, per vostre prez* (xxiii) is the second of two *sirventes* addressed to Alfonso VII of Castile. *Emperaire, per mi mezeis* (XXII), the first, was probably composed in the autumn of 1143 to encourage Alfonso to join the fight against the Almoravids. *Emperaire, per vostre prez* was composed after this, but no later than 1145.[11] In his edition of the two poems Aurelio Roncaglia calls them 'il canto dell'entusiasmo e quello della delusione' (p. 157), but he does not explain why there is a disillusioned tone in the second poem, when Marcabru appears to praise Alfonso in both. Some alternative translations are placed in square brackets.

<blockquote>

I   Emperaire, per vostre prez
e per la proeza qu'avez,
sui a vos venguz, zo sabez,
e no m'en dei ges penedir.

II   Meillz m'en degra lo pels sezer   5
car chai vinc vostra cort vezer,
qu'eu farai loing e pres saber
lo joi que vos es a venir.

III   S'anc per vos demenei orguoill,
tot m'es tornat en autre fuoill;   10
que tals mena bon fait en l'uoill
que no s'en ausa descobrir.

IV   Qui·l sap bon qu'eu sui tant poinenz
als malvaz et als recredenz,
per que n'a serradas las denz   15
e no·n ausa lo criz eissir?

V   Emperaire si ben enquers,
lo reprovers es fis e mers;
ço que donz donz e plora sers,
las lacrimas devon perir.   20

V^bis   Emperaire, si Dieus mi gart   20bis
....
....
....

VI   S'eu me faill al vostre donar,
jamais a gorc qu'auza lauzar
non ira Marcabrus pescar,
c'ades cuidaria faillir.

VII   Per aquella fe qu'eu vos dei,   25
anc mais emperador ni rei
non agron tal merchat de mei
con vos, e Dieus m'en lais jauzir.

VIII   Emperairiz, pregaz per mei,
qu'eu farai vostre prez richir.   30

</blockquote>

I

Emperor, because of your worth and because of the prowess you have, I have come here to serve you, mark my words, and I ought not to repent of this at all.

Marcabru

II

I ought to feel better because I came here to see your court and I will make known far and near the joy which will come to you.

III

If ever because of you I showed pride, my attitude has quickly changed: for the man who knows a good deed when he sees one does not dare to reveal his thoughts about it.

IV

If there is someone who likes the fact that I am so aggressive towards the wicked, why has he closed his mouth about it and why does he not let a cry escape?

V

Emperor, if you examine this closely, the proverb [or reproach] is true and fine: when the master gives something and the servant weeps because of this, the tears are wasted.

V^{bis}

Emperor, if God protects me . . . [rest missing].

VI

If I am ungrateful for your generosity [or if I am disappointed by your generosity], never will Marcabru go fishing in a pond he hears praised, for he would always think himself at fault [or lacking].

VII

By the faith which I owe you, never did an emperor or a king have such a bargain from me as you, and may God grant you joy of it.

VIII

Empress, pray for me [or intercede on my behalf], for I will enrich your worth.

The first two stanzas appear to be straightforward praise. Marcabru then attacks people who do not speak up in defence of righteous men (like himself), magnates who are generous to the wrong people and finally those who are not generous to the right people. In each case the criticism is unstated and merely implied, for example stanza IV is formulated as a question, which makes any insult implicit rather than explicit, and stanzas V and VI make use of proverbs which have an obvious, but unstated moral.[12] Each insult or attack appears to be a moralizing statement with a general application of the kind that abounds in Marcabru's poetry. However, various devices gradually point to the fact that the invective may have a specific, rather than a general application.

Marcabru's use of second person pronouns and verb forms is insistent in this poem (nine times in six stanzas) and he directly apostrophizes Alfonso three times. He only uses impersonal constructions when making a general moralizing statement, otherwise he constantly reminds his audience that the poem is addressed to Alfonso. When, in stanza V, he specifically draws attention to the moral of a proverb, it begins to seem he might be implying that the criticism is directed against him, particularly since *reprovers* can mean 'reproach' as well as 'proverb' (*PSW*, VII, 253). If there is any doubt as to whether the criticism is intended generally or specifically, it is quashed by the ambiguous use of the verb *faillir* in stanza VI:[13] it is unclear whether it is Marcabru or Alfonso who is at fault. The specific mention of *vostre donar*, closely followed by the proverb about the pond, draws unflattering parallels between Alfonso's court and a pond to which troubadours like Marcabru flock to fish, but which proves to be empty: Marcabru had heard Alfonso's court praised, but has himself been unsuccessful there. Mentioning his own name puts the reproach on a personal level. The ambiguity of *faillir* cannot be gratuitous and this, together with the accumulation of insults, which may be general or specific, indicates that it is Alfonso who is being criticized.

Once this has been established, the apparent praise in stanzas I and II can only be interpreted as *ironia*. The opening lines echo those of *Emperaire, per mi mezeis*, the earlier poem addressed to Alfonso:

> Emperaire, per mi mezeis,
> sai, quant vostra proez'acreis,
> no·m sui jes tarzatz del venir;
> que jois vos pais, e pretz vos creis
> e jovens vos ten baut e freis
> que·us fai vostra valor techir. (XXII, 1–6)

Emperor, since your prowess increases, I did not hesitate to come here of my own accord; for joy nourishes you and worth helps you to become greater, and youth keeps you happy and alert, for it makes your valour grow.

This reminder, in *Emperaire, per vostre prez*, of a previous request for patronage may in itself point to the fact that it was not forthcoming.[14] *Zo sabez*, an overstated affirmation of sincerity, may well be a signal to irony; similarly, the use of the modal auxiliary *dever* could be used as a signal to irony, for with the proper intonation it could emphasize the hypothetical nature of the propositions it introduces, particularly in the second instance, where Marcabru's use of the conditional deliberately weakens the assertive value of the proposition.

The final stanza and the *tornada* are similarly double-edged. They appear to praise, but Marcabru draws attention to his ironic intentions when he makes a further protestation of sincerity ('Per aquella fe qu'eu vos dei') which invokes a faith in Alfonso which is being called into question. By saying that it is he, the *joglar*, who is offering a bargain to Alfonso, the Emperor, Marcabru is reversing the usual, and probably real, relationship they must have had. He thus belittles Alfonso, who is ostensibly his patron, but he is also binding up one of the main themes of the poem, which is that Alfonso is not generous enough to Marcabru. The implication is that Marcabru was extremely generous in offering his services to Alfonso, but that Alfonso is not generous enough in return. The address to the Empress could be seen as a sincere appeal for her protection, but in the light of the irony in the rest of the poem, it seems likely that this too is *ironia*.

Marcabru, or the *joglar* performing this song, would no doubt have made it clear that the poem was *vituperatio* in the guise of *laudatio* and the audience would presumably have found it amusing, with the possible exception of Alfonso, of course, although it is hard to imagine a performance in front of him. Roncaglia rightly labelled this song 'il canto . . . della delusione'; it is also an example of a standard medieval rhetorical practice. By crediting Alfonso with qualities he manifestly does not possess, Marcabru highlights his short-comings; by apparently attacking immorality generally when in fact he has a specific target in mind, he mocks him relentlessly.

MARCABRU'S IRONIC SEXUAL METAPHORS

Useful as they are, the Latin rhetorical manuals do not provide an apparatus for discussing every instance of irony in Marcabru's poetry. This is the case whenever there is irony which involves sexual innuendo or obscenity, for the manuals specifically advise the avoidance of obscenity.[15] The question of obscenity and sexual metaphors in Marcabru's work is of some importance: first, because he alludes to sex so frequently, not to say obsessively; secondly, because the condemnation of sexual immorality is such an important part of his moral code; thirdly, because his allusions to sex are often ironic and consequently open to misunderstanding. However, discussing the irony of obscene innuendo raises some important problems.

First, and most obviously, what is obscenity? Secondly, what was considered obscene in the Middle Ages? Finally, what effect would obscenities have had on a medieval audience?

Most cultures attach some degree of taboo to explicit references to the sexual act or to the sex organs. The explicit designation of an organ or an act may be perfectly acceptable when used in private amatory language, but the same word may cause offence in public if some degree of decorum is expected. Obscenity might then be defined as any explicit designation of a sexual organ or act uttered under such circumstances that it might cause offence to someone present. Explicit references to sex are, however, rare, both in literature and in everyday speech, and more often than not a sexual part or act is designated with a metaphor or a euphemism. Once the euphemism or metaphor has been recuperated, it too is generally considered obscene, for it is the designation of the part of the body or act itself which is taboo, not just so-called 'vulgar' words. A distinction nevertheless has to be made between explicit obscenities and euphemisms or metaphors. Whereas an explicit obscenity leaves little room for ambiguity, euphemisms and metaphors are always ambiguous. They can be taken literally, thus observing conventional decorum, and they inevitably lead to irony as they are open to a 'knowing' reading and to a 'naïve' reading.[16]

To argue, as Per Nykrog does, that the medieval conception of obscenity was similar to our own is perhaps to tread on dangerous ground.[17] Is there one 'modern' notion of obscenity? Can we be sure of how a medieval audience might have reacted to any given obscenity or obscene metaphor? However, that a medieval notion of obscenity and degrees of what was considered obscene existed in the Middle Ages is beyond doubt. The striking absence of explicit obscenities in courtly literature is ample testimony to this: eroticism in the troubadour lyric or in the courtly romance is almost always suggested through euphemisms or metaphors.[18] The vocabulary of sex, if not an oblique reference to the act, was certainly taboo in certain types of literature. Guilhem IX and Cercamon may allude to obscenity when they talk of the need to avoid *parlar vilanamens* (VII, 31–6, 'speaking in a vile way') and *mot vila* (III, 32, 'vile words'). Guillaume de Lorris, in the *Roman de la Rose*, warns the lover against obscenity:

> Aprés gardes que tu ne dies
> ces orz moz ne ces ribaudies:
> ja por nomer vilainne chose
> ne doit ta bouche estre desclouse.
> Je ne tien pas a courtois homme
> qui orde chose et laide nome.   (2097–102)

Later, in the section composed by Jean de Meung, the lover reproaches Raison for her use of the word *coilles* ('balls'):

> Si ne vous tieng pas a courtoise
> quant ci m'avez coilles nomees
> qui ne sunt pas bien renomees
> en bouche a courtaise pucele.   (6898–901)

The lover thinks such things should be designated by a euphemism or metaphor ('gloser par quelque courtaise parole', line 6904). Raison riposts that one should call a spade a spade and she particularly singles out for mockery the use of metaphors and euphemisms by women (lines 7137–47). However, Raison's attitude would appear to be exceptional, for other medieval authors refer to the limits prescribed by their sense of decency, albeit sometimes ironically.[19] It is particularly striking that even in a genre which is notoriously scurrilous, such as the *fabliau*, explicit obscenities are comparatively uncommon:[20] there is a constant tendency, as there is now, to respect, and yet at the same time transgress, society's restrictions on references to sex by the use of metaphors and euphemisms, and as a result irony and obscene innuendo often go hand in hand.

The use of explicit obscenities in the Middle Ages would certainly have been calculated to shock some people in most circumstances. What of obscene metaphors? J. N. Adams singles out five factors that determine the reception of explicit obscenities and obscene metaphors in classical literature: the circumstances of utterance and the conventions of the literary genre, the attitude of the speaker to the act in question, the nature of the act, the sex of the speaker, the sex and age of the addressee.[21]

Under what circumstances, then, might a troubadour have chosen to run the risk of outraging some members of his audience with an obscene metaphor or euphemism? It is perhaps possible to define four broad areas where medieval authors might use obscene metaphors: in erotic contexts, in pornography, in burlesque or scatological texts, in moralizing poetry.[22] Of course, the tone and register of obscene metaphors will vary considerably from, say, an erotic poem to a moralizing poem and in any case these categories are not hard and fast. For example, where should the line be drawn between eroticism and pornography? Where does ridicule end and condemnation begin?

Marcabru's poetry clearly belongs to the moralizing register and contains a surprisingly large number of explicit obscenities.[23] He uses these obscenities to shock, to show up a vicious state for exactly what it is. More often than not, however, references to sex in his work take the form of ambiguous sexual metaphors. What is their effect and what do they contribute to his poetry?

The most common semantic field in Latin for metaphors designating the male organ is that of the pointed object or weapon; such metaphors are often accompanied by metaphors of striking or fighting which designate the sexual act.[24] In this respect, as in many others, Marcabru shows himself to be a willing heir to the Latin tradition:

> D'estoc breto
> ni de basto
> no sap om plus ni d'escrimir;
> qu'ieu fier autrui
> e·m gart de lui
> e no·is sap del mieu colp cobrir.　　(xvi, 31–6)

No man knows more than I of breton staff, stick or fencing; for I beat another and defend myself from him, and he does not know how to avoid my blows.

The metaphor of 'striking' with a 'stick' has aggressive overtones and it is interesting that the object of aggression here is masculine rather than feminine, as if the most important aspect of sex, for Marcabru, were the act of aggression against the husband or usual male partner of the woman, rather than any relationship with this woman. The phallus is frequently a symbol of aggression in Latin poetry and Marcabru's use of this motif is revealing of his attitude both to sex and to women. It may also help to explain some hitherto obscure lines:

> Si·ls gilos s'en van seguran
> e li guardador jauzion,
> ges egual no chant e respon,
> qu'ilh van a clardat e ses lum;
> quan vols, t'en pren ab eis lo broc.　　(ii, 16–20)

If the jealous husbands go away feeling safe, and the guardians are joyful, I do not sing the chant and response to the same tune, for they go there in daylight or in the dark; when you want to, he beats you with the stick itself.

> Maritz qui l'autrui con grata
> Ben pot saber que·l sieus pescha
> E mostra com hom li mescha,
> Qu'ab eis lo sieu fust lo bata.　　(xi, 49–52)

The husband who scratches the cunt of another man can indeed know that his own goes fishing and he shows how he is deceived, for he beats him with his own stick.

In each case the verb designating the sexual act is indicative of aggression and has a masculine object: intercourse with a woman is thus seen as an act of aggression against another male. There are, then, two levels of irony in these lines. The first stems from the fact that the words used (*broc, fust, bata*) do not have a primary sexual sense and the second from the substitution of one act for another which reduces the woman's rôle in the sexual act to that of a mere object shunted around between two men.[25]

Other semantic fields used by Marcabru for ironic sexual metaphors are also commonly used in Latin literature: for example, door, passage and hole metaphors to designate the female organs, and eating, drinking, scratching, rubbing, holding and squeezing metaphors, to designate the sexual act[26] However, if some of Marcabru's sexual metaphors belong to a tradition, others reflect his own times or even his own personal obsessions.

One image that seems to have appealed to Marcabru is that of fire. Although the metaphor of fire for lust is well attested in Latin literature, it appears with particular frequency in Marcabru's work:

> De nien sui chastiaire
> E de foudat sermonaire,
> Car pouis la flam'es nascuda
> Del fol drut e de la druda,
> Si·l fols art per l'abrasada,
> Non sui mal meire ni laire.   (v, 31–6)

In vain do I censure and preach about folly, for since the flame is born of the false lover and his mistress, if the fool burns for the burning woman, I am neither a bad harvester nor a robber.

> Fog porti sai
> et aigua lai
> ab que sai la flam'escantir.   (xvi, 52–4)

I carry the fire here and water there, with which I know how to put out the fire.

> D'autra manieira cogossos,
> Hi a rics homes e baros
> Qui las enserron dinz maios
> Qu'estrains non i posca intrar
> E tenon guirbautz als tisos
> Cui las comandon a gardar.   (xxix, 19–24)

There are rich men and barons who are cuckolds in a different manner: they shut them [their women] up in houses so that no stranger may enter, and they keep the churls whom they command to guard them beside the fire.

Marcabru

Aquest intr'en la cozina
Coitar lo fuoc el tizo
E beu lo fum de la tina
De si donz na Bonafo. (xxxi, 55–8)

That man goes into the kitchen to blow on the fire in the embers, and he drinks the perfume from the fountain of his lady Bonafo.

In some of these stanzas the fire or the hearth may on one level represent the comfort of the home. When considered together, however, there appears to be a consistent network of erotic fire imagery.[27] In one poem at least fire is explicitly linked with adultery:

Tant crem'en lo fuoc qu'ieu vos diu,*
La flama la bras'e·l caliu
C'ar de tant se son enferzit
Que bravas en son e braidiu
Las moillers e·il drut e·il marit. (viii, 26–30)

The flames, cinders and embers burn in the fire I am talking of to such an extent that now they have become so furious that wives have become brazen and lovers and husbands impetuous because of it.

Marcabru's fire imagery thus often suggests sexual innuendo, but to what effect? Perhaps the frequency of the fire metaphor is due to the fact that he is also quite deliberately evoking the fires of hell. In *Pus mos coratges* the link is obvious:

Homicidi e traïdor,
Simoniaic, encantador,
Luxurios e renovier,
Que vivon d'enujos mestier,
E cill que fan faitilhamens,
E las faitileiras pudens
Seran el fuec arden engau. (xl, 22–8)

Murderers, traitors, simoniacs, magicians, hedonists and usurers, who live off an evil profession, and those who practise witchcraft and stinking witches will all be equal in the roaring fire.

Whenever Marcabru alludes to fire there may well be two levels of ironic meaning: one suggesting lust and another evoking the fires of hell. This implicit linking of lust and hell adds considerable force to Marcabru's condemnation of promiscuity.

Although sexual metaphors concerning hunting are common in Latin, they also clearly reflect the milieu Marcabru lived in:

En l'autrui broill
chatz cora·m voill
e fatz mos dos canetz glatir,
e·l tertz sahus

eis de rahus
bautz e ficatz senes mentir.

Mos alos es
en tal deves
res mas ieu non s'en pot jauzir.   (XVI, 37–45)

I hunt in another man's hunting ground whenever I want, and make my two little dogs bark, and the third bloodhound rushes forward, bold and fixed on the prey, I assure you.

My allod is so well defended that no man other than myself can enjoy it.

It does not take a great stretch of the imagination to give these lines a sexual sense. The irony would no doubt have been particularly acute for men in Marcabru's audience for whom the private hunting ground (*broill*) and the allod would have been as sacred as their wives' fidelity.[28] Marcabru may also use the hunting metaphor in *Pois la fuoilla*:

Cest trai del mieill la briola
Plen'al maitin et al ser.   (XXXVIII, 29–30)

This man steals the well-stocked hunting ground [?] from the best man in the morning and in the evening.

If *briola* has the same sense as *broill*, Marcabru is again playing on the notion of the churl hunting on somebody else's land and drawing implicit parallels between this crime and the crime the churl commits when he sleeps with another man's wife.

   Not all sexual metaphors can be classified into commonly used semantic fields as easily as those discussed so far. Like many writers, Marcabru often coins his own sexual metaphors, for example:

Puois qu'ieu vei qu'ella non crei castiador,
Anz de totz malvatz pren patz, cals l'a groissor,*
A la den torna soven la leng'on sent la dolor.   (XXIV, 16–18)

Since I see that she does not believe the one who reproaches her, rather she satisfies herself with all the wicked ones, whichever one has the biggest, the tongue often returns to the tooth that aches.

In the last line of this stanza Marcabru may well be playing on a proverb. Compare Morawski, *Proverbes*, 1039, 'la vet la lange ou la denz duet'. However, the previous line makes it clear that this line is heavily laden with sexual innuendo. Toothache, here, is a metaphor for lust; it is painful and impossible to ignore if one is afflicted. By using the proverb, Marcabru shows off his linguistic dexterity and by linking toothache and lust he intensifies his invective.

   Marcabru again coins his own ironic sexual metaphors in his *estornel* poems:

56

Marcabru

De fin'amor dezirada
A una flor pic vairada*
Plus que d'autruna pauzada.
Paucs fols fai tost gran folia.
Perdo·l grat
De l'abat
Saint Privat:
M'ai pensat
Ses cujat
Si·m ditz: mat,
Que l'amors embria.   (xxv, 67–77)

Desired with pure love, she has a changing piebald flower, more so than any other prostitute. The small fool soon commits a great folly. I pardon the gratitude of the abbot of St Privat; I thought without conjecture that if she said to me 'checkmate', love would ensue.

Az una part es partida
Ma fin'amistatz plevida;
Son joc revit, si·l m'envida.
Auzels, per ta conoisensa,
So·l diguatz
Qu'en un glatz
Lev'e jatz,
Desiratz:*
Er l'abatz
An sasatz*
Que n'ajam lezensa.   (xxvi, 45–55)

My pledged, noble love has gone off somewhere else; I revive his game, if he invites me to do it. Bird, with your wisdom, tell him this: the desired one rises and falls in an instant; now may the abbot go away satisfied, as we have the leisure for it.

The interpretation of these stanzas is problematic. According to Roncaglia, the 'abbot of St Privat' has an obscene meaning, although he does not say what it is.[29] It is, of course, possible that Marcabru is referring to a real abbot, but if so, any personal allusion is lost to us for ever. However, it would be entirely in keeping with his constant play on words, his use of ironic sexual metaphors, and with his sense of humour, if there were also a hidden, obscene meaning here. As with the English word 'privates', Occitan *privat* could evoke the sexual organs, and it is therefore tempting to see the 'abbot of St Privat' as a metaphor for the penis, particularly when certain visual similarities between an abbot's mitre and the male organ are considered.[30] This interpretation concords perfectly with the sexual innuendo of the *flor pic vairada*, and with the use of the word *pauzada*. The speaker here is the eager but immoral lover who is sending a message, with the starling, to his lady, who is in fact a prostitute. When he says he pardons 'the gratitude of the abbot of St Privat', he might mean that he always gives in to his lust. Of course, if this interpretation is accepted, the term *fin'amor*, in the first line of the stanza, is used with considerable irony.

This interpretation of the first stanza quoted would seem to be confirmed by the second stanza. The lover/narrator's 'lady' is replying to his message. She echoes the irony of the immoral lover talking of *fin'amor* when she refers to her lust as 'Ma fin'amistatz plevida'. The 'desired one' rising and falling is very probably a metaphor for the sexual act and it would thus seem likely that *abatz* here is also a metaphor for the penis.

Several of Marcabru's *senhals* also deserve mention as ironic sexual metaphors. A *senhal* is usually complimentary because it designates an intimate friend or a lady. Ruth Harvey has shown that Marcabru's *senhals* are often ironic because they are preceded by honorific titles such as *na* or *si dons*, even though they are far from complimentary.[31] The meaning of some of his *senhals*, such as *Cropa fort*, 'Sturdy-rump' (XXXIV, 41), is unequivocal, but often Marcabru adds to the irony of using *senhals* in this way by making their connotations ambivalent, for example:

> Aquest intr'en la cozina
> Coitar lo fuoc el tizo
> E beu lo fum de la tina
> De si donz na Bonafo. (XXXI, 55–8)

That man goes into the kitchen to blow on the fire in the embers, and he drinks the perfume from the fountain of his lady Bonafo.

Deconstructed into its components 'bona fo', the *senhal* would appear to mean 'she was good', or, picking up the imagery of the fountain, 'good fountain'.[32] The honorific *si donz*, which precedes the *senhal*, serves to emphasize how unseemly the lady's behaviour is by drawing attention to her rank. This *senhal* is far from complimentary; on the contrary, its ironic ambivalence considerably enhances the satire of this poem.

The meaning of two other *senhals* with erotic overtones is harder to ascertain:

> Jovens someilla,
> greu prendra mais revel,
> e par q'espeilla
> lo seignor Daucadel;
> tot jorn conseilla
> ab son Don Chaut-Morsel;
> prop del tesel,
> Malvestatz li pendeilla
> al capairo. (XXXII, 73–81)

Youth sleeps and will only stir itself to resistance with difficulty now, and it seems that it is imitating lord Daucadel; every day he whispers with his Sir Chaut-Morsel; near the hook Wickedness hangs from his hood.

Marcabru

Peter Ricketts argues that *tessel* and *capairo* are metaphors for the male organ and the foreskin, that Chaut-Morsel is a *senhal* meaning 'bouchée chaude' and that the *senhal* Daucadel 'est fondé, sans doute, sur l'idée de l'oie qu'on bourre de nourriture pour obtenir du foie gras'.[33] If this interpretation is correct, and I believe it is, I cannot agree with him when he further argues that Marcabru is referring here to 'la pratique solitaire de l'onanisme', for the imagery of the two *senhals* would then be meaningless. For the imagery to make sense, the only sexual activity that can be postulated here is fellatio and given that both *senhals* are explicitly male, the liaison must be homosexual. If the stanza is hard to understand and the irony heavily veiled, this is hardly surprising, given the nature of the aspersions cast.

There are at least sixty ironic sexual metaphors designating some form of sexual act in Marcabru's forty-two poems, at least thirty for the penis and at least fifteen for the female organs. It is, of course, difficult to produce precise statistics, but with an average of at least two such metaphors in each poem, it is clear they make an important contribution to the tone of Marcabru's poetry. Moreover, as thirteen of Marcabru's poems also contain explicit obscenities (II, IV, VI, XI, XII[bis], XVII, XVIII, XXIV, XXXI, XXXVI, XXXVII, XXXVIII and XLI), it is fair to say that sex is a subject which obsesses him. He uses ironic sexual metaphors satirically. It is difficult to gauge accurately just how offensive any given sexual metaphor might have been, but it is perhaps fair to conjecture that there would have been three main effects. First, his ironic sexual metaphors are undoubtedly intended to shock in order to show up a vicious state of affairs for precisely what it is. Secondly, Marcabru's ironic sexual metaphors are often humorous and they thus contribute to his criticism of immoral people, for the audience laugh at them rather than with them. Finally, in a moralizing context, an ironic sexual metaphor highlights hypocrisy by designating a reprehensible act with an apparently innocent word or expression; Marcabru's use of metaphors and euphemisms is thus often tantamount to a condemnation of the way the courtly world he is describing hypocritically masks its promiscuity.

Of course, certain acts would have been more reprehensible than others and it seems likely that references to oral sex, comparisons to animals, implications of homosexuality and *senhals* in which real people may have been identifiable would have been particularly offensive. As Marcabru's poetry probably contains all these elements, it is hard not to suspect that he often deliberately attempts to shock his audience as much as possible.[34] His propensity to shock and outrage is an important element of his personality as he chooses to present it to his audience; it also considerably enhances the entertainment value of his poetry. It is perhaps difficult to understand why patrons and audiences should have enjoyed hearing Marcabru's outraged tirades, and yet enjoy them they must have done, for his popularity and influence are well attested. The obscenities and ironic sexual metaphors strike a humorous note, induce a feeling of moral righteousness and at the same time provide the thrill of the taboo, of transgressing accepted rules.

Troubadours and irony

There is perhaps one more general point worth making about Marcabru's use of obscenities and ironic sexual metaphors. He often portrays sex as an act of masculine aggression perpetrated against another man, whilst generally seeing women's sexuality as either completely passive or utterly voracious, and he is clearly preoccupied with the male organ, its size and its performance. All these are elements which are typical of pornography.[35] Whilst there can be no doubt that Marcabru's attitude to promiscuity is highly critical, it is difficult not to wonder, on another level, whether he was not subconsciously titillated by constantly talking about it. My impression is that the man behind the texts was simultaneously repelled and fascinated by illicit sex, torn between the condemnation of certain activities and a troubling obsession with describing them.

SIGNALS TO IRONY IN MARCABRU'S POETRY

Medieval rhetoricians do not consider the possibility that signals to irony may be present in a text and always refer to detection through delivery. Knox and Green have shown, however, that superfluous affirmations of sincerity, exaggerated professions of belief and the use of verbs such as *credo* in Latin and *cuidier* in Old French are often employed as signals to irony.[36] As Marcabru is the first troubadour to be studied here in detail, it is perhaps appropriate to focus briefly on how signals to irony function in his poems.

Marcabru's use of superfluous affirmations of sincerity is apparent in *Emperaire, per vostre prez:*

> Emperaire, per vostre prez,
> e per la proeza qu'avez,
> sui a vos venguz, zo sabez,
> e no m'en dei ges penedir. (XXIII, 1–4)

Emperor, because of your worth and because of the prowess you have, I have come here to serve you, mark my words, and I ought not to repent of this at all.

The tone of this poem is ironic throughout and Marcabru makes extensive use of the 'false praise topos'. *Zo sabez*, which literally means 'this you know', but which might be translated more appropriately by an idiomatic expression such as 'mark my words', adds nothing to the meaning of the sentence. It is a superfluous affirmation of sincerity and therefore draws attention to the proposition it purports to reinforce whilst simultaneously undermining it because of its redundancy.

Similar techniques occur elsewhere in Marcabru's work, for example:

> Doncs no pairejon li derrier,
> en totz bos sens ab los faducs?
> el og! si Cozer e Sarlucs
> valon Toloz'e Monpeslier! (III, 33–6)

So, will people now not take after their forefathers in all ways, both good and foolish?
Yes, indeed, if Cozère and Carlux are worth as much as Toulouse and Montpellier.

The question in lines 33–4 is ironic because it implies a proposition, that is that people do now take after their forefathers, which is undermined through the comparison with another proposition which is patently absurd, that is that two completely insignificant towns, of which many people might not have heard, are worth as much as Toulouse and Montpellier.[37] Why does Marcabru reinforce his statement with a superfluous affirmation of sincerity, *el og*? This redundant overstatement was probably intended as a signal to irony, as a way of prodding the audience in the right direction. In this case the intended meaning communicated to the initiated is that people do not now take after their forefathers; in other words, Marcabru is reiterating one of his favourite contentions, that is that moral standards have declined. There may also be a veiled reference to the bastard children of noble women and their servants whom Marcabru so despises and whom he claims to see all around him; if people no longer take after their forefathers, this may be because their parentage is not quite what it seems.

In *Hueymais dey esser alegrans* (xxxiv), a superfluous affirmation of sincerity again acts as a signal to irony:

> v Ja Dieus no·l sia perdonans
> Qui las vol onrar ni servir,   30
> Estas putas ardens cremans
> Pejors que ieu no·us saubra dir;
> Tan lor sap bo lo clau copar,
> Que non hi guardon dreg ni tort,
> Mas selh que mielhs las sap ronsar!   35
>
> vi Qui anc fon prezats ni amans
> Per dompnas, ben s'en deu gequir!
> Qu'aytan s'en aura us truans
> O mais, si mais li pot bastir;*
> Et ieu poiri'o ben proar   40
> Per ma domna na Cropa fort
> Mas ja no la vuelh decelar.
>
> vii Messatge[s] cortes, ben parlans,
> Vai t'en en Urgel ses falhir,
> E sias del vers despleyans   45
> A'n Cabrieira, que lo remir,
> E potz li dir senes gabar
> Qu'en tal loc ai tornat ma sort
> On elh poiria pro muzar.

v

May God not be forgiving to anyone who wants to honour or serve them, these burning, ardent whores who are worse than I can say; they like striking the nail so much that they look at neither right nor wrong, but only at the man who knows best how to lay them on their backs.

VI

He who was ever esteemed or loved by ladies must indeed give this up. For a scoundrel will have just as much from them, or more, if he can get more; and I could indeed prove this through my lady Sturdy-rump, but I do not want to reveal her identity.

VII

Oh, courtly, eloquent messenger, go to Urgel without fail and recite my poem to lord Cabrieira, so that he might contemplate it, and you can say this to him, without boasting, that I have placed my destiny in the hands of someone before whom he could wait in vain for a long time.

Marcabru insults the 'lady' he purports to court in stanza VI in no uncertain terms. First, he designates her with an unflattering *senhal*, and secondly, he implies that he can prove the existence of all the debauchery he describes in stanza V by citing her as an example. In stanza VII, Marcabru asks a *joglar* to assure the dedicatee of the poem, the lord Cabrieira,[38] that he has placed his 'destiny in the hands of someone before whom he [Cabrieira] could wait in vain for a long time'. In other words, Marcabru is maintaining that the lady he is courting would not listen to the entreaties of any other suitor. However, given that he has insulted his lady and all but accused her of being one of 'these burning, ardent whores', his ostensible trust of her in stanza VII must be ironic and *senes gabar* (line 47), a superfluous affirmation of sincerity, may well therefore be a signal to this irony. Marcabru is telling Cabrieira about a lady who he believes will not keep him waiting too long at all! If a real lady were recognizable in the *senhal*, Marcabru's poem must have been particularly inflammatory, his irony unusually acerbic even by his standards.

If Marcabru uses superfluous or exaggerated affirmations of sincerity, as signals to irony, what of his use of the verb *cuidar*? According to John Marshall, the Occitan verb *cuidar* often means 'to imagine' or 'to intend to do something (which one fails to accomplish)'.[39] Clearly, the verb can give these senses, but perhaps a finer distinction should be made between denotation and connotation if the use of the verb is to be understood properly, particularly in Marcabru's poetry.

Unless *cuidar* is used intransitively or the infinitive as a noun, it introduces a proposition. In some cases it serves to affirm this proposition and it would thus seem that its semantic denotation is 'to believe/think something is so':

> Qui ab fals'amor dentelha
> se mezeys me cuich que·s tuoilla
> e camja per autrui pelha
> sa dreytureira despuoilla.
>
> (Bernart de Venzac, IVᵃ, 25–8)

I believe that the man who consorts with false love steals from himself and he changes his rightful attire for another's clothes.

> Car soven, so cug, badalha
> Qi s'aten a l'autrui be.
>
> (Cercamon, VIII, 26–7)

For I believe that the man who depends on another's wealth is often wasting his time.

> Mais vuelh trenta dezonors
> q'un'onor, si lieys mi tuelh,
> q'ieu suy hom d'aital natura,
> no vuelh l'onor que·l pro lays.
> Ni ges no·m laissa·l paors,
> don mos cors non s'asegura,
> qu'ades cug qu'autre la·m tuelha.
>
> (Peire Rogier, I, 36–42)

I would rather be dishonoured thirty times than have one sign of honour, if it takes her away from me, for I am the kind of man who does not want the honour a worthy man casts aside. Nor does fear leave me, wherefore my heart is uncertain, for now I believe another takes her from me.

More frequently, however, *cuidar* introduces a proposition which the speaker may not wish to affirm, but which he or she either explicitly denies or implicitly undermines. When the proposition is explicitly denied, it is clear that the semantic denotation of *cuidar* is still 'to believe/think something is so':

> Ai, las! tan cuidava saber
> d'amor, e tan petit en sai!
>
> (Bernart de Ventadorn, XLIII, 9–10)

Alas! I thought I knew so much about love, and I know so little.

In these lines Bernart says he believed something to be so at one time but that he now realizes he was wrong. The denial of the proposition which *cuidar* introduces is performed not by the verb itself, but by another clause.

When the proposition it introduces is implicitly undermined, *cuidar* still denotes 'to believe/think something is so', but it draws attention to the fact that the proposition it introduces is a proposition, in other words a matter of opinion and not a statement of fact. It introduces into the text the possibility that what is believed is not necessarily so, as in the following instances from Marcabru:

> Tals cuid'esser ben gardaire
> De la so'e de l'autrui laire.   (V, 25–6)

Such a man thinks he can guard his own wife and steal another's.

> E segon que ditz Salamos,
> Non podon cill pejors lairos
> Acuillir d'aquels compaignos
> Qui fant la noirim cogular,
> Et aplanon los guirbaudos
> E cujon lor fills piadar.   (XXIX, 25–30)

And according to what Solomon says, these men could not welcome worse thieves into their houses than those companions, who bastardize the offspring, and they caress the little churls and think they are pitying their own sons.

> Non puosc sofrir qu·als moilleratz
> Non diga lor forfaitz saubutz;
> Non sai la cals auctoritatz
> Lor mostra c'om los apel drutz;
> Semblan fant de l'ase cortes,
> C'ab son seignor cuidet bordir,
> Cant lo vic trepar ab sos ches. (xxxix, 50–6)

I cannot stand not telling husbands about their notorious crimes; I do not know what authority tells them that they can be called lovers; they are like the courtly donkey who thought he could dance with his master when he saw him playing with his dogs.

In each of these examples a proposition is introduced by *cuidar* which someone believes to be true: the denotation of the verb is thus still 'to believe/think something is so'. The connotation, on the other hand, is that the proposition is not true. There is an opposition between intended and pretended meaning in the statements following *cuidar* which might be tabulated thus:

Poem	Proposition (pretended meaning)	Intended meaning
v	He can guard his wife and steal another man's	He cannot
xxix	The churls are the barons' sons	They are not
xxxix	The donkey may dance with its lord	It may not

In each case the use of the verb *cuidar* makes the opposition possible; it is thus acting as a signal to irony. Although it obviously does mean 'to imagine', 'to be in error in thinking that' or 'to intend to do something (which one fails to accomplish)', these meanings of *cuidar* are always implied, depending on connotation rather than denotation, and its literal meaning is always 'to believe/think something is so'.[40]

It is, of course, possible for any troubadour to use *cuidar* as a signal to irony, but no word can per se become a signal to irony: irony always depends on context and what may be a signal in one context may not be in another. Nevertheless, it is noteworthy that Marcabru uses *cuidar* as a signal to irony with remarkable consistency. He uses the verb transitively twenty-eight times in his extant poems, and in all but five cases it acts as a signal to irony.[41] Moreover, these five exceptions confirm the rule, for in four of them Marcabru uses the verb negatively, for example:

> Non cuich que·l segles dur gaire
> Segon qu'escriptura di. (xvii, 3–4)

I do not think the world can last much longer, according to what the scriptures say.

64

When used negatively *cuidar* explicitly denies a proposition and so it cannot act as a signal to irony. The hypothesis that Marcabru habitually uses *cuidar* as a signal to irony is also confirmed by the fact that when he wishes to introduce a proposition which he does not intend to undermine through irony or when he simply wants to indicate that someone rightly believes something, he uses the verbs *creire* and *saber*.[42]

Textual signals to irony are relatively frequent in Marcabru's poetry. One reason for this is that he is a satirist: he wants his audience to understand the message he tries to convey and as irony can nearly always lead to a misunderstanding, he sometimes feels the need to push his listeners in the right direction.

In many instances, however, obvious textual signals to irony could easily spoil the effect the ironist is striving for; the audience's sense of satisfaction as it laughs at those who take the irony at face value must not be destroyed. One area where obvious textual signals to irony would clearly be detrimental to the text is parody. There may, however, be signals to irony of a different order in parodies.

MARCABRU AND PARODY

When a poet adopts a style or a persona which is recognizably not his own and which he proceeds to undermine, this may well be a signal to the fact that the text is a parody. In *D'aisso lau Dieu* (xvi), the *estornel* poems (xxv/xxvi) and *L'autrier jost'una sebissa* (xxx), Marcabru appears to be parodying with satirical intention types of poetry he would usually condemn. I shall not dwell on these texts as they are among the most frequently studied in Marcabru's corpus and their interpretation is now relatively uncontroversial. I propose, rather, to examine a form of parody in Marcabru's poetry that has attracted less critical attention, namely his parodies of courtly nature openings.

Marcabru's attitude to nature is closely linked to what he himself calls *trobar naturau*, in Linda Paterson's words, 'the art of composing according to an understanding of what is natural and unnatural, and of the moral truths nature reveals'.[43] Although Marcabru's nature imagery is not totally consistent, it is possible to talk about general trends: images of nature in his poetry imply a moral order and he often attributes to certain creatures inherent moral qualities. What are his ideas on nature? More particularly, what is his attitude towards the seasons?

On the whole Marcabru seems to dislike summer and to prefer winter. He likes to sing in winter when the cold quietens the outpourings of creatures he associates with pride and decadence;

> Lo vers comens quan vei del fau
> ses foilla lo cim e·l branquill,
> c'om d'auzel ni raina non au
> chan ni grazill,

ni o fara jusqu'al temps soau
que·l vais brondill. (XXXIII, 1–6)

I start the verse when I see the branch and the top of the beech tree without leaves, for neither song nor croaking of bird or frog is heard, nor will it be until the sweet season when the nut tree has new leaves.

In *Per l'aura freida* (XXXVI), the absence of the distractions afforded by summer allows him to concentrate on more important issues:

I Per l'aura freida que guida
 L'invern qu'es tant plens d'iror,
 L'auzeill qu'us no·n brai ni·n crida
 Sotz foilla ni per verdor,
 Car l'estiu, a bell'aizida, 5
 Mesclon lor joia certana.

II Non auch chant ni retentida
 Ni non vei brondel ab flor,
 Empero si ai auzida
 Una estraigna clamor, 10
 De Joi que·is plaing, ses ufana,
 Cui Malvestatz disciplina.

I
Because of the cold wind which guides winter which is so full of anger, the birds, of which not one sings or cries out under the leaf or in the greenery, because summer rests, adulterate their certain joy.

II
I do not hear the songs or the sound of singing, nor do I see a branch in flower, but I have heard a strange protest from Joy, who complains, without pretence, as Evil torments him.

In *Al prim comens* (IV), he thinks that true prowess can only be seen and tested in winter, that summer corrupts people who might otherwise be steadfast:

I Al prim comens de l'ivernaill
 Qand plovon del bosc li glandutz,
  Vuoill c'om s'engaill
 De Proeza, que non tressaill,
 E que n'esti'amanoïtz 5
 Aissi cum s'era·l temps herbutz.

II Ladoncs quecs avols hom se plaing
 Qand ve·l temps frei e las palutz,
  Contra·l regaing,
 Que·is avil'e met en bargaing 10
 Qu'en estiu que non es vestitz
 Pot anar d'una peilla nutz.

Marcabru

I

At the very beginning of winter, when acorns rain from the trees, I want men to vie with each other in Prowess, without faltering, and that they should be prepared for this as if it were the grassy season.

II

Then the vile man complains when he sees the cold weather and the marshes appearing instead of the late harvest, for he debases himself and offers himself up for sale, because in the summer when he is not dressed, he can go about without a tunic.

In *Pois la fuoilla* (xxxviii), Marcabru expresses his opinion on the seasons explicitly and at length:

I Pois la fuoilla revirola
  Que vei d'entre·ls cims cazer,
  Que·l vens deromp e degola,
  Que no·is pot mais sostener,
  Mais pretz lo freich temporau   5
  Que l'estiu plen de gandill
  Don nais puti'et enveia.

II Lo pics e la rossignola
  Tornon lor chant en tazer,
  Si·s fa·l gais e l'auriola,   10
  Don l'inverns fai son plazer;
  E l'orgoills torn'en canau
  Per garssos plens de grondill
  Qu'en estiu contradenteia.

III Graissans ni serps que s'amola 15
  No·m fant espaven ni mau,
  Mosca ni tavans que vola,
  Escaravait ni bertau,
  Aquest malvatz volatill*
  Non sent bruir ni oler,   20
  Don francs inverns nos neteia.

I

Since the leaf, which I see falling from among the treetops, and which the wind tears off and decapitates so that it cannot hang on any longer, twists in the air, I prefer the cold season to the summer, which is full of subterfuges, and which gives birth to whoredom and lust.

II

The woodpecker and the female nightingale become quiet, as do the jay and female oriole with which the winter does its pleasure; and pride, which bears its teeth in summer, falls into the gutter because of surly churls.

III

Neither swollen toad nor snake frightens me or harms me; flying insect nor horsefly in flight, beetle nor hornet; I neither hear nor smell any of these evil flying things of which honest winter cleanses us.

Not only is winter seen here as *francs* and summer associated with 'whoredom and lust', but the creatures Marcabru uses to depict summer are seen to be guilty of the worst crime of all in his eyes, cross-breeding.[44] In the light of these lines, any poem where Marcabru apparently likes summer, or prefers it to winter, may contain elements of incongruity or contradictions that might indicate irony, and such poems should perhaps be scrutinized closely.

The nature opening is conventional from the start of the troubadour tradition. Although Marcabru is by no means alone in using winter or autumn openings, it is a testimony to the fact that spring openings are the most common and popular variety of nature opening that 'début printanier' has so often been used as a blanket term by critics: spring and summer are understandably the favoured seasons of courtly poets. In the nature opening the seasons usually reflect how the lover feels: happy because it is summer and he is in love or unhappy because it is winter and his love is unrequited. A common variation on this is a contrast between the season and the lover's feelings: he is unhappy even though it is summer or happy despite the weather. Alternatively, the lover might feel moved to sing by nature or completely indifferent to it. With its many variations the nature opening is a common motif and an integral part of the poetics of *fin'amor*.[45] Whenever a nature opening in Marcabru's poetry is ironic, it is thus likely that he is deliberately parodying a courtly convention, adopting a style, only to hold it up for mockery.

When Marcabru claims to like summer, this is frequently followed by an abrupt change of mood:

> Assatz m'es bel del temps essuig,
> Quand la douz gem a la fonz bruig
> E son li prat reverdezit,
> Pesa·m de Joven car s'en fuig,
> C'a penas troba qui·l convit. (VIII, 1–5)

The dry season is very pleasing to me, when the spring groans and the fountain makes a noise, and the meadows are green again, I am unhappy about youth because it flees, for it can hardly find anyone to welcome it.

Throughout the rest of the poem Marcabru bemoans the decline of moral values and criticizes the people whom he holds responsible. The switch from feeling happy because of the summer to despairing of 'fleeing youth' is so abrupt and crude that it is as if Marcabru cannot bear to make any concessions to courtly taste at all. The two emotions described here are clearly incompatible and it would thus seem likely that the nature opening is ironic.

Similar switches in mood probably indicate irony in other poems:

> Hueymais dey esser alegrans
> Pus l'aura doussa vey venir
> *Et* auch lays e voutas e chans
> Dels auzelhs que·m fan esbaudir;
> Lo gen[s] temps me fai alegrar,
> Mas per Joven me desconort

68

Marcabru

Quar totz jorns lo vey sordeyar.
D'una ren suy meravelhans
Qu'ades vey granar e florir
Escassetatz, oc! et Enjans.   (xxxiv, 1–10)

Henceforth I must be happy since I see the gentle wind coming and hear songs, chirpings and melodies of birds, which make me joyful; the noble season makes me happy, but I am disconsolate because of youth, for I see it getting worse every day.

I am amazed by one thing: that now I see avarice and cheating growing and flowering, yes!

Pois l'inverns d'ogan es anatz
E·l douz temps floritz es vengutz,
De moutas guisas pels plaissatz
Aug lo refrim d'auzels menutz;
Li prat vert e·il vergier espes
M'ant si fait ab joi esbaudir,
Per qu'ie·m sui de chant entremes.

Totz lo segles es encombratz
Per un albre que·i es nascutz,
Autz e grans, brancutz e foillatz,
Et a meravilla cregutz.   (xxxix, 1–11)

Since this year's winter has departed and the gentle flowery season is upon us, I hear the refrain of the little birds sung in many ways along the hedgerows; the green meadows and the lush orchards have made me so happy with joy that for this reason I have undertaken to sing.

The whole world has been taken over by a tree that was born there, tall and large with branches and leaves, and it has grown miraculously.

In both these poems the switch in mood indicates that the spring opening is intended as irony and parody. The irony in each case is reinforced by the fact that immediately after the spring opening, the growth of evil is described in terms reminiscent of descriptions of spring and burgeoning nature: avarice and cheating grow and flower and the evil tree is covered in branches and leaves.

The opening of A l'alena (11) is equally sophisticated:

i   A l'alena del vent doussa
que Dieus nos tramet, no sai d'on,
ai lo cor de joy sazion
contra la dousor del frescum
quan li prat son vermelh a groc.   5

ii   Belh m'es quan son ombriu li mon,
e·ls auzels desotz la verdon
mesclon lurs critz ab lo chanton,
e quascus, ab la votz que an,
jauzis son parelh, en son loc.   10

69

III   De say sen um pauc de feton,
      que lai torna·l pel al bussa:
      qu'encaritz son li guasta-pa,
      quais per elh son gardat li don,
      qu'estrayns mas lo senher no·y toc.   15

I

With the breath of the sweet wind, which God sends us, I know not from where, my heart is sated with joy before the sweet coolness, when the meadows are scarlet and yellow.

II

It pleases me when the mountains are shady and the birds underneath the greenery mix their cries with their singing, and each one, with his own voice, enjoys his mate in the place where it is most fitting.

III

From here I can smell a slight stench, which over there sets a man's groin on fire [?], for the cuckolders are favoured and so the ladies [?] are guarded by them so that no stranger, except the lord of the house, may touch them.

Marcabru appears to be enjoying the coolness of late summer here. The light, delicate tone and the soft, rounded rhymes (-on, -um, -an) combine with the sensuous images of soft breezes, cool meadows and shady mountains to create an atmosphere of languid well-being. The spectacle of all the birds with their partners introduces an element of erotic expectation. Suddenly, in the third stanza, the spell is broken. Marcabru weaves this change in mood into the images he has been using: the wind which he had found so sweet and refreshing in the opening stanza now paradoxically brings with it a stench which kindles lust. The discreet, but erotic, overtones of the word *jauzir* are juxtaposed to crude explicitness. Moreover, the rest of the poem continues in the same vein and the idyllic mood and setting of the opening are entirely forgotten. This nature opening is a parody of the conventional spring opening of the courtly *canso*. Quite apart from the comic effect which the spectacle of Marcabru, or the *joglar* performing the song, imitating the performance of a conventional nature opening might have had, the force of the following invective would have been considerably intensified. He is linking the *gausta-pa* and the *senher*, the men he despises, to the season he despises and he is undermining the conventions of the poetry they use to mask their immorality.

It is easy to see why Marcabru should parody conventional nature openings. What better way to attack a society he considers immoral than to satirize the conventions of its poetry, particularly when that poetry seems, in Marcabru's view at least, to have played such an important rôle in the maintenance of the hypocrisy he so condemns? Marcabru's attitude towards courtly society predisposes him towards using the conventions of courtly poetry ironically, and this, together with his attitude towards nature, which tends to go against courtly platitudes, accounts for the high frequency of ironic nature openings in his work.

Marcabru

When Marcabru parodies the conventional nature opening, the parody is usually only sustained for one stanza, two at the most, but as with *D'aisso lau Dieu* (xvi), the *estornel* poems (xxv/xxvi) and *L'autrier jost' una sebissa* (xxx), the poems which are sustained parodies, the effect of the parody can only be fully appreciated if performances of the songs are imagined.

If he was to be successful in the courtly arena, each troubadour had to ensure that his poems bore the mark of his own stage personality, which may or may not have coincided with his real-life personality. Otherwise, it would not be possible to distinguish the work of different poets, and no professional performer, or troubadour composing poems for public performance, can have relished the thought of having his work confused with that of another poet.[46] In Marcabru's poems the presence of what Vincent Pollina calls 'a strong and unforgettable author-*persona*' is pervasive to say the least.[47] Indeed, although he tells us virtually nothing about himself, Marcabru's personality, as presented to us in his poetry, can make other troubadours seem weak and insipid in comparison: he goes out of his way to insult his audience, accusing people of immoral or deviant sexual practices and meanness. His *vidas* are an indication of just how notorious he was:

E fo mout cridatz et ausitz pel mon, e doptatz per sa lengua; car el fo tan maldizens que, a la fin, lo desfeiron li castelan de Guian[a], de cui avia dich mout gran mal.

(*A*, §6)

And he was talked of and heard all over the world, and feared because of his tongue; because he was so slanderous, in the end, the castellans of Guyenne, of whom he had spoken badly, killed him.

We shall never know if Marcabru really met the end which the scribe of manuscript *A* attributes to him, but a reading of his poems certainly makes such a death credible. As if to add to his flamboyant flouting of convention, Marcabru constantly uses his name when he is at his most provocative and outrageous, deliberately making sure that neither the name nor the image of himself he is presenting is forgotten.[48]

There are obvious reasons why Marcabru should apparently risk making enemies in this way; he is attempting to make his style instantly recognizable and his name acts as a kind of copyright. As far as we know, Marcabru was a professional troubadour and *joglar*. He may have had other professional activities, other sources of income, but he could still not afford to have his songs passed off as anyone else's.[49] He himself points out that no one should try to tamper with his songs (IX, 1–4); using his name is a further safeguard.

As a *joglar*, Marcabru's main function would have been to entertain an audience and given that his chosen subject matter is not, at first glance, ideal material for this, he has recourse to all kinds of devices to enhance the dramatic qualities of his work and to make his moralizing pill easier to swallow. He might illustrate his point of view with little scenarios in which real people may have been recognizable (poems xxxi and xxxii), or ironically praise a great lord or lady (poems XXIII and XXXIV); he could introduce ironic sexual metaphors to make his audience laugh, or seek to impress with his formal, rhythmic or rhetorical dexterity; alternatively, he might parody the conventions of courtly poetry, again to make his audience laugh.

Whenever Marcabru chose to parody a convention taken from courtly poetry, such as the nature opening, the humour of this would have been sharpened by the fact that the audience would probably have been familiar with Marcabru's usual stance and with the personality he usually presented. The spectacle of Marcabru, the virulent moralist, noted for his vulgar and violent language, imitating a pining courtly lover inspired to sing by the twittering birds and leafy boughs of spring must have been hysterically funny.

MARCABRU'S IRONY AND THE INTERTEXT

Marcabru's taste for parody indicates that he felt himself to be part of a group of poets. Even if he casts himself in the rôle of critic of other troubadours, he clearly writes from within the troubadour tradition and he participates in the 'dialectic' of *trobar*. On several occasions he goes further than criticizing types of poets or parodying conventional devices and genres and actually names, or has an exchange with, another poet. Such poems are heavily laden with irony, at the expense both of the poets concerned, namely Alegret (XI), Ugo Catola (VI), Audric del Vilar (XX/XXbis) and Jaufre Rudel (XV), and of their work. I propose to focus on two of these texts, first, in order to suggest that Marcabru, who, like Bernart de Ventadorn, generally appears to take his subject matter seriously, is capable of playful and ironic distance from his work, and secondly, in order to show how an awareness of the rôle irony can play in the intertext can radically alter our reading of a poem.

Amics Marchabrun (VI) is a *tenso* with a poet called Ugo Catola.[50] Their dialogue is about the nature of love: Ugo finds it ennobling and good, whilst Marcabru characteristically takes the opposite point of view and starts to moralize. Although Marcabru uses the term *faus' amistat* in the second stanza, throughout the rest of the poem the protagonists use the same word, *amors*, to designate something they define quite differently. This gives Ugo a chance to ironize at Marcabru's expense:

> Marcabrun, si cum declinaz,
> qu'amor si ab engan mesclaz,
> dunc es lo almosna pechaz:
> la cima devers la raïz.   (25–8)

Marcabru, if, as you declare, you adulterate love with cheating, then alms-giving is a sin and the world is upside down.

Ugo mimics Marcabru's style here and ironically states his adversary's point of view.[51] He draws attention to his ironic intentions by comparing his initial proposition, that is that love is adulterated with cheating, to two patently absurd and untrue propositions; he uses the construction *si cum . . . dunc* to emphasize this. The two propositions in lines 27–8 are thus *ironia*, because Ugo clearly believes their opposite to be true and intends his audience to realize this. The intended meaning of the stanza is that, unlike Marcabru, Ugo does not consider love to be adulterated by cheating and the effect of the *ironia* is to ridicule Marcabru, who is stupid enough to believe something so patently absurd.

Similar *ironia* occurs in Ugo's next speech:

> Marcabrun, amistatz dechai
> car a trobat joven savai;
> eu n'ai al cor ir'et esclai
> qar l'en alevaz tan laiz criz. (33–6)

Marcabru, friendship goes to ruin because it has found youth to be base; I am so upset and horrified by this because you make such an awful noise about it.

Ugo mimics Marcabru's lamentations on the decline of courtly values, but the statement of his opponent's point of view is again immediately shown to be *ironia* by the following lines in which Ugo indicates that he is not unhappy because courtly values are declining, but because Marcabru makes such an awful noise about it. Once again Marcabru is ridiculed.

The apparent hostility which the two poets show each other in *Amics Marchabrun* is not indicative of real hostility. The complicity which the joint composition of the poem must have involved surely indicates to some degree at least that the hostility is feigned for dramatic purposes and that the relationship between the two poets can best be described as playful.[52] Irony, or 'la bonne conscience ludique', as Jankélévitch called it, underpins the tone of the whole poem. The fact that Marcabru, despite his apparently deeply held convictions, allows himself to be ridiculed shows his willingness to participate in the playfulness that is implicit in so much troubadour poetry from Guilhem IX onwards.[53]

The most famous troubadour whom Marcabru names in his work is Jaufre Rudel. The poem he sends to Jaufre (xv) is not typical of his style:

> I Cortesamen vuoill comensar
> un vers, si es qui l'escoutar,
> e puois tant m'en sui entremes
> veirai si·l poirai afinar,
> qu'era vuoill mon chan esmerar   5
> e dirai vos de mantas res.
>
> II Assatz pot hom vilanejar
> qui cortesia vol blasmar,
> que·l plus savis e·l mieills apres
> no·n sap tantas dire ni far   10
> c'mon no li puosca enseignar
> petit o pro, tals hora es.

III   De cortesia·is pot vanar
      qui ben sap mesur'esgardar;
      e qui tot vol auzir quant es   15
      ni tot quant ve cuid'amassar
      lo tot l'es ops amesurar
      o ja no sera trop cortes.

IV   Mesura es en gent parlar
      e cortesia es d'amar;   20
      e qui no vol esser mespres
      de tota vilania·is gar,
      d'escarnir e de folejar,
      puois sera savis, ab que·ill pes.

V   C'aissi pot savis hom reignar   25
      e bona dompna meillurar;
      mas cella qu'en pren dos o tres
      e per un no s'i vol fiar,
      ben deu sos pretz asordejar
      e sa valors a chascun mes.   30

VI   Aitals amors fai a prezar
      que si mezeissa ten en car;
      e s'ieu en dic nul vilanes
      per lieis, que m'o teign'a amar:
      be·ill lauzi fassa·m pro musar,   35
      qu'ieu n'aurai so que·m n'es promes.

VII   Lo vers e·l son vuoill enviar
      a·n Jaufre Rudel outra mar,
      e vuoill que l'aujon li Frances
      per lor coratges alegrar,   40
      que Dieus lor o pot perdonar,
      o sia pechatz o merces.

I

I want to start a song in a courtly fashion, if there is someone to listen to it, and since I have made such an effort, I will see if I am able to refine it, for now I want to perfect my singing and I will tell you of many things.

II

A man who wants to blame courtliness can indeed make himself vile, because the wisest and the most educated man does not know how to say or do so much about this that sometimes one cannot teach him either a little or a lot.

III

He who knows how to restrain himself properly can boast of courtliness; and yet the man who wants to hear everything that there is, and who thinks he can gather for himself everything he sees, must restrain himself in everything, or he will never be worthy.

IV

Restraint comes from speaking in a gracious manner and courtliness from loving, and he who does not wish to be blamed must avoid all unworthy behaviour, deceit and folly; then he will be wise, as long as he thinks about it.

V

For thus can a wise man reign, and a good lady improve herself; but she who takes two or three lovers, and does not want to put her faith in one, must indeed make her worth and merit grow always more vile.

VI

The kind of love that holds itself dear is to be prized; and if I say anything base about it because of it, let this be considered due to false love in me: I advise her to keep me waiting in vain a long time, for I will have from it what has been promised me.

VII

I want to send the poem and the tune to Sir Jaufre Rudel, over the sea, and I want the French to hear it, to make their hearts happy, for God can forgive them for this, whether it is a sin or a good deed.

The dedication of this poem to Jaufre Rudel has allowed scholars to date its composition precisely: late 1148, shortly after Jaufre's arrival in the Holy Land on the Second Crusade. The adoption of the smooth, limpid style, so different from Marcabru's own, has traditionally been attributed to the fact that he is sending the poem to Jaufre; scholars have thought that Marcabru was couching his usual virulent moralizing in a more acceptable style and language out of deference to Jaufre, and a close poetic relationship has been postulated between the two men.[54]

In a recent study of the poem Ruth Harvey puts forward a new interpretation of several of its elements. She notes that the two main themes of the poem are the importance of *mesura* (lines 13–14) and the attack on the promiscuous woman who does not know how to restrain herself and takes two or three lovers; she also points to parallels between lines in *Cortesamen* and lines from poems by Cercamon with whom Marcabru probably had a close poetic relationship.[55]

Harvey finds the resemblance between lines 27 of Marcabru's poem, 'mas cella qu'en pren dos o tres', and the second line from this stanza of Cercamon's *Ab lo pascor* particularly striking:[56]

> Non a valor   d'aissi enan
> Cels c'ab dos ni ab tres jai.
> E tal enqer lo cor Tristan
> Qe Dieus tan falsa non fetz sai.
> Miels li fora ja non nasqes
> Enanz qe failliment feses
> Don er parlat tro en Peitau.

The woman who lies with two or three men is henceforth without worth. There is a woman who seeks the heart of Tristan who is falser than any woman God made here [any pagan woman]. It would be better had she never been born rather than commit the error which will be talked about as far away as Poitou.

Rita Lejeune argues that Cercamon's poem was composed in the Holy Land and that he alludes here to the alleged misconduct of Eleanor of Aquitaine in

1148 at the court of Antioch; more recently John Marshall has commented that Cercamon's allusion to 'Peitau' cannot be gratuitous and he accepts 'without hesitation' that this stanza 'makes oblique but specific reference to the alleged misconduct of Eleanor'.[57]

What did Eleanor do? Whilst she and her first husband, Louis VII of France, were on the Second Crusade, Eleanor, apparently already tiring of Louis, who was later to divorce her, expressed her intention to stay with her uncle, Raymond of Antioch, instead of continuing with the French to Jerusalem. She had to be kidnapped in order to be made to stay with Louis and she is criticized for her behaviour by every chronicler to mention the incident, John of Salisbury, Gervase of Canterbury, William of Tyre and Gerald of Wales, to name but a few. The 'Antioch incident' was often cited to justify Louis' separation from Eleanor. According to Amy Kelly, the rumours that Eleanor and Raymond actually had an affair are dubious because they are all from French sources, but she nevertheless points out that 'the custody of Eleanor made it very apparent that something very dreadful had occurred in Antioch', and she concludes her chapter on the subject: 'the rumours pursued the Duchess of Aquitaine to the end of her days'.[58]

If it is accepted that Cercamon alludes to the Antioch incident in *Ab lo pascor*, then, as Ruth Harvey suggests, Marcabru's *Cortesamen* may also contain a specific allusion to Eleanor's conduct at Antioch. She does not base her argument solely on the fact that both poets use the formula 'two or three lovers'. Why should Marcabru single out the French as the audience he most wants to hear his song in the last stanza? Does not the dating of the poem concord perfectly with the hypothesis that Marcabru is alluding specifically to Eleanor?[59] The hypothesis that Marcabru's *Cortesamen* conceals an oblique attack on Eleanor of Aquitaine's behaviour at the court of Antioch is certainly plausible, but if it is accepted, the tone of the poem may need to be reconsidered. Does Marcabru really adopt this apparently more delicate style out of deference to Jaufre?

Maria Luisa Meneghetti suggests in passing that the very fact that Marcabru's style in *Cortesamen* seems so different from his usual style is suspicious and that he may therefore be chastising Jaufre for deviating from the true courtly ideal, rather than offering the poem as a tribute to him. Her interpretation thus differs from the traditional view of this song, but if Marcabru is attacking Jaufre rather than honouring him, the poem is obviously heavily laden with irony.[60] A closer reading of the text bearing in mind Harvey's elucidation of the historical context of the poem and Meneghetti's suggestion about the tone is perhaps in order. What, for example, is the significance of the first line of the poem, 'Cortesamen vuoill comensar'?

The abstract noun *cortesia* occurs three times in Marcabru's work apart from in *Cortesamen*. It always designates a good quality, for example:

> Qui ses bauzia
> vol amor albergar,

Marcabru

de cortesia
deu sa maion jonchar. (xxxii, 55–8)

The man who wants to shelter love without cheating must strew his house with *cortesia*.

The adjective *cortes*, on the other hand, often seems to lend itself to irony in Marcabru's poetry:

D'Amor(s) vos dirai com es:
Si valiatz un marques
Ja no·us fasatz *cortes*,
Pos d'aver non auretz ges. (vii, 33–6)

I will tell you what love is like: even if you are as worthy as a marquis, do not style yourself courtly when you will have no money.

Non sai que faire
tant fort sui entrepres,
q'entorn l'araire
si fant vilan *cortes*
e·il just pechaire
d'aisso q'en lor non es;
si m'ajut fes,
tals mil en auzetz braire
c'anc res no·n fo. (xxxii, 19–27)

I do not know what to do, so embarrassed am I, for around the plough peasants become courtly, and the upright sinners because of things that have nothing to do with them; by my faith, you will hear a thousand of them cry out in this way that it never was so.

Non puosc sofrir qu·als moilleratz
Non diga lor forfaitz saubutz;
Non sai la cals auctoritatz
Lor mostra c'om los apel drutz;
Semblan fant de l'ase *cortes*,
C'ab son seignor cuidet bordir,
Cant lo vic trepar ab sos ches. (xxxix, 50–6)

I cannot stand not telling husbands about their notorious crimes; I do not know what authority tells them that they can be called lovers; they are like the courtly donkey who thought he could dance with his master when he saw him playing with his dogs.

Although Marcabru uses the adjective *cortes* to describe people he apparently does believe are courtly, in these, and possibly in other examples, *cortes* is used ironically to designate people or creatures who only have the outward appearance of *cortesia*, but who are not really courtly at all.[61] When this and the subject matter of *Cortesamen*, that is the criticism of promiscuous women and particularly of Eleanor, are born in mind, it would seem possible that

77

Marcabru is using the adverb *cortesamen* ironically in the first line of this song.

There is a clash in *Cortesamen* between the style, which is not Marcabru's and might be more appropriate to a poet who sings of his love for a lady, and the content, which has elements typical of Marcabru's moralizing work. Marcabru may indeed begin his poem *cortesamen*, but the aspersions he casts are just as provocative as those in his other apparently more outspoken poems. Could he be mocking the people who give the outward appearance of *cortesia*, whilst in fact behaving in a reprehensible manner, by imitating the style of poetry they appreciate? It is difficult to imagine how this smooth, pleasant-sounding poem might have been sung, given that the style and content are so incongruous. If, however, the style is pastiche, the problem posed by this incongruity is resolved. A performance of *Cortesamen* would have been as funny as one of Marcabru's parodies, the first word, *Cortesamen*, being intoned with a good deal of irony.

Eleanor of Aquitaine's taste in poetry is well known. She liked the smooth, polished love poetry of Bernart de Ventadorn.[62] Bernart may already have been active as a poet in 1147, when *Cortesamen* was composed, but the best-known composer of smooth, polished love poetry amongst Marcabru's contemporaries was surely Jaufre Rudel, not, perhaps, the best exponent of *mesura*:

> D'aquest'amor sui tan cochos
> que quant ieu vau ves lieis coren,
> vejaire m'es qu'a reversos
> m'en torn e qu'ela·s n'an fugen.   (vi^b, 8–11)

I desire this love so ardently that when I go running towards her/it, it seems to me that I am going backwards, and that she/it is fleeing.

Marcabru draws the attention of both the French and Jaufre Rudel to his song. Why should the French be happy to hear a song about their immoral queen? There may be a touch of sarcasm in Marcabru's tone here and it is thus possible that Jaufre Rudel is also being attacked for singing of what Marcabru believes to be an immoral love. Perhaps Jaufre is the 'wise and educated' man mentioned in line 9 of *Cortesamen*: he might think himself courtly, but he still has a lot to learn about the fickle and deceptive ways of the world. Perhaps it is Jaufre's limpid style that Marcabru is mimicking and at the same time condemning as a front for immoral behaviour.

If *Cortesamen* is read in this way, it is a polemic and ironic attack, not only on Eleanor and Jaufre Rudel, but also on the style of poetry they represent for Marcabru. Elsewhere Marcabru attacks schools or types of troubadours:

> Ja non farai mai plevina
> Ieu per la troba n'Eblo,
> Que sentenssa follatina
> Manten encontra razo;

Marcabru

Ai!
Qu'ieu dis e dic e dirai
Quez amors et amars brai,
Hoc,
E qui blasm'Amor buzina.   (XXXI, 73–81)

Never more will I pledge myself to the poetic school of Sir Eble, which maintains mad ideas instead of reason. Ah! For I said and say and will say that true love and lust clash loudly, yes, and he who blames true love in this talks nonsense.

Trobador ab sen d'enfanssa,
Movon als pros atahina,
E tornon en disciplina
So que veritatz autreia,
E fant los motz, per esmanssa,
Entrebeschatz de fraichura.   (XXXVII, 7–12)

Some childish troubadours cause trouble for the worthy and make torment out of what truth grants and they deliberately interweave their words with fragmentation.

Although he clearly sets himself apart from his peers, Marcabru is very much a part of the 'dialectic' of *trobar*. He denigrates and ridicules his contemporaries, but by communicating with them and referring to them in his own work he indicates that their work was a context for his. It is characteristic of Marcabru's polemic stance that intertextual play in his songs involves irony, but this irony serves as more than a tool for Marcabru's moralizing. Irony makes songs like *Cortesamen* amusing and entertaining; it indicates that Marcabru could be as playful in his approach to poetry as Guilhem IX, though to different ends and with a different effect.

CONCLUSION

Irony is an important aspect of Marcabru's *eloquentia*. As a satirist he uses irony as the classical and medieval Latin rhetorical manuals suggest one should, to mock, criticize and denigrate, and his irony may bear the mark of their influence; as a moralist, one of his major preoccupations is clearly to make sure his message is understood and this explains his use of signals to irony. However, Marcabru was an entertainer as well as a moralist. He had to amuse if he was to be allowed to continue preaching and irony must have been one of his chief tools as a public performer. His ironic sexual metaphors, his use of parody, his ability to laugh at himself, his ironic attacks on immoral people and on other troubadours all add to the dramatic qualities of his poetry and make it engrossing, convincing and entertaining.

3

Bernart Marti

Bernart Marti is one of the most perplexing troubadours of the early period. In some of his songs he seems to have been influenced by the style and ethics of Marcabru; in others he appears flippant and cynical, if not amoral. Was Bernart a disciple of Marcabru, as some scholars have thought, or one of the 'trobador ab sen d'enfanssa' Marcabru criticized? Ernest Hoepffner concluded his study of Bernart:

> ici c'est le persiflage, la moquerie légère; là la satire mordante. Il semble ne rien prendre au sérieux. Le même spectacle qui arrache à Marcabru ses invectives furieuses, ne provoque chez Bernart qu'un sourire amusé.[1]

I propose to take a closer look at Bernart's 'sourire amusé'. It is not always a happy smile, but it is frequently ironic, constantly inviting Bernart's audience to question the apparent or pretended meaning of his utterances.

Bernart's poetry poses serious problems of interpretation, often surviving in only one manuscript in a form that is clearly corrupt. The nine poems which can be attributed to him with any certainty were edited by Hoepffner in 1929 and by Fabrizio Beggiato in 1984.[2] I have chosen not to refer to either of these editions for two reasons. First, I found a small, but nevertheless significant, number of discrepancies between their readings of the manuscripts and my own. Secondly, neither scholar hesitates to correct the manuscripts in places where it may not in fact be necessary, often without justifying his decision to do so.[3] I have consequently re-edited from the manuscripts all the poems I discuss, though I do not consider the versions I offer as definitive critical editions, rather as attempts to make sense of difficult texts without rewriting whole sections. Although many textual problems remain unresolved, I believe there is sufficient basis for the interpretations which follow. I have retained Hoepffner's numbering of the texts.

AMAR DEI

Nowhere does Bernart's 'sourire amusé' offer a more subtle invitation to probe his poetry for layers of meaning than in *Amar dei* (1). He is often an introspective poet, and his self-analysis in this poem indicates an acute awareness of the parodoxes human emotion can involve:

Bernart Marti

I Amar de*i*
que ben es mezura
lanquan vei
lo tems en verdura,
e l'aura es dousana   5
e refrinh lo chan pels plais
que l'auzels demena,
e·ill nueitz aserena
e floris la mora.

II Dun*c* dompnei   10
color en peintura,
mas be vei
en plan ma rancura;
cui sa dona engu[a]na
tan no·s pagua ni s'irais –   15
que ia m'en sovenha!
D'elir amor terrena
soven chant'e plora.

III Ges no·l nei,
que sa forfaitura   20
no·ill plaidei
tot per nueit escura
ab leis ses luguana;
mas, la·*m v*ailla Dieus, la bais,
gardan, de mal plena,   25
que·l plait destremena
e d'als non labora.

IV L'aer correi
qu'es com folatura,
leis non grei   30
si·l veils quers peiura
. . . .
lassa, que·s fara iamais?
Tan greu cug revenha,
tant ha blava vena   35
c'uns veillums langora.

V Leis mercei,
d'eisa sa tortura
senhorei;
si vas mi·s meillura   40
non es tant trefana,
pero ges ieu no·m n'esmai
del ben que·m n'avenha;
gen baizan m'estrena,
de que m'asenhora.   45

VI Lonc eslei
fis d'amor segura;
cui m'autrei
tant es fin'e pura

grail'e grass'e plana   50
que dedins lo cor me trais
gran ir'e greu pena
ab ioi que·i amena
que iamais no·i fora.

VII   Non a rei   55
el mon, tan com dura,
   meils estei,
ricx de mezura
[e] d'onor *mondana*
ab sol una vetz que·m bais;   60
e no l'es contena
mai s'amor retenha,
no sei quant ho cora.

I

I must love, for it is a sign of restraint when I see the green season has arrived and the wind is sweet, and the song which the bird makes resounds along the hedges, and the night is serene and the blackberry bush is in flower.

II

So I pretend to pay court, but I can see my cause for complaint only too clearly; the man whose lady deceives him is not so satisfied nor so sorrowful – may I remember this! He often sings and weeps from having chosen worldly love.

III

Indeed I do not deny it, for I do not contest her crime when I am with her in the dark night without a light; but, rather, may God help me in this, I kiss her, watchfully, full of evil though she may be, for she concludes the case and works at nothing else.

IV

I beat the air, which is like madness, may it not grieve her if an old hide gets worse ... miserable, what will become of her henceforth? I think she is unlikely to recover because she has such bad blood that old age is made to languish.

V

Thanks to her I rule, even when she tortures me; if she treats me better she is not so perfidious, but I am certainly not dismayed about the good thing that may come to me from her; she gratifies me by kissing me sweetly, which makes her rule over me.

VI

I was tested in certain love for a long time; the person to whom I grant myself is so fine and pure, delicate and shapely and smooth, that she causes me great anger and harsh pain in my heart, along with the joy which she brings to it, which would not have been there otherwise.

VII

There is no king in the world, as long as it lasts, better off than I, who am rich in restraint and worldly honour, so long as she kisses me just once; and she does not quibble about granting me her love, I know not where or when.

The poem evokes the turmoil love can produce, the constant oscillation between elation and despair. Bernart is reworking the *odi et amo* theme: no one is either so frustrated or so satisfied as he is (lines 14–15); he juxtaposes torture and elation (lines 38–9), joy and pain (lines 52–3), and he laments that worldly love causes him not only to sing often, but also to weep (lines 17–18). At one stage he is so confused that whilst realizing his lady is *de mal plena*, 'full of evil', all he can think of doing is kissing her (lines 24–5), as if at any one time he is incapable of deciding between two extremes of emotion. Shortly after this crucial point, Bernart actually gives in to madness (lines 28–9); the tone is one of resigned despair.

Bernart's resignation is obvious from the very first line of the poem, 'Amar dei'. His love is not induced by his lady's good qualities nor by his desire to improve himself; on the contrary, he loves because it is expected of him, because it is the social norm.[4] It is spring again and so he had better fall in love. There are no fine speeches about the lady's *pretz* or *valor* or any of the usual qualities that might inspire the courtly lover: love has become a duty, and not necessarily a pleasant one.

The element of constraint in the opening line (*dei*) undermines the emotive aspect of falling in love and this leads to a slight irony in tone, which encourages the listener or the reader to ask questions about the text. Can Bernart's love really live up to the expectations created by the spring opening when it has been ridiculed in this way? Is not the spring opening made slightly ridiculous in any case by Bernart's apparent willingness to take an often banal poetic formula to extremes? He is not merely saying 'Spring makes me happier in love than I might have been', but, with a resigned tone, 'I must love because it is spring.' Compare this spring opening with lines from Bernart's *Lancan lo douz temps* (IX):

> Las, non es dregz domneiaire
> qi ia nul mes met en soan,
> qar genars non val meins gaire
> q'abrils e mais q'es vertz e blan. (43–6)

Alas, the man who despises any given month is not truly courtly, for January can hardly be worth less than April or May, which is green and sweet.

It is hard to believe, in the light of these lines, that the exordium of *Amar dei* is simply a conventional nature opening. Bernart is as unhappy about the conventional and trite nature opening as Marcabru, but instead of parodying it, he undermines it, with an irony which is perhaps more subtle, by feigning total submission.

Any irony here hinges on the force of the word *dei*. However, the word *mezura* is also striking in its dominant position at the second rhyme. As the poem progresses, it becomes apparent that love, which Bernart elects as a way of life because it is a sign of *mezura*, induces actions and feelings which are hardly compatible with *mezura*. As if to emphasize this, all these undesirable qualities rhyme with *mezura*: *peintura* (indicating pretence and illusion), *rancura*, *forfaitura*, *folatura*, *peiura* and *tortura*. The effect of this is intensified by the alternation of three- and six-syllabic lines in the first four lines of each stanza, which draws attention to all the rhyme words in these lines, particularly since the rhymes are all either diphthongs or feminine rhymes spanning two syllables. The notion of *mezura* is thus undermined throughout the poem, but the irony this produces is not of the kind that offers a specific alternative meaning. Bernart's attempt in this poem to follow the precepts of *mezura* is shown to lead to feelings that are incompatible with it, to paradox and to tension. The paradox which Bernart highlights through his ironic play on the word *mezura* is perhaps intrinsic to all troubadour love poetry,[5] but his cynicism takes his meditation out of the realm of pure 'poetic' paradox and into that of irony. We realize that *mezura* is not necessarily an infallible principle by which one can govern one's life, but we are left unclear as to whether Bernart is suggesting any alternative; surface meanings are thus dissolved and dispersed, but nothing replaces them. The irony here suggests, through tone and juxtaposition, that Bernart Marti, the poet, is creating a distance between himself and Bernart Marti, the lover. It allows him, armed with his 'sourire amusé', to point out his own weaknesses, passions and internal contradictions.

Along with all this inner turmoil Bernart looks at his relationship with his lady, which he portrays as being based on pretence. He implies that she cheats him by comparing his own misery to that of a man whose lady cheats and by then talking of his lady's 'crime' (lines 14–15, 20); he admits to having to use pretence in order to pay court to her, thus indicating that he cannot give himself up whole-heartedly to something he does not really believe in. As his poem is the means of paying court, 'dompnei / color en peintura' (lines 10–11) may also refer to the way in which his poem pretends to be a courtly poem.

Bernart's plight is made insupportable by his lady's *forfaitura*, but what frustrates him most is that he himself is incapable of reproaching her: he cannot 'contest her crime' when 'with her in the dark night without a light' (lines 21–3). The power of sex is a central theme of *Amar dei* and the legal metaphor which expresses the idea that Bernart is powerless to control his desire adds an ironic note of cold detachment (stanza III). He talks of the power his lady has over him because of sex (lines 42–4),[6] how it can make him feel wretched (line 52), then exalted (lines 53–63); Bernart's lady is described in sensual, evocative terms (line 50) and it appears that his predicament can only get worse as he grows older (lines 30–1). It is the theme of powerlessness in the face of sexual desire that provides coherence to the poem as a whole. Bernart is cynical about love because in his experience it reduces itself to sex and to a kind of power struggle. There is a tissue of imagery concerning power towards the end of the poem (*senhorei*, line 39, *asenhora*, line 45, *rei*, line 55, *ricx*, line 58, *onor*, line 59), and it is on this note that Bernart ends his poem, clearly anticipating victory.

If the power of consuming lust is seen as the central theme of *Amar dei*, the whole poem may be understood as an ironic play on the word *mezura*. However, the irony is possibly even more pervasive than this. Every hint of cynicism undermines the poem's *raison d'être* as a love song and creates that

Bernart Marti

most intangible of qualities: ironic tone. Bernart's irony here differs considerably from Marcabru's. Whereas irony in Marcabru's poetry leads the audience to discover a specific alternative meaning, Bernart suggests no alternative. He undermines the literal meaning of his poem, but he suggests nothing to replace it. In Jankélévitch's words, the type of irony Bernart uses 'charge l'absurde d'administrer lui-même la preuve de son impossibilité'.[7] In this case the 'absurd' offering proof of its own impossibility is that mainstay of the 'courtly consensus': *mezura*.

QUAN L'ERB'ES

There is humour in *Amar dei*, but the poem is hardly comic. In his other love poems (II, III, VII, VIII, IX), Bernart is less intense and introspective, but he is nevertheless particularly adept at self-examination and his constant quest for self-knowledge leads to irony. Consider, for example, *Quan l'erb'es* (VII):

I   Quan l'erb'es reverdezida
els pratz delonc lo vivier
e·l rossinhol brai e crida,
e son flurit li vergier,
adonx par que·l tems s'esclaire   5
quant hom au las ranas braire
el mares e per lo riu.

II   Si ai amor encobida
e mes tot mon consirier,
que ia no vueill a ma vida   10
mon grat far autre mestier,
c'anc pos nasquei de ma maire
no volgui autr'obra faire,
ni d'autre labor no viu.

III   Mas ieu n'ai una chauzida   15
que no m'en fai destorbier,
mas be m'a sa fe plevida
et ieu iurat a mostier
... don no·m puesc estraire,
tan li soi fizels amaire,   20
ses faillir, so·ill iur e·ill pliu.

IV   Dormit ha, si no·s reisida,
en oblit un an entier
e no pretz s'ila m'oblida
mais tot lo mon un denier;   25
ara la·m gart Sains Salvaire
c'om no la·m puesca sostraire,
ni per autre no·m esquiu.

V   S'ila·m fai breu consentida
d'aquo don ai dezirier –   30
que la bai nuda ho vestida –

ia autra ricor non quier;
assatz val mais qu'enperaire
si desotz son mantel vaire
iosta son bel cors m'aiziu.   35

VI   Blanca e graila et escafida
es, ses coratge leugier,
dousa e fresca, colorida
com flors de mai en rozier,
corteza e de bon aire,   40
e non soi de ren gabaire,
c'asatz n'es plus qu'ieu non diu.

VII   Una gancha trassaillida
me fon dig que·m fes l'autrier;
s'es de bel mentir garnida   45
e mon ver mi fai mensongier,
los forfaitz, qu'ieu non pres gaire,
no vueill auzir ni retraire
per c'om no m'aia per auriu.

VIII   Car si·n fauc fol'esbrugida   50
e trop gran vertat l'enquier,
si auran m'amor delida
e vieillas e lauzengier;
qui·s vol s'en fassa ianglaire
mas mi apel quan repaire   55
son bon amic senhoriu.

IX   N'Eblon man ves Marguarida
lo vers per un mesatgier,
qu'en lui es amor iauzida,
de don'e de cavalier,   60
et ieu soi sai aiustaire
de dos amicx d'un veiaire,
N'Aimes e·n l'Estrebesquiu.

X   N'Aimes e·n l'Estrebeschaire
son dui amic d'un veiaire   65
. . . . ab l'Entrebeschiu . . .

I

When the grass in the meadow beside the pond has turned green again and the nightingale sings and cries and the orchards are in flower, then it seems that the weather grows brighter when one hears the frogs singing in the marshes and along the stream.

II

I have so desired love and devoted all my thought to it that I do not ever want willingly to have another occupation, for never since my mother bore me have I wanted any other work, nor do I live off any other labour.

III

But I have chosen a lady who does not cause me any trouble, since she has pledged her faith to me and I have sworn in church [an oath] I cannot break, because I am such a faithful, unswerving lover to her, this I swear and pledge to her.

86

Bernart Marti

IV

She has lain dormant, without stirring, in my memory for a whole year, and I care nothing for the world any longer if she forgets me; now may the Holy Saviour stop another man taking her away from me and prevent her from abandoning me for another man.

V

If she quickly grants me what I desire of her, that is that I kiss her naked or clothed, then I do not want any other riches; I would be more worthy than an emperor if underneath her fur cloak I find pleasure beside her beautiful body.

VI

She is white and smooth and delicate, and without a fickle heart, sweet and fresh and coloured like flowers in a rose garden in May, courtly and of noble birth, and I am not boasting at all, for she is far better than I can say.

VII

I was told that the other day she played a dirty trick on me; if she indulges in sweet lying and makes my truth into lies for me, I do not want to hear or tell of her misdeeds, for which I care nothing, so that no man may think me a fool.

VIII

For if I were to spread gossip foolishly about her and demand the whole truth from her, then old women and slanderers would have destroyed my love; let whoever wants to do so become a gossip about it, so long as she calls me her good, sovereign friend when I return.

IX

I send the poem by messenger to my Lord Eblon towards Marguarida, for in him the love of ladies and knights is made joyful, and here I bring together two friends of the same opinion, Sir Aimes and Sir l'Estrebesquiu.

X

Sir Aimes and Sir l'Estrebeschaire are two friends who agree about something [?] . . . with the interlacing . . .

In some ways this poem can be treated like a short narrative. After an apparently conventional nature opening and an elaborate declaration of his devotion to love, Bernart insists throughout a whole stanza on the bond between his lady and himself and on his own fidelity (stanza II). The tone, however, is perhaps a little too insistent, for Bernart repeats his affirmation of fidelity no less than six times in four lines (lines 18–21). Immediately after this he admits that he forgot about his lady for a whole year, a somewhat bizarre proof of his unswerving fidelity. He goes on to talk of what he wants from his lady in terms that leave no doubt as to the physical nature of his desire (line 31: 'que la bai nuda ho vestida') and he describes her in sensual, evocative terms similar to those used in *Amar dei* (line 36, 'Blanca e graila et escafida'). Spiritual qualities are tacked on as if they were afterthoughts (line 37, 'ses coratge leugier', line 40, 'corteza e de bon aire') and words like *ricor* and *aiziu* (lines 32 and 35) are heavily laden with erotic innuendo.

In the next two stanzas (VII and VIII), Bernart admits that unpleasant rumours circulate about his lady and her attitude to him. His immediate reaction is to hide his head in the sand: he does not wish to hear about her 'misdeeds', for if people know he is aware of them, and he carries on courting his lady, he can only be considered a fool (lines 45–9). The implication is that he does not mind being duped, as long as this is not public knowledge. After rounding on the *lauzengiers* and old women for trying to destroy his love (lines 50–3), Bernart makes his position even clearer, in a way that shocked Hoepffner for its cynicism:[8] let people say what they like, all he wants is to be his lady's *bon amic senhoriu*, in other words her lover (line 56). His vocabulary makes it clear that once again he considers the game of love a power struggle.

The poem is rife with contradictions. Given the lady's *gancha trassaillida*, her 'dirty trick' (line 43), which the poet at no point denies, all her good qualities are undermined and the poet's profession of faith in her (lines 15–17) would also seem to be ironic. Moreover, the exaggerated affirmation of sincerity which accompanies the description of her good qualities (line 41, 'e non soi de ren gabaire') may well be a signal to irony. This irony is not, however, just at the expense of the lady. Given his ability to forget her for a whole year and his apparent blindness to her infidelity so long as she sleeps with him, the poet's devotion to his lady as expressed in stanza III is also undermined and his total commitment to love (stanza II) is subverted to say the least.

With all these strings pulling against each other it is difficult not to suspect irony in the first stanza of the poem. The two creatures Bernart mentions here in order to typify spring are both linked with pride and sterile verbosity in Marcabru's poetry,[9] and given that Bernart makes it clear elsewhere that he despises courtly platitudes on the seasons, it would seem likely that the nature opening of *Quan l'erb'es* is ironic and intended to be perceived as parody.

The ending of the poem is obscure. Bernart talks of 'bringing together two friends of the same opinion' and the identity of these friends can only be guessed at. It would seem, however, that Bernart is changing the subject completely, and whilst this is not unusual in the troubadour lyric, his lady can have felt none too flattered by this 'love song' which casts aspersions about her virtue, makes it quite clear that the poet is only interested in one thing, and then seems to forget all about her.

It is almost as if Bernart will not allow himself to be duped by his own poetry. He is able to compose in the courtly style which may have been expected of him, as the first three stanzas of the poem show, but he will not forget that his love is not as pure as it perhaps ought to be. In *Quan l'erb'es*, Bernart once again portrays himself as consumed by unrequited lust, but his tone is light-hearted, often verging on the cynical, and his critical examination of his own failings appears refreshingly honest.

Bernart Marti

BERNART AND THE *AUTOBIOGRAPHICAL ASSUMPTION*

Implicit in my examination of both *Amar dei* and *Quan l'erb'es* is the assumption that Bernart's poetry can be interpreted, on one level at least, as autobiographical. Such an assumption jars somewhat with the ideas of several schools of modern scholars who would see the first person subject of a medieval lyric poem variously as a representative of a social class, as a character invented for dramatic purposes, or as a purely grammatical figure representing anyone who chose to perform the song.[10] The adoption of any one of these premises as an infallible key to the interpretation of medieval poetry could only be reductive and Marcabru's poetry perhaps demonstrates the point. Marcabru may well sometimes represent the views or interests of a social class, but he is by no means consistent in this; his poetry is marked by his own personal obsessions and a rigid sociological approach cannot deal with the ambiguities of his position, or with his rôle as an entertainer. His poetry *is* marked by the constant presence of a strong author–persona who in some ways could be seen as a dramatic creation of the poet, but on the other hand, Marcabru goes out of his way to link his style of poetry to his name so that his personality, name and poetry are inextricably associated in the minds of his audience and any fiction in his presentation of himself is thus deliberately made to merge with reality. Finally, if the 'I' of a medieval poem were really just a grammatical figure, why should Marcabru take such trouble to attack other troubadours and to distinguish their work from his own?

In a recent article Sarah Kay examines the problem of rhetoric and subjectivity in troubadour poetry and concludes:

I think it . . . reasonable to associate the lyric 'I' of a troubadour song with an individual historical figure, the association varying, according to the context of performance, from one with the physical presence of a celebrated performer, with a troubadour known but absent and represented by his spokesman, or at least with a certain reputation. This assumption, which I shall call the *autobiographical assumption*, has been a constant of the reception of troubadour poetry from the thirteenth century to the mid-twentieth, in the context of which the 'more sophisticated than thou' glosses of sixties and seventies criticism appear an aberration.[11]

A troubadour might adopt conventional attitudes, play a rôle of his own invention or pretend to be in a certain situation in order to create a desired dramatic effect, but he may also be relating his own personal experience. Bernart Marti's introspection and his portrayal of himself as a flawed character would seem to indicate that his poems can be read as autobiographical; not, of course, in the sense that they are factual narrations of real events, but simply inasmuch as they may be seen as an attempt to articulate real feelings. In *Amar dei* and *Quan l'erb'es*, he highlights the paradoxes which love involves, undermining, through irony, various feelings in order to indicate how love can induce startling shifts in emotion. His irony offers no definite point of view, as Marcabru's does, and it is often directed against himself as much as against his lady. He feels that the constraints placed upon the courtly lover by *mezura*, by the presence of the *lauzengiers* in the courtly world, and by courtly convention in general, are unrealistic, for the truly ardent lover always wants his desire to be consummated. Bernart is aware that he is unable to live up to his own ideals and whilst this might be thought cynical, it is also perhaps honest. The result of his meditations on his own position regarding love is poetry that is strikingly individual and subjective.

Bernart does not always portray himself as consumed by unrequited lust. In two of his other love poems, *Qant la plueia* (VIII) and *Lancan lo douz temps* (IX), he talks of fulfilled physical love. He nevertheless indicates, with characteristic irony, that the man who claims totally pure motives in love is deluding himself:

> Anc mos cors ni mos cossiriers
> d'amor non fo vencutz ni laz,
> que d'als non es mos cors entiers,
> ni autre tresaur no amas,
> ni autre ricor non deman;
> que qi l'ha, ni tor ni castel,
> eu m'ai mon bel palaïs el forn. (VIII, 8–14)

Never has my heart or mind been vanquished or sad in love, for in nothing else is my heart whole, nor do I gather any other treasure or ask for any other riches; for, whoever has a tower or a castle, I have my beautiful palace in the oven.

> Qan de ma dona sui laire,
> ges no·m tenc per malvatz afan;
> qan sui nutz e son repaire
> e sos costatz tenc e mazan,
> ieu non sai null emperador
> vas me puesca gran pres cuillir
> ne de fin'amor aver mais. (IX, 15–21)

When I 'steal' my lady, I do not consider that I suffer greatly; when I am naked in her chamber and hold and caress her sides, I know of no emperor who could have more worth or pure love than I [or 'who could get more out of/profit more from pure love than I'].

In the first instance Bernart uses a common ironic sexual metaphor to designate the female organs. On the literal level the comparison between the oven (in other word the kitchen) and the tower and castle works perfectly well: Bernart knows his place and does not envy wealthier men. On an ironic level Bernart is boasting of sexual fulfilment and the tower and castle become symbols of the impregnable defences of virtuous ladies. In the second stanza quoted, the syntax allows the last line to be ambivalent, open to two apparently incompatible readings. On one level Bernart is reiterating a commonplace about the worth and status to be had from *fin'amor*: that through love he is as worthy as an emperor; on an ironic level he is again boasting of sexual fulfilment and it would thus seem likely that he is using the term *fin'amor*, generally used to designate a pure emotion, ironically, as here it affords him physical gratification.[12]

Bernart Marti

Bernart's propensity for introspection and self-examination is equally evident in his moralizing poetry. He does not, like Marcabru, indulge in general invectives; his grievances are usually specific and he concentrates on the aspect of a problem that affects him personally (poem II):

v   Lengua forcat traversan   25
si·ll metetz deniers davan
far vos ha de gossa quan,
e d'eisa guiza levar
lo dia tro lendeman
tan son savi del mesclar.   30

vi   Si·l cuiatz el ponh tener
e·l avetz dat vostr'aver,
el ho fara assaber
a l'autre, que·ill volra dar,
per so que sapcha tener   35
lo tort contra·l dreit baisar.

v

If you put money before an evil, fork-tongued man, he will make a bitch into a dog for you, and in the same way make the day into the next, so good are they at confusing.

vi

If you think you have him under your thumb and have given him all your money, he will tell the other one about this, for he will want to give to him so that he might stop evil losing ground to rectitude.

Farai un vers ab son novel
e vuelh m'en a totz querelar,
qu'apenas trobi qui m'apel
ni sol mi denhe l'uelh virar:
trobat m'an nesci e fadelh
quar no sai aver aiustar.   (vi, 1–6)

I will compose a verse with a new tune and I want to quarrel with everyone because of this, for I can hardly find anyone to summon me or even to deign to look at me: they have found me so foolish and idiotic because I do not know how to make money.

Bernart plays the rôle of the victim of immorality rather than its supreme judge. This may be a device to incite pity or a way of moralizing by inverse example, but Bernart lacks Marcabru's satirical bite. His main concern is with an individual's predicament rather than with the morals of the outside world and poems like *A senhor* (II) and *Farai un vers* (VI) should perhaps be understood, like *Amar dei* and *Quan l'erb'es*, as subjective.

In *D'entier vers far* (v), the poem in which Bernart attacks Peire d'Alvernha for boasting of being the first to compose *vers entiers*, 'whole poetry', Bernart spells out his message unequivocally; he is criticizing Peire's vanity from a moral and poetic point of view.[13] He contends that an important prerequisite of the modesty, poetic and moral integrity he advocates is self-knowledge:

x   E selh no par ges cortes,   55
qui·s lauza ni·s glorifia,

quar eys Dieus nos anuncia –
'qui trop s'yssaussa mens es
bayssan, e selh levatz es
qui segon so s'umilia'.   60

XI   So dis, qu'om si conogues,
      e qui aisso gardaria,
      ia no·s sobrelauzaria,
      que sobrelaus follesc es
      e pareys be si pros es   65
      ia el mezeis non o dia.

X
And he who praises or glorifies himself does not make a courtly impression at all, for
God himself announces to us: 'he who exalts himself too much is humbled and a man is
exalted in as much as he humbles himself'.

XI
He [God] says this, that one should know oneself, and he who observes this would not
praise himself too highly, for over-praising oneself is folly and if one is worthy, this is
apparent without one saying so oneself.

It is perhaps self-knowledge that Bernart is striving for above all in his poems,
and irony is frequently a tool to this end, highlighting the disparity between
courtly ideals and reality.

COMPANHO, PER COMPANHIA

Companho, per companhia (IV) stands apart from Bernart's other moralizing
poems. First, it is partly a love song: Hoepffner even classifies it as a *canso* in
his edition and at the end of the poem Bernart clearly turns away from
moralizing towards the type of introspection that characterizes *Amar dei.*
Secondly, although rhetorical irony of the kind Marcabru uses is absent,
Bernart's 'sourire amusé' is definitely present. He again constantly invites his
audience to question the sincerity of what he says.

I   Companho, per companhia
         de folor
      soi d'amor en gran error:
      laidament romp e deslia
      e·l iovens qu'en leis se fia   5
         vai marritz
      pels amadors apostitz.

II   Ma part ai en la folia,
         chantador,
      quar anc fui proatz d'amor,   10
      c'al comensar me fon pia,
      mas era·m torn'en bauzia
         tot quan ditz
      per que·m tenc per avelitz.

III   Mas ab bels mentir[s] prendia   15
         ses clamor,

92

no tem mais escarnidor
qu'ela ditz ver quan mentia
et ieu ment can ver dizia;
a envitz   20
rema lo drutz esbaïtz.

IV   Pos a trichamen saillia
trichador,
trichem tug dompneiador,
que·l trichars abaisaria   25
mas lo trichament; ceria
feblezitz
lo tric de la trichairitz.

V   Mas a engan se vezia
ses paor   30
....
enguanat enguanaria
enguanatz; de felonia
vai garnitz
com enguan'enguanairitz.   35

VI   Pero per conseill faria
la leuior
Bernart Martin lo pintor
que ditz a trai guirentia:
greu er amor ses putia   40
camiairitz
tro que·l mon sia fenitz.

VII Uzatges es c'om en ria
o qu'en plor:
anc nuils hom a dezonor   45
non fes plag en drudaria,
per qu'ieu penrai de la mia,
totz aunitz,
lo be que·m n'es escaritz.

VIII Eu n'aurai la senhoria   50
en pascor
quan so·l ram carguat de flor;
tals pot esser l'escaria
qu'encaras reverdiria
la raïtz   55
e·l verguan estes floritz.

I

Companions, because of the companionship of folly I am in great perplexity concerning love: it breaks and destroys in an ugly manner and the young man who trusts in it is made miserable by false lovers.

II

I have played my part in the folly, singers, as ever was I tested in love, for it behaved well towards me to start with, but now it turns everything it said into falsehood, because of which I consider myself dishonoured.

III

Since it stole with sweet lies and without fuss, I no longer fear the person that mocks, for it tells the truth when it used to lie, and I lie when I used to tell the truth; the lover remains dumbfounded reluctantly.

IV

Since it used to make the cheater cheat, let all us lovers cheat, for cheating would lower cheating even more; the cheating woman's cheating would then be weakened.

V

But it [love] saw itself wrongly without fear ... the cheated would cheat the cheated; he goes around armed with treachery as he cheats the cheating woman.

VI

But he would advisedly follow the frivolity of Bernart Marti, the painter, for he says and guarantees: love can rarely exist without fickle whoredom, until the world ends.

VII

It is customary that one laughs about it or cries about it; no man was ever dishonoured by making a pact with love, wherefore I, all covered in shame, will take from mine the good thing that has fallen to my lot from it.

VIII

I will rule over it at Easter, when the branches are covered in flowers; fate can be such that the root may turn green again and the rod may flower.

Bernart begins his song on a heavy moralizing note reminiscent of Marcabru. The assonance *folor/amor/error*, which is accentuated by the rhyme, leaves no doubt as to his feelings: love is destructive and evil. The song is directed to Bernart's *companho* and although this formula is used by Guilhem IX, it is not used here in the same way. Whereas Guilhem was a powerful lord addressing his entourage, Bernart is presumably addressing his equals and the opening of this poem is thus nearer in spirit to Marcabru addressing his *compaignier*, or the other *soudadier*. Moreover, the dedication of this song to Bernart's *companho* suggests that the song was intended for an exclusively male audience and consequently that its ethos is not that of the *canso*, which requires the notional presence of a woman, even if she is fictional and effectively excluded from the poetic discourse.

The second stanza is also reminiscent of Marcabru, who on two occasions admits to having been duped by carnal love or to having sung with 'foolish troubadours' (VII, 15–18, XXXI, 73–6). Here Bernart says he has played his part in the 'folly', in other words he has sung of love without realizing the trap he set himself. Like Marcabru's *puta* (XLIV, 9–11), Bernart's *amor* is kind to start with, but soon shows its true colours: it turns everything into falsehood, and Bernart continues in this vein throughout the third stanza.

The first three stanzas could almost be by Marcabru. The tone then suddenly changes in stanza IV, first because of the word-play on *trichar* and secondly because of the content. In this seven-line stanza there are seven variations on the one radical, *trichar*. The technique of playing on one radical like this was common in the late Old French dramatic monologues and the effect in performance was clearly humorous.[14] The alliteration and assonance here alter the tone considerably and Bernart suggests in this jaunty manner that since cheating is so common, everyone should cheat, as this is the only way to hold one's own and to combat the cheating of others. He plays the same game with *enguanar* in the next stanza and although he describes the participants in his *ronde* as 'armed with treachery' the tone of the previous stanza is maintained.

However, it is not just in tone that stanzas IV and V contrast completely with the first three stanzas. They appear to advocate precisely what one might expect Bernart to condemn. These lines provoked Hoepffner to comment that Bernart accepted 'l'état des choses', Roncaglia to suspect he was one of the 'trobador ab sen d'enfanssa' whom Marcabru condemns, and Jean-Charles Payen to attribute to Bernart 'un immoralisme latent'.[15] However, Bernart immediately indicates that he intended his words ironically. The advice he has just given is 'Bernart Marti's frivolity' and not to be taken seriously: the joke is on the people who believe he intends every word to be taken literally and this is underlined by the rest of stanza VI which is in the form of a sententious declaration against love.

If stanzas IV and V are to be understood ironically, are they to be understood *per ironiam*? In other words, is the intended meaning the opposite of the literal meaning? In stanza VII, Bernart evokes emotions which he explores more thoroughly in *Amar dei*, ironically praising *drudaria* and saying 'I, all covered in shame, will take from mine the good thing that has fallen to my lot from it.' As in *Amar dei*, Bernart is playing on the meaning of the word *ben*, which usually has spiritual connotations, but which here is charged with sexual innuendo. If Bernart's lady, who interestingly enough is not mentioned in the poem, is as virtuous as might be expected, why should he be 'covered in shame'? If he is as morally upright as the tone of the first three stanzas suggests, why should he carry on consorting with her? Does not his *leuior* refer not only to his frivolous advice, but also to his own misdemeanours, past, present and future? The poem need not, of course, be a narration of actual events, but in his representation of his feelings in this poem Bernart finds himself joining in the *ronde*, just as he does in *Amar dei* and *Quan l'erb'es*, despite his apparent lucidity regarding love.

The irony in stanzas IV and V does not, therefore, amount to outright condemnation through *ironia*. It might be Bernart's frivolous advice, but in the light of his subsequent admission to being as guilty as the next man, it also has the effect of showing that such matters are not as simple as one might at first think. The last stanza must consequently also be understood as ambivalent. Again Bernart sees love as a power struggle: he wants to rule over love and by extension over his lady. The images of Easter and spring symbolize renewal, both spiritual and physical, but the connotations of the flowering *verguan*, 'rod', are surely more erotic than spiritual. The poem ends on a note of erotic expectation which is incongruous with the moralizing tone of the first three stanzas and the last part of stanza VI. It is, however, entirely compatible with Bernart's admission of his own weakness, and, juxtaposed as it is to the shame of the previous stanza, it contributes to the ironic tone of the whole poem.

Such irony would be alien to a troubadour like Marcabru. Capable of adopting his adversaries' point of view or style in order to parody them, he never admits to taking part in the debauchery he condemns, unless it is to further his aims as a moralist. Marcabru wants above all to moralize; Bernart seems to want to examine his own reactions to the moral and emotional problems with which he is confronted.

CONCLUSION

Bernart Marti is not an immoralist whose ideas are opposed to Marcabru's. He accepts the triangular nature of conventional *fin'amor*:

> Dona es vas drut trefana
> de s'amor pos tres n'apana;
> estra lei
> n'i son trei,
> mas ab son marit l'autrei
> un amic cortes prezant. (III, 10–15)

A lady is disloyal in love towards her lover if she gives it to three men; it is against the law that there should be three of them, although I do allow her one worthy friend as well as her husband.

But this in itself does not make him an immoralist. Marcabru too condones a lady taking a lover and does not condemn adultery, only promiscuity. The difference between Marcabru and Bernart does not lie in their moral standpoints: the two are in fact very close in this respect.[16] It lies rather in Bernart's introspection and in his questioning of the feasibility of the moral standards he has set himself. These differences are reflected in the use the two poets make of irony: Marcabru uses it as a weapon and as a device to entertain, Bernart as a means of undermining his own utterances.

If I am correct in my view that Bernart Marti's work is intensely personal, this may go some way towards explaining his apparently marginal status in the troubadour tradition. Beggiato suggests that so few of Bernart's poems have survived because he was not a professional troubadour. He believes Bernart's work has all the qualities of an amateur poet, that it is often clumsily obscure, and he attributes his unusual, ironic treatment of the conventions of *fin'amor* to the fact that he was not a 'full-time' troubadour.[17] Yet Bernart's poetry is hardly unsophisticated and it is equally possible that his marginal status in the tradition stems from the fact that he chose to take an individualistic, subjective line, subverting conventions in a manner that may have been as disturbing for his contemporaries as it has been for some modern critics.

4

Peire d'Alvernha

Peire d'Alvernha admired Marcabru and did not mind being seen to imitate him:

> Chantador, lo vers vos fenis:
> aprendetz la comensansa.
> Marcabrus per gran dreitura
> trobet d'altretal semblansa. (XIII, 36–9)

Singers, I finish the verse for you: learn the beginning. Marcabru, through great rectitude, composed in a similar way.

There are, however, fundamental differences between Peire's poetry and Marcabru's, differences which affect considerably the use the two poets make of irony.

Marcabru is concerned more with truth and meaning than with eloquence. Unquestionably proud of his own skills, he mistrusts eloquence which can be put to the service of evil and explicitly condemns obscurity. There are, of course, different levels of meaning in Marcabru's poetry, but they are distinct and discernible; his chief concern is to convey a message, and ambivalence, where it exists, is intended to enhance rather than confuse his exposition of the moral issues at stake.[1]

Peire, on the other hand, delights in eloquence for its own sake. In his love lyrics, he extols the quality of his poetry, not, like Bernart de Ventadorn, in order to illustrate how it is inspired only by the quality of his love, but because he wishes to demonstrate his superiority as a poet:[2]

> Ab fina ioia comenssa
> lo vers qui bels motz assona
> e de re no·i a faillenssa;
> mas no m'es bon qe l'apreigna
> tals cui mos chans non coveigna,
> q'ieu non vuoill avols chantaire,
> cel que tot chan desfaissona,
> mon doutz sonet torn'en bram. (III, 1–8)

With sincere joy the verse, which makes beautiful words pleasant sounding, begins, and there is nothing at fault in it; but it is not pleasing to me that someone for whom my song might not be suitable should learn it, for I do not want a vile singer, of the kind that deforms all singing, to turn my sweet tune into roaring.

Similarly, in his moralizing poetry, there are indications that Peire is more concerned with his *eloquentia* than with any message he is trying to convey:

> Que cum l'aurs resplan e l'azurs
>   contra·l fer ros
>   *de*sobre *l*os escutz
> mi det do, tro lai ont es Surs,
>   qu'ieu sobriers fos
> als grans et als menutz
>   dels esciens
> de trobar ses fenhs fatz,
>   don sui grazens
> ad aquelh don m'es datz.*   (v, 61–70)

For just as gold and azure shine against the rusty steel on shields, it has been given to me, from here to Tyre, to be superior to the great and the small amongst all those who know how to compose without foolish presumptions, wherefore I am grateful to the one through whom this is given to me.

This text no doubt has a moral element,[3] but it is Peire's pride in his own eloquence that prevails, for this is the last stanza of the poem. Thus it comes as no surprise that he ends another moralizing song by boasting about his *trobar*:

> Peire d'Alvernha mot quera
> qui acomtos us'a concas:*
> e per aqui hom lo sabra,
> car del fin trobar non roncas,
> ans n'as ben la flor plus belha:
> detorz e l'art e l'aparelh,
> e no·i a motz fals que rovelh
> ni sobredolat d'astelha.   (xv, 57–64)

Peire d'Alvernha will search for a way of speaking which uses embellishments by the bushel load; and through this men will know it, for you do not wait a long time for fine poetry, rather you indeed have its finest flower; I display the art and the tool and there is no false, rusting word, nor any excessive planing away of splinters.

For Peire it would seem that eloquence was an end in itself and he appears to take great pleasure in the use of 'colours', as if at times he were striving for deliberate ambiguity.[4]

De Riquer believes Peire is ironic when he boasts of his superiority as a poet,[5] but with the exception of his claim to be 'maïstres de totz' at the end of *Cantarai d'aqestz trobadors* (xii, 82), which is clearly humorous, such boasts are not undermined in any way that would indicate irony. Peire may exaggerate and have an inflated view of his talents, but he clearly does believe himself to be a great poet:

Peire d'Alvernha

Sobre·l vieill trobar e·l novel
vueill mostrar mon sen als sabens
qu'entendon be   aquels c'a venir son
c'anc tro per me   no fo faitz vers entiers.   (XI, 1–4)

Upon the old and new ways of composing poetry I wish to show my wisdom to the wise, so that those who are yet to come might understand that never, before me, was a 'whole' song composed.

The fact that Bernart Marti, Peire's contemporary, took this boast seriously and saw no irony in it is surely evidence enough that Peire intended it unequivocally.

It is in keeping with Peire's own view of his poetry that deliberate ambiguity in his moralizing songs does not lead to irony. He uses ambiguity to embellish, to suggest further levels of meaning, all of which are plausible and possible. No one interpretation is valid to the exclusion of others: there is no ironic meaning that deliberately undermines for an initiated audience the literal meaning of the statement.[6] It is also in keeping with Peire's *eloquentia* that, with the exception of poems in which he appears to be parodying the style of other troubadours, he wants his poetry to be taken seriously. Peire refers over and over again to his *sen* and *saber*:[7] he is a serious poet and wants no one to forget it. He is also a confident poet, as his claims about his poetry show: there is no room for the self-examination that leads to irony in Bernart Marti's songs.

Peire nevertheless has recourse to irony for very specific purposes: he is ironic when writing political satire and when he wishes to be comic. His love poems, his devotional songs and his general, sententious moralizing poems abound with 'artful' ambiguities, but these do not subvert the literal meaning. I shall examine individually the poems where I believe Peire is ironic: II, XIII, XIV, IV, XII:

AL DESSEBRAR DEL PAÏS

This interesting poem has attracted very little critical comment.[8] To my knowledge, the only critic to have provided an extensive analysis of it is Leslie Topsfield: he discerned a close pattern of intertextual play between *Al dessebrar* (II) and songs by Jaufre Rudel, involving rhyme sounds (*-is*, *-ays*, *-onia*), key words (*alegre, irays, camis, Sarrazis, vezis*) and the device of a refrain word. For Topsfield, Peire and Jaufre share a commitment to an abstract ideal they call 'love':

Jaufre in *Belhs m'es* rejected the confusion and burden of sensual or 'close' love and turned to *Fin'amors*, and in *Lanquan li jorn* he sought joy in separation from 'close' love and the illumination of the mind through the memory of distant love. Peire finds joy in freedom from dominant 'close' love, but he also sees danger in too great a delight in human love, and the line *que paors es de perir* (39) implies that earthly love which is too pleasing may lose a man his hope of salvation. Peire demands distance in love in order to preserve his mental, social and spiritual self.[9]

99

Troubadours and irony

As Topsfield suggested, *Al dessebrar* is closely connected to Jaufre Rudel's small canon of seven poems. However, is it true that Peire and Jaufre are both finding *joi* by rejecting a 'close' love? Is Peire really developing Jaufre's themes, or is he reacting against them?

In Topsfield's view, Jaufre needed distant love in order to maintain the purity and quality of his feelings. A key poem in his interpretation of Jaufre's corpus is *Belhs m'es* (v). Topsfield sees one stanza of this poem as crucial to an understanding of Jaufre's *amor de lonh*. He quotes it as follows, from Jeanroy's edition (iv), with the following translation:

> Mas per so m'en sui encharzitz,
> Ja no·n creyrai lauzenjador,
> Qu'anc no fuy tan lunhatz d'amor
> Qu'er no·n sia sals e gueritz.
> Plus savis hom de mi mespren,
> Per qu'ieu sai ben az escien
> Qu'anc fin'amors home non trays. (29–35)

Since by this means I have improved my standing [my self-respect], I will nevermore believe the slanderer, for never was I so distant from love that now I may not be saved from it and cured of it. A wiser man than I can fall into error, and for this reason I know truly that *Fin'Amors* never betrayed a man.

For Topsfield, 'Jaufre is rejoicing at freeing himself from a love which he calls *Amors* and which, as he says, was not "distant" enough and caused him grief and confusion of mind.'[10] In his view, this stanza shows that Jaufre rejected close, venal love in favour of a higher spiritual love (*Fin'amors*): Jaufre's view of love, though expressed in different terms, is thus, for Topsfield, identical to Marcabru's.

In a recent article Pol Skårup demonstrates that this interpretation of lines 29–35 of *Belhs m'es* is based upon an incorrect translation of lines 31–2:

> cette construction est constituée par les éléments suivants: verbe accompagné d'une négation + *tan* + *que* + *no* + subjonctif . . . Dans notre construction, c'est la subordonnée dépendant de *tan* qui porte l'information principale. En la traduisant, on peut rendre la principale par une subordonnée concessive du type: 'quelque . . . que' et la consécutive par une principale, en supprimant les deux négations: 'quelque profondément que j'aie dormi, je me réveillais par peur' . . . Et dans le passage qui nous intéresse: 'quelque *lunhatz d'amor* que j'aie été, j'en suis maintenant sauf et guéri', c'est-à-dire qu'il a été effectivement très *lunhatz d'amor*, mais malgré cela, il en est à présent sauf et guéri.[11]

In other words, after having been distanced from love, Jaufre is now cured of this and 'close' to love again. Skårup suggests that *Mas per so* (line 29) is grammatically related to *Que* (line 31) and that line 30 can only be an interjection. He proposes the following punctuation:

> Mas per so m'en sui encharzitz
> (Ja no·n creyrai lauzenjador):
> Qu'anc no fuy tan lunhatz d'amor

Peire d'Alvernha

Qu'er no·n sia sals e gueritz.
Plus savis hom de mi mespren,
Per qu'ieu sai ben az escien
Qu'anc fin'amors home non trays.

But through this I have raised my worth (never will I believe a slanderer in this): never was I so distanced from love that now I am not safe and cured of this. A wiser man than myself can err, wherefore I know truly that pure love never betrayed anyone.

Fin'amors betrays no one in this stanza because Jaufre is brought back to *amor*. There is no dichotomy here between *fin'amors* and *amor*; they are one and the same thing. Jaufre is not choosing a 'distant' love and rejecting a 'close' love; on the contrary, the type of love he desires is clearly 'close'.[12]

In fact, Jaufre continually yearns to approach his *amor de lonh*:

> Amors de terra lonhdana
> per vos totz lo cors mi dol.
> E no·n puosc trobar meizina
> si non vau al sieu reclam
> ab atraich d'amor doussana,
> dinz vergier o sotz cortina
> ab dezirada companha. (III, 8–14)

Oh, love from a distant land, my entire heart grieves because of you; and I find no cure for this, if I do not go to her bait, drawn by sweet love, in a garden or behind a screen, with a desired companion.

> Ben tenc lo Senhor per verai
> per qu'ieu veirai l'amor de lonh;
> mas per un ben que m'en eschai
> n'ai dos mals, quar tan m'es de lonh.
> Ai! car me fos lai pelegris,
> si que mos fustz e mos tapis
> fos pels sieus belhs huelhs remiratz! (IV, 29–35)

I indeed believe the Lord to be true, wherefore I will see the distant love; but for every good thing that befalls me, there are two bad things, because she is so far from me. Ah! If only I were a pilgrim there, so that my staff and my carpet might be seen by her beautiful eyes.

The force of Jaufre's poetry, the appeal that his *amor de lonh* still has to this day, are derived from the fact that he is unable to approach his love, despite his desire to do so. He does not wish to remain distant:

> Car nulhs autres jois tan no·m plai
> cum jauzimens d'amor de lonh.
> Mas so qu'ieu vuelh m'es atahis,
> qu'enaissi·m fadet mos pairis
> qu'ieu ames e non fos amatz. (IV, 45–9)

For no other joy pleases me as much as the possession of a distant love. But what I want is not permitted me, for thus was I cursed by my godfather, that I should love and not be loved.

Jaufre's love is unrequited and distant (though this may be a metaphor), but he laments this and does not accept it. Only in *Belhs m'es* does Jaufre manage to achieve his goal of reaching his *amor de lonh*. In this song he is triumphant, restored, in the place where he wishes to be:

> Er ai ieu joi e sui jausitz
> e restauratz en ma valor,
> e non irai jamais alhor
> ni non querrai autrui conquistz. (v, 8–11)

Now I have joy and am given joy, and I am restored to my worth, I will never go anywhere else, nor will I seek another conquest.

Jaufre's constant desire is to be with his *amor de lonh*. In this one poem he achieves his aim.

In *Al dessebrar*, Peire d'Alvernha cannot, then, be developing Jaufre's themes in *Bels m'es* or in any other poem. Jaufre is always moving towards distant love; in *Al dessebrar*, Peire deliberately distances himself from love as much as possible, with, I believe, heavy irony at Jaufre's expense. I have re-edited the poem.

> I Al dessebrar del païs
> on m'avi'amors conquis
> aprendetz, si no·us es fays,
> so don m'alegr'e m'irays
>   on que·m vir;   5
> mas tan cum suy ab gent conia
> no·m dey per ira marrir
> qu'on mays puesc apres non ponia.
>
> II Mas ves un'amor fuy fis
> tro qu'a lieys plac que·m giquis   10
> e quar al sieu tort mi trays
> ben fazen e .   .   .   .   .
>   ab den dir,
> quar de doussa terra conia
> mi trays e·m fetz dessalhir,   15
> mas, quan que tric, l'er vergonia.
>
> III Anc non aniey tans camis
> ves Francs ni ves Sarrazis,
> on mielhs fos demandatz iays
> ni plus amatz pretz verays   20
>   ab servir;
> e·ls gens qu'es cortez'e conia,

sill que·m veiran tart venir,
ta mal m'es qui m'en deslonia.

IV Si l'amor don fuy vezis,   25
dont ara m'esfredezis,
amer'ieu plus que Roays,
e si no·m fos per fols brays
   trassalhir
et a la mia doussa conia   30
si m'eschai e ses mentir,
vos agratz d'aital messonia.

V D'esser hueymais m'esbaudis
pus amars m'enamarzis;
qu'ara·m sent de totz assays   35
vertz e blancs e brus e bays;
   e m'albir,
e dic vos d'amor nems conia
que paors es de perir
lai on li es ops que lonia.   40

VI Ar am ses cors e fals ris
tot aisi cum l'abelhis;
qu'ieu mi gurp de lieys e·m lays
e mi no veyra iamais.
   A partir   45
m'ave de la terra conia:
si no·m fos per que·s n'azir,
mes mi for'en la canonia.

VII Senher n'Estrieu, qui s'aconia
de trop human ioy iauzir,   50
mal fai qui non lo calonia.

I

As I leave the land where love had conquered me, learn, if this does not burden you, what makes me happy and what saddens me, wherever I go; but as long as I am with charming people, I must not be saddened by anger, so that afterwards I might not be able to censure where I am able to do most.

II

But I was faithful to one love until it pleased her to abandon me, and because she betrayed me unjustly through her good deeds, . . . with kind words, the greater will be her shame, however much she cheats/delays, for she sent me forth and made me leave a charming land.

III

I have never been along so many roads, towards Franks nor towards Saracens, where joy was more in demand, nor true worth more loved with service; and the people who are courtly and pleasant, the ones who will not see me for a long time – I certainly dislike anyone who distances me from them.

IV

Indeed, I would have loved more than Edessa that love to which I used to be close, and which now leaves me cold, and if I did not have to transgress by braying foolishly, and if I grant myself to my sweet, charming lady, and that without lying , you would have such a lie.

V

Henceforth I rejoice in living, since false love makes me bitter; for now I feel green, white and brown and bay regarding all tests; and I take stock and I say to you concerning love that is too attractive: there is a danger of perishing in that place from which one needs to distance oneself.

VI

Now I love without haste or false laughter exactly as it pleases her; for I leave her and give up and she will never see me again. It is fitting that I should leave the sweet land: if I did not have to annoy her, I would put myself in a canonry.

VII

My lord Estrieu, it would be wrong not to challenge a man who attaches himself to the pleasures of too human a joy.

As Topsfield points out, the stylistic device of a refrain word, the use of certain key words and the occurrence of certain rhymes in this song echo Jaufre too closely for there not to be deliberate intertextual play intended. Moreover, Peire opens the poem by announcing his departure from the country where love had conquered him, a deliberate reversal of the direction Jaufre takes, metaphorically or otherwise, in all his poems. Peire claims he ought not to give in to his *ira* when with charming people, but as he concentrates on his *ira* throughout the poem, this is ironic. He expresses his desire to censure: like Marcabru he is a *castiador*, and the rhyming of *ponia* and *conia* surely undermines the deceptively gentle tone which the use of *conia* as a refrain word might otherwise set.

In stanzas II and III, Peire explains why he is leaving this land of 'courtly and pleasant people' and 'true worth' (lines 17–22), although, as in Jaufre's poetry, any image of distance or movement may be metaphorical. His lady betrayed him; she may have appeared to act kindly, but her good deeds and kind words were deceptive (lines 11–13). Hence Peire reproaches her personally, bitterly and explicitly.

The ironic force of the poem is concentrated into the next stanza. By this stage, an initiated audience would certainly have recognized the reversal of the *amor de lonh* theme: the last word it has heard is, after all, *deslonia*. The first line of stanza IV again evokes Jaufre: Peire was close (*vezis*) to this love; now it grows cold within him. Whereas Jaufre's desire increases with distance, Peire's diminishes. He presents as a hypothesis that he might have loved his lady (or his love) more than Edessa, but this is undermined and shown to be ironic by the rest of the stanza, in which it is made clear that to maintain this would be lying. What does Peire mean by *fols brays* in line 28? He could mean courtly platitudes. In courtly terms, however, Peire is guilty of uttering *fols brays* in this poem because he is criticizing love. He is therefore using the term ironically here. He will indeed continue with his *fols brays*, although he, of course, does not think they are foolish. He refers to his lady as *la mia doussa conia*, which, in the light of his criticism of her in stanzas II and III, can only be understood *per contrarium*. It is thus no accident that *conia* rhymes with *messonia*.

In stanza V, Peire rejoices because love made him bitter. He feels strong as he distances himself from love and the end of the stanza must again evoke Jaufre for the initiated audience because of the word *lonia*. Indeed, the last lines of this stanza only make sense if they are understood as an explicit rejection of the type of love Jaufre advocates.

The final stanza restates the criticism of Peire's former lady and reaffirms that he is abandoning love; he would put himself in a canonry, but he wishes to annoy his former love, and doing so would give her the victory in their conflict. He now gives the impression that he is happy and relieved to leave this *amor nems conia* and this too may be an intentional play on Jaufre's work:

> Iratz e jauzens m'en partrai
> s'ieu ja la vei, l'amor de lonh. (IV, 15–16)

Glad and joyful will I leave her/it, if I see her/it, the distant love.

The *envoi* of the poem addresses a lord Estrieu, who has not been identified, but it seems likely that the *envoi* is ironic. Peire is not openly accusing Estrieu of not speaking out against those who achieve human joy, he is merely drawing his attention to a moral platitude. However, this technique is widely used by Marcabru to attack immoral people and Peire may well be ironically criticizing Estrieu here.

The constant reversal of Jaufre Rudel's themes in this poem, without ever mentioning his name, creates a pervasive irony at Jaufre's expense. There may, however, be a further level of meaning. In stanza IV, Peire refers to Edessa (*Roays*). It was the fall of Edessa on Christmas Day, 1145, that provoked the Second Crusade and among the Occitan contingent of the Christian armies that left for the Holy Land was Jaufre Rudel.[13]

Peire says he might have loved his lady 'more than Edessa', but he has already stated that his lady has betrayed him and that he has left her; moreover, he undermines this proposition, explicitly stating three times that to say he loved his lady more than Edessa would be a lie (lines 28–32). To mention Edessa at all evokes the reasons for the Second Crusade; to mention it in this way, implying that Edessa is certainly much more important than love, must surely indicate that the fall of Edessa was still a topical issue at the time *Al dessebrar* was composed. It would therefore seem likely that Peire composed this song between 1146 and 1150 at the latest, which does not radically conflict with what is known of his career, for one other song was probably composed before 1149.[14]

If Peire composed this song before 1150 in ironic criticism of Jaufre, he probably knew Jaufre was leaving, or had left, on the Crusade: Marcabru certainly knew Jaufre was 'outremer' in 1148 (XV, 37–8). For some, Jaufre's *amor de lonh* is a metaphor for the crusading ideal, but he only proclaims his devotion to this ideal once explicitly, and elsewhere the latent eroticism of his poetry would seem to belie this interpretation.[15] Given that Peire criticizes Jaufre's notion of 'distant love' throughout *Al dessebrar*, it is possible that this reference to Edessa is also intended as a criticism of Jaufre. According to Peire, the man who puts love above all else is wrong (lines 38–40); the crusading ideal is more important and worth abandoning love for (lines 25–32). Could Peire mean that the Crusade, for which Edessa is a synecdoche, is more important than Jaufre's *amor de lonh*, or even, that in his view, Jaufre puts love above the Crusade?

Unfortunately, we shall never know the answer to this question, nor whether Peire's poem dates from before or after Jaufre's departure for the Holy Land. It is interesting, however, that in the one poem where Jaufre explicitly proclaims the crusading ideal, he also claims to abandon love in a way that echoes Peire in *Al dessebrar*:

> Amors, alegre·m part de vos
> per so quar vau mo mielhs queren (VI[b], 29–30)

Love, I leave you happily, for I go to seek what is better for me.

These lines, and the commitment to the Crusade which follows (lines 36–42), represent a change in the poem's direction, for, until this point, it has been a love song typical of Jaufre's corpus. It is as if Jaufre, like Peire, has given up love for a higher ideal. Whether or not these lines are a response to Peire's poem is a question which is likely to remain unanswered. It does seem, though, that Peire's *Al dessebrar* may be an extended metaphorical statement of the crusading ideal.[16]

BEL M'ES, QUAN LA ROZA FLORIS

Critics have generally confined themselves to commenting on the last stanza of *Bel m'es*, which is considered proof that Peire admired Marcabru.[17] It has not, to my knowledge, been considered as a whole. Does the reference to Marcabru at the end of the poem affect in any way the text as a whole? Why should Peire cite Marcabru in this song in particular? I have re-edited the poem, number XIII in del Monte's edition.

> I Bel m'es, quan la roza floris
> e·l gens terminis s'enansa,
> fas'un vers a ma ventura,
> don mos cors es en balansa,
> pel dous chan del rossinhol
> c'aug chantar la nueit escura
> per los verdiers e pels plais.
>
> II Reis, per Crestians faillis,
> quar Masmutz nos faun sobransa:

coms ni dux non senh sentura   10
mieills de vos feira de lansa;
per l'emperador me dol,
c'a moutas gens fai fraitura:
tals en plora que n'a iais.

III   Vostre coratges s'esclarzis,   15
qu'ar n'avetz bon'esperansa;
sobre paguans, gens tafura,
cavalguatz cenes duptansa;
premiers penretz Labadol,
e si anatz ab dreitura   20
tro a Marroc feiran lais.

IV   Sel que·l ioi del setgle delis
vei que son pretz dezenansa;
fils es d'avol criatura,
que fai avol demostransa,   25
e per tan no·n baisa·l col
qu'ar gitatz es a noncura.
E'stai mais entre·ls savais.

V   Per mi non dic, tan m'abelis,
quan vei molt gran alegransa;   30
amors vol calonia dura;
e no pot aver fizansa
se·l carnal amar non vol;
quar vei que cors non a cura
mas de senhor que engrais.   35

VI   Chantador, lo vers vos fenis:
aprendetz la comensansa.
Marcabrus per gran dreitura
trobet d'altretal semblansa,
e tengon lo tug per fol   40
qi no conois sa natura
[q]e no·ill membre per qe·s nais.

I

It pleases me when the rose flowers and the sweet season advances that I should compose a verse for my good fortune, about which my heart is uncertain, because of the sweet song of the nightingale which I hear singing in the dark night in the gardens and along the hedgerows.

II

Oh, King, it is because of Christians you have failed, since the Muslims are overpowering us: there is no count or duke who girds his sword who could strike better than you with a lance; I grieve for the Emperor, who is missed by many people: some weep about this who [in reality] have joy because of it.

III

Your heart lightens, for now you have good hope from this; ride against pagans, the base people, without fear: first you will take Badajoz, and if you go on with rectitude, they would lament as far as Morocco.

IV

I see the worth of the one who destroys worldly joy declining; he is the son of a vile creature, for he behaves badly and for all that does not bow his head, so that now he is despised. And he remains ever more amongst the evil ones.

V

I do not say this for myself, so happy am I when I see great rejoicing; love wants harsh strife; and it cannot feel secure unless it wants carnal love, for I see that the body does not take care of anything except that its lord should grow fat.

VI

Singers, I finish the verse for you: learn the beginning. Marcabru, through great rectitude, composed in a similar way, and they all consider him a fool who does not know his nature because he does not remember why he is born.

Zenker's dating of this song between August 1157 and August 1158 is convincing. Peire refers to a king and to an emperor who has died; the song was clearly composed in Spain. The only emperor this can refer to is Alfonso VII of Castile and Leon, who died in August 1157. His son, Sancho III, inherited his domains, but was known as King, not as Emperor. Sancho died young, in August 1158.[18]

At first glance the poem appears diffuse. It begins as an exhortation to Sancho to fight the Moors, but the last three stanzas do not mention the *reconquista* at all. They strike a moralizing tone, reminiscent of Marcabru, and end with a statement of solidarity with his *dreitura*. Peire also ironically attacks Marcabru's adversaries; in his view it is they who are the fools, not Marcabru as they hold. How does this stanza affect the meaning of the rest of the poem?

Ostensibly stanza IV is an attack on the destroyer of worldly joy. Elsewhere Peire defends one type of worldly joy (VI, 25–36), and the stanza may thus be read as a diatribe against the destroyer of this *entier* worldly joy. However, this is difficult to reconcile with his attack on *amors* and *carnal amar* (possibly synonyms for *lo ioi del setgle*) in the following stanza. Moreover, there seems to be no dichotomy here between two joys, one good, one bad, or between *fin'amor* and *fals'amor*.[19] Perhaps *Sel* (line 22) designates a particular person.

Given that Peire evokes the opinions of Marcabru's critics in order to praise him and condemn them in the final stanza, he may well be doing the same here. The one who destroys worldly joy could then be Marcabru himself. He was, after all, a well-known critic of worldly pleasure, feared for his sharp tongue. If *Sel* does designate Marcabru, it is easy to see why his reputation is declining: everybody (except Peire, of course) considers him a fool. Following this interpretation, in lines 24–8, Peire is ironically evoking the opinions of Marcabru's critics, possibly playing on lines from Marcabru's own poetry:

> Marcabrus, fills Marcabruna,
> fo engenratz en tal luna
> Qu'el sap d'Amor cum degruna. (XVIII, 67–9)

Marcabru, the son of Marcabruna, was conceived under such a moon that he knows how love casts its seed.

The use of the word *demostransa* (line 25) may be a reference to Marcabru's *Al son desviat*:

> L'amors don ieu sui mostraire
> Nasquet en un gentil aire. (v, 49–50)

The love I advocate was born of a noble line.

If *Sel* does refer to Marcabru, lines 26–8 are also ironic; the intended meaning for the initiated is that Marcabru has every good reason to hold his head high and that those who despise him and lower his reputation should be chastised.

If this interpretation is accepted, stanza v opens on a reassuring note for those whom Peire is attacking, the uninitiated audience who believes he is criticizing Marcabru sincerely: he ironically distances himself from the 'one who destroys worldly joy'. But the gentle tone of lines 29–30 makes the invective of lines 31–5 harsher, more violent, and the switch in tone could have produced a formidable impact in performance. Peire adopts the virulent and vituperative tone of Marcabru. Love wants harsh strife: it cannot feel secure unless it desires *carnal amar*. These lines involve *ironia per contrarium: fizansa* implies a good quality, but the kind of confidence this love has is, according to Peire, superficial and worthless, for it is inspired by *carnal amar*. This *ironia* is immediately followed by Peire's declaration of solidarity with Marcabru's ideals.

However, the reference to Marcabru is more than just a general statement of solidarity. Peire says 'Marcabru . . . composed in a similar way', wording which is surely not gratuitous, and which could mean 'Marcabru composed a song like this.' The first three stanzas are an exhortation, addressed to Sancho III, son of Alfonso VII, to fight a crusade against the Muslims in Spain. Marcabru himself addressed two songs to Alfonso (xxii and xxiii) and it is also possible that *Al son desviat* (v) commemorates Sancho's engagement as a child.[20] As de Riquer points out, in *Bel m'es*, Peire is evoking the songs in which Marcabru offered similar exhortations to the Spanish Emperor.[21] But to which of Marcabru's two *sirventes* to Alfonso does Peire allude? To *Emperaire, per mi mezeis* (xxii), which appears to be a straightforward exhortation, or to *Emperaire, per vostre prez* (xxiii), which is an ironic attack on the Emperor? Obviously the question is crucial to the interpretation of *Bel m'es*.

If Peire alludes to *Emperaire, per mi mezeis*, he is simply using Marcabru's name in order to support his plea to Sancho to fight the Muslims: Marcabru was, after all, well known as an advocator of the *reconquista*.[22] If, however, Peire is hoping to remind his audience of *Emperaire, per vostre prez*, the poem is open to an entirely different interpretation. By recalling Marcabru's ironic 'false praise', Peire could be warning Sancho that his praise could be considered ironic if Sancho does not act in the manner described in stanza iii. If this is the case, then certain words throughout the poem may be 'coloured', if not ironic. For example, *fai fraitura* (line 13) most obviously means 'is missed', but if Peire is deliberately recalling Marcabru's criticism of Alfonso the expression could equally well mean 'is at fault' or 'is lacking'.[23]

Similar irony may occur in stanza IV. *Faire avol demostransa* (line 25) can mean 'to behave badly', but it may also have its literal meaning of 'to give a vile proof'. Could Marcabru's 'vile proof' be his praise, or ironic praise, of Alfonso? It may be no coincidence that *demostransa* is reminiscent of the word used in Latin rhetorical manuals to denote 'praise and blame':[24] 'demonstrativum est quod tribuitur in alicuius certae personae laudem vel vituperationem' (*ad Herennium* I.2.2: 'the epideictic is devoted to the praise or censure of some particular person'). Marcabru's *avol demostransa* could thus be one of two things: first, his praise of Alfonso (in which case Peire is attacking Sancho in *Bel m'es*, as he is implying Marcabru's praise of Alfonso was unjustified); secondly, his criticism of Alfonso (in which case Peire's praise of Sancho may be sincere as he may be attacking Marcabru for criticizing Alfonso, his father).

It is not possible to tell from the text of *Bel m'es* to which of Marcabru's *sirventes* Peire is referring. It is even possible that the poem is intentionally ambiguous. Sancho's reign was brief, so whenever Peire composed the song, the King was a relative newcomer. No one knew how he was going to behave and Peire's song may well be designed to test Sancho's reactions. Will he be like his father, one of the men who consider Marcabru a fool? Or will he fulfil Marcabru's expectations as expressed in *Al son desviat*? The irony of the poem does not provide us with one intended meaning, but leaves these questions unanswered.[25]

Whatever the motivation of the song, one thing is clear: Peire admired Marcabru. It is thus interesting that Marcabru is referred to in the present tense throughout this song: *tengon, conois, membre*, and, if my interpretation of stanza IV is correct, *delis, dezenansa, es, fai, baisa*. The only verb used in relation to Marcabru which is in the past tense is *trobet*, which in any case refers to songs composed some fifteen years previously. Could *Bel m'es* be an indication that Marcabru was still alive in 1158? The evidence is slight, but the close link between Peire's *rossinhol* poems and Marcabru's *estornel* poems, the possibility that *Al dessebrar* may have been composed as early as 1146 and for a troubadour to whom Marcabru also addressed poetry, and this hint that Peire may have known Marcabru still to be alive in 1158, combine to suggest not only that their careers overlapped, but that the two troubadours actually knew each other.

BELH M'ES QUI A SON BON SEN

In *Bel m'es, quan la roza floris* Peire may deliberately allude to a poem in which Marcabru attacks Alfonso VII through ironic false praise, but it is not clear whether or not he himself uses the 'false praise *topos*'. In *Belh m'es qui a son bon sen* (XIV), as del Monte points out, there seems to be little doubt that his praise is ironic.[26]

I   Belh m'es qui a son bon sen
        qu'en bona cort lo prezen,
        q'us bes ab autre s'enansa
        e ricx mestiers conogutz,
        lai on pus es mentaugutz,   5
        val mais qu'a la comensansa.

II   Doncx aissi·m dei far parven,
        ieu que venc novellamen,
        e mostrar en detriansa
        lo saber que·m ne's cregutz,   10
        quar qui vas dos loc s'esdutz
        leu l'en sort grans alegransa.

III   Per que d'est comte aten
        de Barsalon'un don gen,
        que pro·m fass'e lluy onransa;   15
        e cre, si de dar non dutz,
        qu'en sa cort, on suy vengutz,
        es fams e vera mermansa.

IV   De baron m'es avinen
        qu'a verguonhos pessamen;   20
        tals o conoys que romansa:
        ans que s'en leu mager brutz,
        aitals afars trop saubutz
        non es grans mas per semblansa.

V   Ara·us es ops, e non len,   25
        efforsar contra joven,
        qu'us encombriers vos sobransa
        de sai, on lo solelh lutz,
        en que seretz deceubutz,
        s'acortz no ven deves Fransa.   30

VI   Qu'ab un iovencel valen
        avetz lai guerr'e conten,
        tal que fier si de sa lansa,
        que d'aquelhs Engles coütz
        ni dels vostres esternutz   35
        non a paor ni duptansa.

VII   Lai es lo vers remazutz
        on espazas sobr'escutz
        penran del forfag venjansa.

Troubadours and irony

I

It is pleasing to me that whoever has good sense should present it in a good court, for one good thing improves with another, and a noble craft, which is recognized as such in the place where it is most celebrated, is worth more than at the beginning.

II

Wherefore I must be quite open, I who have arrived recently, and show distinctly the knowledge which has grown in me from this, for the one who goes towards a sweet place can easily derive great happiness from this.

III

Wherefore I expect a gracious gift from this count of Barcelona, which may advance me and bring him honour, and I believe, if he does not behave generously, that there is hunger and true deprivation in his court, to which I have come.

IV

It seems pleasing to me that barons should have modest thoughts; a man who sings in romance knows this: before more noise is made, such a deed that is too well known is only great in appearance.

V

Now you must gather forces against youth, for an obstacle, here where the sun shines, is superior to you; you will be deceived in this if an agreement does not come from France.

VI

For there you make war and battle on a worthy young man so that he so strikes with his lance that he is neither afraid nor fearful of those be-tailed Englishmen, nor of your sneezing.

VI

The verse has come to an end where swords on shields will take vengeance for the crime.

This song contains references to two historical characters: Raymond Berengier IV of Barcelona, the count mentioned in stanza III, whom Peire addresses in stanza V, and his enemy, Raymond V of Toulouse, the *iovencel* of stanza VI. It dates from between 1158 and 1162.[27]

The first four stanzas of the poem appear to praise Raymond Berengier and give the impression that Peire has come to his court to seek patronage. In stanza V, Peire addresses the Count directly, but at the same time he actually begins to praise Raymond V of Toulouse, his enemy, and he continues to do so until the end of the poem. Raymond V's forces are designated by the word *joven*, which cannot be used in a troubadour lyric without evoking all kinds of courtly virtues generally associated with *Joven* personified. For Marcabru, *Joven* is 'the father of the world' (v, 37–9); Peire too extols its virtues:

> En estiu, qan crida·l iais
> e reviu per miei plais
> joven ab la flor que nais,
> adoncs es razos c'om lais
> fals'amor enganairitz
> als volpillos acropitz. (IX, 1–6)

Peire d'Alvernha

In summer, when the jay cries out and youth loves again amongst the hedges with the blossoming flower, then it is right that one should leave treacherous false love to the vile cowards.

For Marcabru the slayers of youth are the cause of all evil (XI, 17–40) and if Raymond Berengier is fighting against *joven*, the courtly virtue, stanza V is a harsh indictment; this is probably picked up in stanza VI where Raymond V is referred to as a *iovencel*.

If we read stanzas V and VI as harsh criticism of Raymond Berengier, the praise of him in the first part of the poem must be ironic. But where then did Peire compose this song? More importantly, where did he intend it to be performed? For del Monte, he must already have been at the court of Raymond V when he composed the poem, but stanza III, in which Peire claims he has just arrived at Raymond Berengier's court, would seem to belie this.[28] On the other hand, if the poem is intended as criticism of Raymond Berengier, is it likely that the song was composed and performed at his court as Peire claims? In fact, the *bona cort* of the first stanza, where Peire hopes to perform his songs, is not designated with any precision, nor is the 'sweet place' in stanza II. Is he being deliberately playful? The *tornada* has the tone of a parting shot. If Peire did not actually compose this poem as a caustic commemoration of his leave-taking, he certainly wishes to give this impression.

If *bona cort* is understood to designate Raymond Berengier's court, it is *ironia per contrarium* and we must assume that *ricx mestiers* are singularly lacking there. If, however, the *bona cort* is Raymond V's, Peire is implying that a much better court awaits him. Stanza II is also ambivalent. On the one hand, Peire appears to use the conventions of traditional panegyric, on the other is he not implying, through irony, that his welcome in Barcelona left a lot to be desired?

Stanza III offers the first textual hint that Peire's praise is not straightforward. He only expects a gift from the Count, he has not actually received one. The use of the word *cre* (line 16) may well be a signal to irony here and Peire's intended meaning is surely that hunger and true deprivation *do* reign at the Catalan court. *Mermansa*, in its strong position at the last rhyme, ironically recalls *alegransa* of the previous stanza as well as *onransa* (line 15).

In the next stanza the 'falseness' of the praise becomes more apparent. Peire adopts Marcabru's technique of drawing an individual's attention to a moral platitude. This has the effect of accusing this person of the fault described. Ostensibly, Peire is chastising nobles who boast generally, but the ironic meaning is that Raymond Berengier never realizes his boasts. The word *verguonhos* (line 20) is particularly ambiguous, for it can mean both 'shameful' and 'restrained'. If it means the former, Peire's claim that shameful thoughts please him is ironic; if it means the latter, it contributes to his ironic praise of Raymond Berengier. *Verguonhos* may also imply meanness in certain instances. If this is the case here, Peire's otherwise obscure allusion to 'a man who sings in romance' indicates that this stanza is also an oblique and ironic allusion to the Count of Barcelona's lack of generosity to troubadours and *joglars*.

Belh m'es qui a son bon sen is a prime example of 'false praise' as described by the Latin rhetorical manuals. It provides yet another indication that Peire has a sound knowledge of rhetoric and that its influence is clearly discernible in his poetry.[29]

PEIRE AND PARODY

Marcabru parodied both genres and the style of other poets. Peire's surviving poems show no trace of irony at the expense of genres of poetry, but he does seem to enjoy parodying the style of other troubadours and the butt of his humour would seem to be invariably Bernart de Ventadorn.

One song where Peire clearly imitates Bernart is *Chantarai pus vey* (IV), but are critics such as Appel and del Monte right to see it as a sincere love poem?[30]

I   Chantarai pus vey qu'a far m'er
d'un chant nou que·m gronh dins lo cays;
chantars m'a tengut en pantays,
cum si chantes d'aytal guiza
qu'autruy chantar non ressembles,   5
qu'anc chans no fon valens ni bos
que ressembles autruy chansos.

II   Belh m'es quan l'alauza se fer
en l'ayr, per on dissen lo rays,
e monta, tro li·s bon que·s bays   10
sobre·l fuelh que branda·l biza,
e·l dous temps – qu'anc bona nasques! –
entruebe·ls becx dels auzelhos,
don retin lur chans sus e ios.

III   Qui a donc amor e l'enquier,   15
et amors brot'e bruelh'e nays,
e qui l'es humils e verays,
en breu d'ora l'a conquiza;
q'umilitatz la vens ades
e belhs semblans ab gent respos,   20
qu'estiers no·n es hom poderos.

IV   Mays de mi, las!, qu'enayssi·l ser
e re no·n ai mas quan lo fays:
ayso meteys m'es lo grans iays,
maier que qui·m dava Piza;   25
e s'a lieys plagues qu'a sos pes
vengues ves lieys de ginolhos
e·lh disses un mot amoros! . . .

V   Amors, saber volgra quon er
de nos dos, si·us plazi', hueymais,   30

que per re engrayssar no·m lays,
mas quar no sai ma deviza;
e podetz aver cor engres
ves mi, qu'ieu non l'aurai ves vos,
tro que·l cors rest de l'arma blos.   35

VI   Ab sol qu'en aiso non esfer,*
non reblan gelos ni savays,
que ia nulh dan, si be·s n'irays,
no·l pretz una pauca briza.
M'en puesca tener luenh ni pres,   40
sia lauzengiers o gilos,
sol qu'ela·m sia a mos pros.

VII Sol sia que mos cors s'esmer,
que ves autra part non biays!
Qu'un'amors ad autr'enquier plays,   45
si·n sabi'esser auciza;
e sapchatz, s'ieu tant non l'ames,
ia non saupra far ni vers ni sos,
e non o feira, s'ilh no fos.

VIII Peire d'Alvernhe l'er cofes   50
tant de servir e d'orazos,
tro que li·n venha guizardos.

I
I will sing since I see that I must compose a new song which grumbles in my throat;
singing has worried me, as if I were singing in such a way that it did not resemble
another's singing, for never was a song worthy or good that resembled another's song.

II
It pleases me when the lark takes flight into the air where the ray of sunlight falls, and it
rises until it pleases it to descend on to a leaf, which the wind makes shiver, and the mild
weather, the like of which has never been seen before, opens the birds' mouths, from
whence their song resounds high and low.

III
The man who has love then and seeks it, in whom love grows and flourishes and is
born, and who is humble and true towards it, has soon conquered it, for humility
vanquishes it at once, and a seemly appearance with sweet conversation, for in no other
way is one powerful.

IV
But as for me, alas! For thus do I serve her and I have nothing but suffering: this in itself
gives me more joy than if I had been given Pisa; and if only it pleased her that I should
come to her feet, on my knees, and say a loving word to her! . . .

V
Love, I would like to know what is to become of us henceforth, if it pleased you, for I
do not allow myself to grow fat on anything because I do not know my lot; and you
can have a harsh heart towards me, for I will not feel harshly towards you, until my
body is deprived of its soul.

VI

As long as she is not annoyed by this, I do not serve a jealous or wicked one, for he does not care about harm at all, however much it may annoy him. Let her keep me distant or close, whether or not there are slanderers or jealous men, as long as she is working for my advantage.

VII

As long as my heart improves and does not veer off to some other place! For one love seeks to quarrel with another if it knows it can be destroyed by it; and know this: if I did not love her so much, I would not know how to compose poems and tunes, and I would not do so if it were not for her.

VIII

Peire d'Alvernha will be a debtor as much with serving as with prayers, until he gets a reward from it.

Rita Lejeune returned to the problem of Peire's imitation of Bernart in the second stanza of this poem and concluded that Peire was imitating Bernart ironically. She bases this interpretation on lines 3–7, of which she comments: 'C'est par antiphrase qu'il se vantait de composer un chant original.' Ulrich Mölk and Jörn Gruber also believe Peire is boasting in these lines that he will not sing a song that resembles any other. Mölk comments that this is the first instance where a troubadour claims explicitly to strive for originality; Gruber criticizes Mölk for being unaware of Appel's comments on Peire's poem and argues that his imitation of Bernart in the second stanza indicates that lines 3–7 are ironic; for Gruber Peire is attempting to outdo Bernart's poem and the subtlety of this is masked by the irony of lines 3–7.[31] Gruber appears to be unaware of Lejeune's comments on Peire's poem.

In fact, Lejeune's translation of lines 4–5 belies her interpretation:

comme si je chantais de telle façon à ne ressembler chant d'autrui.[32]

Neither Mölk nor Gruber translate the stanza. The lines are ambiguous: the collocation *cum si* may indicate purpose, giving 'so that I might sing . . .', but it can more plausibly be translated, following Lejeune, 'as if . . .', giving 'singing has worried me, as if I were singing in such a way that it did not resemble another's singing'. In other words, Peire is not claiming to be original; on the contrary, he has no need to worry about this song because it *is* going to be like someone else's. The last lines of the stanza indicate, through irony, that this song will be neither *valens* nor *bos*.

Lejeune draws parallels between lines of this song and songs by Bernart de Ventadorn, Giraut de Borneil, Bernart Marti and Cercamon.[33] In my view, however, the most striking parallels that can be drawn between *Chantarai pus vey* and songs by other poets are all with songs by Bernart de Ventadorn. The opening stanza, for example, with its repetition of words with the radical *chan*, evokes and 'outdoes' the opening stanza of one of Bernart's most famous songs:

Peire d'Alvernha

Chantars no pot gaire valer,
si d'ins dal cor no mou lo *chans*;
ni *chans* no pot dal cor mover,
si no i es fin'amors coraus.
Per so es mos *chantars* cabaus.   (xv, 1–5)

Singing can hardly be worth anything if the song does not come from the heart, and a song cannot come from the heart, if there is no sincere, pure love there. Because of this my singing is perfect.

Other parallels could be tabulated thus:

8–10   Can vei la lauzeta mover
         de joi sas alas contral rai,
         que s'oblid'e·s laissa chazer
         per la doussor c'al cor li vai.   (xliii, 1–4)

15–16   ab l'autre joi, qu'eu ai en mo coratge
         dobla mos jois e nais e creis e brolha.   (xlii, 3–4)

17–19   Tan er gen servitz per me
         sos fers cors durs e iratz
         tro del tot si'adoussatz
         ab bels dihz et ab merce;
         qu'eu ai be trobat legen
         que gota d'aiga que chai,
         fer en un loc tan soven
         tro chava la peira dura.   (xvi, 33–40)

22–3   on plus la prec, plus m'es dura   (xxx, 33)

25   car en loc de sa ricor
         no volh aver Piza   (xliv, 23–4)

26–8   Mas mas jonchas li venh a so plazer,
         e ja no·m volh d'a sos pes mover,
         tro per merce·m meta lai o·s despolha.   (xlii, 40–2)

26–8   Mal o fara, si no·m manda
         venir lai on se despolha,
         qu'eu sia per sa comanda
         pres del leih, josta l'esponda,
         e·lh traga·ls sotlars be chaussans,
         a genolhs et umilians,
         si·lh platz que sos pes me tenda!   (xxvi, 29–35)

29–32   Amors, e que·us es vejaire?
         Trobatz mais fol can me?
         Cuidatz vos qu'eu si'amaire
         e que ja no trop merce?   (iv, 1–4)

Many of these parallels involve courtly commonplaces, but Bernart de Ventadorn was the first troubadour to adopt courtly conventions whole-heartedly, and at such an early stage in the tradition as this, Peire's use of the *topoi* would have evoked Bernart de Ventadorn's style rather than anyone else's. Peire's song is a banal imitation of this style and ironic because it is ostensibly a serious love song. The initiated audience would have realized this, if it were not made clear in performance through tone and gesture. First, the nonchalant tone of the beginning of stanza VII, 'As long as my heart improves and does not veer off to some other place!', undermines the sincerity of the love expressed throughout the poem and by extension casts aspersions on Bernart's sincerity. How are we to take Peire's impassioned declarations if he acknowledges that his affections can be so easily diverted? Secondly, the last part of this stanza is a hollow imitation of Bernart's boast to be the best singer because of the quality of his love:

> Non es meravelha s'eu chan
> melhs de nul autre chantador
> que plus me tra·l cors vas amor
> e melhs sui faihz a so coman. (XXXI, 1–4)

It is no wonder if I sing better than any other singer, for my heart draws me more towards love, and I am better fashioned to do its bidding.

Given that Peire has obliquely hinted in the opening stanza that his song will be neither *valens* nor *bos*, his use of the 'I sing well because I love well' *topos* also undermines the sincerity of his love poem, indicating ironic tone throughout. *Sapchatz* (line 47) may well be a signal to this irony, whilst the use of the word *cofes* in the *tornada* could be a veiled acknowledgement that the poem is parody. To whom and for what is Peire a debtor? Could he mean a debtor to Bernart de Ventadorn for the style he adopts in this poem? 'Serving and prayers' could well be metaphors for poetry, particularly for Bernart's style of poetry.

Peire's mocking of Bernart is not, however, unfriendly. The tone is humorous and playful, not satirical. It is interesting that the Peire who composed the *tenso Amics, Bernartz de Ventadorn*, who may or may not be Peire d'Alvernha, should strike precisely the same note:[34]

> Amics Bernartz de Ventadorn,
> com vos podetz de chant sofrir,
> can aissi auzetz esbaudir
> lo rossinholet noih e jorn?
> Auyatz lo joi que demana!
> Tota noih chanta sotz la flor.
> Melhs s'enten que vos en amor. (XXI, 1–7)

Bernart de Ventadorn, friend, how can you stop yourself singing when you hear the nightingale rejoicing thus, night and day? Listen to its joy! All night it sings beneath the flower. It devotes itself better to love than you.

Bernart evokes the nightingale no less than eight times in opening stanzas. It is always associated with *joi*:[35]

> Bel m'es qu'eu chan en aquel mes
> can flor e folha vei parer,
> et au lo chan doutz pel defes

del rossinhol matin e ser.
Adoncs s'eschai   qu'eu aya jauzimen
d'un joi verai   en que mos cors s'aten,
car eu sai be que per amor morrai.   (x, 1–7)

It pleases me that I sing in this month, when I see the flower and leaf appearing, and I
hear the sweet song of the nightingale, morning and evening, along the walls. Then it
befalls me to possess a true joy, to which my heart aspires, for I well know that I will
die through love.

Peire deliberately mocks Bernart by adopting commonplaces and themes that
abound in his poetry. If the audience did not know Bernart's poetry and his
usual persona, the *tenso* would be dull and of little interest: its effect depends
upon the initiated audience realizing that Peire is adopting Bernart's usual
stance, and thus ironically mocking him. The spectacle of Bernart then
rejecting his usual persona in his part of the *tenso* would presumably have
caused much hilarity to members of the audience who were used to hearing his
love songs.[36]

In *Cantarai d'aqestz trobadors* (XII), Peire mocks other troubadours,
mostly by hurling insults at them. If Walter Pattison is correct in thinking that
the twelve troubadours he sings of would have been present at the first
performance of the song, the tone of the poem is one of friendly and playful
joking.[37] This is certainly the impression the poem itself gives, for Peire ends it
by ironically mocking himself:

> Peire d'Alvernge a tal votz
> que canta de sus e de sotz,
> e lauza·s mout a tota gen;
> pero maïstres es de totz,
> ab c'un pauc esclarzis sos motz,
> c'apenas nuils hom los enten.   (XII, 79–84)

Peire d'Alvernha has such a voice that he sings high and low and praises himself greatly
in front of everyone; but he is the master of them all, if only he would make his words a
little clearer, for hardly anyone can understand them.

Peire's words evoke his claims to be the best poet, but he undermines any
claim to that effect here by drawing attention to the aspect of his work which
his own colleagues might mock: his ambiguity and obscurity.

Most of the insults Peire directs at his colleagues are explicit, or at least
appear to be so. Some may conceal irony depending on intertextual play, but
as not all the troubadours Peire sings of are known to us, such irony is not
discernible.[38] The stanza devoted to Bernart de Ventadorn is, however,
certainly ironic:

> E·l tertz, Bernartz de Ventedorn,
> qu'es menre de Borneill un dorn,
> en son paire ac bon sirven
> per trair'ab arc manal d'alborn*

119

e sa mair'escaldava·l forn
et amassava l'issermen. (19–24)

And the third, Bernart de Ventadorn, who is shorter than Borneill by a hand, had a good servant in his father, skilled at shooting with a laburnum bow, and his mother heated the oven and gathered the kindling wood.

The first two lines of this stanza are ironic because of their ambivalence: they may refer to physical height or to poetic skill. As Aurelio Roncaglia points out, Peire then plays on Bernart's apparently humble origins, the *arc manal* and the *forn* being, in all probability, ironic sexual metaphors.[39]

CONCLUSION

Irony is not an essential part of Peire's *eloquentia*. In the majority of his poems he is allusive and ambiguous, but this does not lead to irony, for he has no desire to subvert the literal meaning of his words. He is ironic when he parodies the style of other troubadours or when he composes poems which represent, in some way, an intervention in political and worldly affairs: *Al dessebrar*, if it does evoke the style of Jaufre Rudel and reject his *amor de lonh* in favour of the crusading ideal, belongs to both categories. When intervening in political affairs, Peire uses irony, like Marcabru whom he admired, to denigrate and attack and the influence of rhetoric is perceptible in such poems.

Peire prides himself on being a serious poet; it is thus all the more interesting that he too should have recourse to irony in his poetry and particularly that in his poetic encounters with Bernart de Ventadorn he should see the act of composing poetry as a game, with irony as the principal tool.

5

Raimbaut d'Aurenga

Raimbaut d'Aurenga's poetry is the largest corpus by an amateur poet to have survived from the early years of the troubadour tradition.[1] Unlike troubadours such as Marcabru or Bernart de Ventadorn, he did not have to develop a style which was recognizably his own, for which audiences might turn to him, and him alone. He composed now in one style, now in another; he adopts one persona, then another. He mocks labels and composes his poetry however and whenever it pleases him. His work, unlike that of Marcabru or Bernart de Ventadorn, resists systematization, whether critics are attempting to study his style, the content of his poems, or the man behind the facade. Virtually the only unifying factor that runs through the corpus is an appealing lack of respect for convention, which often manifests itself through a relentless sense of humour.

Medieval rhetorical manuals are consistent in linking *ironia* with mockery and criticism. The kind of biting irony they prescribe is perhaps best typified by Marcabru's virulent moralizing. It is hardly surprising that a poet as capricious as Raimbaut should have little or no use for such devices. Confident, even complacent, in his position as a young noble, Raimbaut has no need to criticize the social order or to lament his position in it; his tongue is usually firmly in his cheek. He does not use rhetorical irony as Marcabru does, and yet his poems are perhaps more strikingly ironic than those of any other troubadour. More often than not his irony is directed at the conventions of *fin'amor* and as these are literary as well as social, he enjoys flouting conventions and foiling expectations in both the way he composes and what he composes about. His purpose is rarely to expound a higher truth or to moralize: it is always to entertain, but to entertain with scant respect for the tastes of any one section of his audience. Irony is so pervasive in Raimbaut's corpus that my study is necessarily selective: I shall begin by examining Raimbaut's irony when he comments on style. Sections will then be devoted to irony dependent on the intertext and to Raimbaut's use of parody. Finally, I will examine a poem which is the cornerstone of the work of Luigi Milone, the scholar who has devoted most attention to Raimbaut in recent years, as I believe his views may be coloured by the fact that he frequently fails to recognize irony.

Troubadours and irony

Raimbaut's poetic career probably spanned no more than eleven years, for he died young in 1173.[2] During that period the debate as to how and why one should compose poetry intensified: Peire d'Alvernha's boast of being the first troubadour to compose *vers entiers* provoked a reply from Bernart Marti, and Raimbaut himself engaged in a *tenso* with Giraut de Borneil as to whether or not the *trobar clus* was superior to the *trobar leu*. Raimbaut's attitude to style has been analysed in detail by Linda Paterson. She begins her study by pointing out that 'Raimbaut's style and intentions are so varied and capricious, his statements so often loaded with humour, that his comments on style can only be examined in the context of his individual works.' She concludes:

Raimbaut defends *clus* and *car* styles as the most valuable and most calculated to satisfy a personal ambition to compose the most worthwhile poetry, whatever the general public may think. But he takes a great many different approaches to style, always looking for a new and whimsical way of expressing and guarding his individuality.[3]

In *Ara·m platz* (XXXI), the *tenso* with Giraut de Borneil, Raimbaut does indeed appear to defend the *trobar clus*. He despises the type of poem that everyone can compose and understand and seeks a small, discerning audience, wanting his songs to be judged only by those he deems worthy to do so. Although this stance reflects his social position inasmuch as he can afford to go against popular tastes, his arguments are, as Paterson suggests, literary rather than social; nowhere does he expound deliberate hermeticism in order to exclude social inferiors.[4] Moreover, as Sarah Kay has recently argued, the *tenso* is probably not to be taken seriously; she suggests that both Raimbaut and Giraut adopt in this poem the style they purport to criticize, that the entire text is a literary joke.[5] Thus, although Raimbaut ostensibly presents himself as the defender of the *trobar clus*, his attitude to style in this *tenso* may not be as cut-and-dried as it suggests at face value.

As might be expected, whenever Raimbaut mentions the 'easy' style, he is disparaging and this is usually expressed through irony. In *Pos trobars plans*, for example, he appears to give in to public demand for the easy style:

> Pos trobars plans
> Es volguz tan
> Fort m'er greu s'i non son sobrans:
> Car ben pareis
> Qi tals motz fai
> C'anc mais non foron dig cantan,
> Qe cels c'om tot jorn ditz e brai
> Sapcha, si·s vol, autra vez dir. (XVI, 1–8)

Since the plain style is desired so much, I will be very annoyed if I am not the best in it: for it seems right that he who can put words together in such a way as they had never been sung before should know, on another occasion, how to say words that everyone says and shouts all the time, if he so desires.

Raimbaut d'Aurenga

Köhler argues that this stanza is a clear indication that Raimbaut was interested in public acclaim.[6] On the surface he seems to want to excel at all styles and yet the opposition between what is rare and precious and what is commonplace and vulgar is as present here as it is in *Ara·m platz*. The implication is that if Raimbaut can compose exceptional and unusual poems, he can certainly churn out the type of song everyone wants to hear. The words *si·s vol* make the act of composing such songs seem casual and effortless – hardly worth Raimbaut's trouble. He may be attempting to pander to public taste and to excel at everything, but he makes it clear to an initiated audience, through irony, that he does not respect his wider audience's opinion.

His tendency to mock the *leu* audience is even more marked elsewhere. In *Assaz m'es belh* this is expressed through *ironia*:

> Assaz m'es belh
> Que de novelh
> Fassa parer
> De mon saber
> Tot plan als prims sobresabens
> Que van comdan
> Qu'ab sen d'enfan
> Dic e fatz mos captenemens;
> E sec mon cor
> E·n mostri for
> Tot aisso don ilh m'es cossens. (XVII, 1–11)

I am very pleased to show my wisdom again quite openly, to the refined, over-clever people, who are saying that I speak and conduct myself in a foolish manner; and I follow my heart and only show outwardly as much of it as she allows me to.

Tot plan implies the easy, open style, yet Raimbaut says that he will follow his heart, do as he pleases and show outwardly only what his lady allows, which would seem to imply discretion and therefore veiled meanings. He talks later in the poem of his *sen novelh* and *saber ver*, again in terms which would seem to imply the *clus* style:

> Ab sen novelh
> Dic e favelh
> Mon saber ver
> E·l fas parer
> Lay on tanh que sia parvens. (23–7)

With new wisdom I speak and pronounce my true knowledge and I make it apparent there where it is fitting for it to be seen.

His song in fact turns into an erotic boast:

> Don d'amar dic:
> Qu'am si ses tric
> Lieys qu'amar deg,
> Que·l miels adreg

123

Troubadours and irony

(S'eron sert cum l'am finamens)
  M'irion sai
  Preguar hueymai
Que·ls essenhes cum aprendens
  De ben amar;
  E neus preguar
M'en venrion dompnas cinc cens.   (34–44)

Because of this I say of loving that I love so guilelessly the lady I ought to love, that the most adept (if they could be sure how truly I loved her) would come here henceforth to beg me to teach them as students how to love well; and even five hundred ladies would come to beg me about it.

If this is the *saber* Raimbaut has alluded to, then it is quite clear that he is mocking the *prims sobresabens* (the audience of *plan* poetry) and that he believes them and not himself to have the *sen d'enfan*. The words *prims sobresabens* must consequently be understood as having the opposite of their literal meaning.[7]

In *Aissi mou*, Raimbaut once again appears to concede to public demand for a *Chansson leu*:

Aissi mou
Un sonet nou
On ferm e latz
Chansson leu,
Pos vers plus greu
Fan sorz dels fatz.
Qu'er er vist,
Pos tan m'es quist,
Cum sui senatz;
Si cum sol,
Fora mos cors vesatz;
Mas chamjar l'ai pos quex o vol.   (XVIII, 1–12)

Thus I begin a new little tune in which I enclose and bind an easy song since a more difficult verse makes the fools deaf. Now it will be seen, since it is so often asked of me, how wise I am; my heart would be joyful in its usual way, but I will change it since this is what everyone wants.

He makes it quite clear, however, that he is descending from loftier heights to give the public what it wants. The word *fatz* is unequivocal, but it is implicit that it is the *fatz*, the people who are too stupid to understand a *vers plus greu*, who enjoy listening to a *Chansson leu*, and this casts an ironic shadow over Raimbaut's use of the term. Despite his wisdom he will give the fools one of these trivial little songs (*sonet*) if this is what they want.

If he is consistently ironic and disparaging about the easy style, Raimbaut might be expected, given his apparent attitude in *Ara·m platz*, to champion the *trobar clus*. However, this is not the case. He does compose one serious *clus* poem, *Cars, douz* (I), but the only other poem in which allusiveness, rarity of rhyme and technique unite to suggest the *clus* style, *Ar vei* (X), turns out to be burlesque and ribald when the surface is scratched.[8] In *Lonc temps* he makes a mockery of *clus* terminology:

> Lonc temps ai estat cubertz,
> Mas Dieus no vol qu'ieu oimais
> Puosca cobrir ma besoigna,
> Dont mi ven ira et esglais.
> Ez escoutatz, cavallier,
> S'a ren ai obs ni mestier.   (XXVIII, 1–6)

For a long time now I have kept my thoughts to myself, but God no longer wants me to hide my deficiency, because of which sorrow and fear afflict me. And listen, knights, if I am in need or lack anything.

The words *cubertz* and *cobrir* are indicators of the *trobar clus*. Although the fact that Raimbaut addresses his audience as *cavallier* may be sufficient to suggest that the song will be scabrous, this is not clear when the words are used in lines 1–3. The audience soon realizes, however, that the poet is covering up not meanings, but the fact that he has been castrated (or so he ironically claims): *cubertz* and *clus* are ironic, suggesting one thing to the uninitiated and quite another to the initiated. Raimbaut seems to have a marked lack of respect for the style he claims elsewhere to consider superior to all others.

Raimbaut often steers a course between the 'easy' and the allusive style, with humour and irony to the fore. In *En aital rimeta prima*, for example, he claims to compose spontaneously and with *lieu mot*:

> En aital rimeta prima
> M'agradon lieu mot e prim
> Bastit ses regl'e ses linha,
> Pos mos volers s'i apila.   (II, 1–4)

In such a subtle little poem, light and smooth words, built without rule or form, please me, since my desire wants it thus.

The song may be easy to understand, as the *leu* terminology suggests, but it is certainly not built without rule or form. The rhyme scheme, though not unique, has derivative rhymes, some of which are very rare, and this provides a rigorous formal framework.[9] Again Raimbaut is laughing at the expectations of his audience, promising it a *leu* song, but using a *clus* technique.[10] His claim to be composing without rule or form is clearly ironic since it is contradicted by the poem itself.

In *Una chansoneta fera*, Raimbaut mixes together *clus* and *leu* terms in a topsy-turvy manner:

> Una chansoneta fera
> Voluntiers laner'a dir;
> Don tem que m'er a murir
> E far l'ai tal que sen sela.
> Ben la poira leu entendre

> Si tot s'es en aital rima;
> Li mot seran descubert
> Al quec de razon deviza. (III, 1–8)

I would willingly compose a little song to be sung in a low way; but I'm afraid it will be the death of me and I will make it so that it hides meaning. It will be easily understood even if it is in such a rhyme; the words will be unveiled to anyone who expounds it with reason.

For Mölk this song is 'obviously' *leu*, but he is probably falling into the trap Raimbaut intended for his contemporaries, for as Paterson says, he is punning on the meaning of *laner*, 'low' or 'base'.[11] Although *laner* implies the easy style, Raimbaut's intentions are expressed in the conditional (*fera*), and he quickly goes on to say that he will hide meaning in terms that imply the *trobar clus*. However, the *clus* style is also undermined, for Raimbaut is not unveiling a higher moral truth, he is composing a boasting poem full of ironic sexual metaphors:

> Bo·m sap car tan m'apodera
> Mos cor que non puesc sufrir
> De mon talan descubrir;
> C'ades puech a plena vela
> (Qui que veya joy dissendre)
> Per que no·y puesc nulh'escrima
> Trobar; ans ai trop suffert*
> De far parer ma conquiza. (9–16)

I am happy, for my heart so controls me that I cannot suffer from revealing my desire; for now I rise to my full extent (no matter who sees joy diminishing), wherefore I cannot find a screen for it; before I suffered too much from allowing my conquest to be seen.

It is now clear why Raimbaut's song is 'low'. The first three lines of this stanza might be acceptable in any courtly context, but they are at once revealed as ironic. Raimbaut cannot help 'revealing' his 'desire' (*talan*), because he 'rises to his full extent'. The sexual innuendo must have been clear even to the pure-minded, and the incongruity of using a word from the courtly register to designate a sexual organ makes the irony sharper. The heaviest irony derives, however, from the use of the word *descubrir*, a word evocative of the *trobar clus*, to designate the 'unveiling' of Raimbaut's 'desire', and this only four lines after the past participle has been used in a *clus* context. Once again Raimbaut refuses to take seriously the style he appears to defend so ardently in *Ara·m platz*.

If Raimbaut was more attracted to the *clus* and *car* styles than to the *trobar leu*, more often than not he manages to stay aloof from the whole argument and to ironize at everyone's expense. Raimbaut was not the defender of an aristocratic, closed style of poetry; he successfully avoids allying himself with either camp and it is irony that allows him to do this.

Raimbaut d'Aurenga

Frequent references to style in Raimbaut's work would seem to imply not only that such matters were considered to be of some importance in his day, but also that he actively engaged in discussing them with other troubadours. He obviously knew Giraut de Borneil and Peire Rogier; with a lesser degree of certainty scholars assume that he had contact with Bernart de Ventadorn, Peire d'Alvernha and Gaucelm Faidit. It has even been advanced that he may have known the northern French *trouvère* and *romancier* Chrétien de Troyes.[12]

Intertextual play in Raimbaut's work alluding to some of these poets has already been pointed out by scholars, and recently Gruber has shown how he adapted the rhyme schemes of earlier poets such as Marcabru and Cercamon.[13] The considerable volume of critical writing on Raimbaut's allusions to other poets makes a detailed account of intertextuality in his work superfluous. I shall, however, examine one instance which has either gone unremarked or been misinterpreted. Needless to say, Raimbaut's irony and sense of humour are as present in his interventions in the troubadour literary *Dialektik* as they are elsewhere in his work.

Linda Paterson suggests that the opening stanza of Raimbaut's *Amors, cum er?* (XIX) is a parody of Bernart de Ventadorn's *Amors e que·us es vejaire?* (IV). She shows how Raimbaut makes fun of Bernart's use of rhetorical questions in the opening stanza of his poem and points out that Bernart's song is sent to Tristan, a *senhal* Bernart uses for Raimbaut.[14] Indeed, there are thematic and structural parallels between the two songs, suggesting that Raimbaut's parody extends beyond the first stanza, but what interests me in Bernart's song is the *envoi* in which the *senhal* Tristan occurs:[15]

> Ma chanson apren a dire,
> Alegret; e tu Ferran,
> porta la·m a mo Tristan,
> que sap be gabar e rire.   (61–4)

Learn my song, Alegret; and you, Ferran, take it for me to my Tristan, who knows how to joke well and laugh.

Appel and Jeanroy suggest that Bernart's Alegret may be the troubadour Alegret.[16] Only two poems by this troubadour have survived, but he is also mentioned by Marcabru in *Bel m'es* (XI). This song has been dated 1145 and Alegret is consequently considered to have been active as a poet in the middle of the twelfth century. Little can be learnt about Alegret from his own poems: one is a fragmentary and banal love song and the other an obscure moralizing poem, very much in the style of Marcabru. Marcabru parodies the latter in *Bel m'es* and, with heavy irony, accuses Alegret of being a hypocrite, a cuckolder, a flatterer and a cheat.[17]

It is, of course, highly possible that Bernart de Ventadorn knew the troubadour Alegret. Bernart's poetic activity is thought to have begun in 1147 at the latest, only two years after the composition of *Bel m'es*.[18] Moreover, the name Alegret is only recorded three times in troubadour poetry: when Alegret names himself in *Ara pareisson*, in *Bel m'es* and in *Amors e que·us es vejaire?*[19] It is therefore not unreasonable to assume that the same man is designated. The lines in which Bernart mentions Alegret are ambiguous: he may be asking Alegret and Ferran (another *joglar*) to learn his poem and intending Alegret to take it to Tristan, or he may be asking them both to learn his song and intending Ferran to take it to Tristan. In either case the mention of Alegret and Tristan in the same *envoi* introduces a serious possibility that Raimbaut too knew Alegret, particularly since the description of Tristan here makes the *senhal* so easily identifiable as Raimbaut.

Such an encounter is not impossible. Supposing Alegret were a young man of twenty in 1145 when he composed *Ara pareisson*, he would have been thirty-seven in 1162, when Raimbaut is thought to have started composing poetry, and forty-eight in 1173 when Raimbaut died. Is there anything in Raimbaut's poetry to suggest that he knew Alegret?

Pattison goes to great lengths in order to argue for the existence of a *joglar* named Palharet in Raimbaut's entourage. He bases his argument on a stanza which he edits as follows:

> Palharet, non ges grans palhiers,
> D'aquest vers ompli tos paniers
> E porta tot ton col cargat
> A'n Girart, de cuy ai peccat,
> A Perpinhan part Laucata.
> E di·l (per que m'aia comprat)
> Qu'el cassa·s e'n desbarata.　　　　　　　　(xxxvii, 57–63)

Pattison identifies this Palharet with 'one of the witnesses of Raimbaut's oral will, in all probability a member of his household . . . a man called Pallerius, which is the latinized form of *palhier*, "straw stack", apparently a nick-name'. He argues for a pun on this nickname: Raimbaut's 'fancy jumps from *palhier* to *palhard* "rascal", which he softens by adding a diminutive. Thus the whole line translates "Little rascal, not big straw stack", but with an untranslatable pun.'[20]

Pattison's argument is tenuous to say the least and it is seriously undermined by the confused state of his edition of the text. In his text the name, which only occurs in one manuscript (*a*), reads Palharet, in his variants he says it reads *pailhairet* and in his notes to the text *pailharet*. Whilst the version he prints in his text is a possible Occitan derivative of the Latin Pallerius, neither of the others is. What is in the manuscript? According to Appel it reads *pailhairet*, and my own reading of the manuscript confirms this.[21] In any case, the dimunitive of the Occitan *palhart* would be *palhartet*, not *palharet* as Pattison suggests, and the pun is obviously so untranslatable that Pattison fails to convey its meaning. Moreover, Pattison bases his text on just one manuscript (*a*), discarding the readings of five other manuscripts. According to both Pattison and Appel, line 57 reads as follows in other manuscripts:

Raimbaut d'Aurenga

A	Alegrat monges grans parliers
I	Alegrar monies grans parliers
K	Alegrar non ges grans parliers
N²	Alegrar monies grans parliers
C	Por lairatz non ges grans parliers

The resemblance between the first word of the line in *AIKN²* and Alegret's name is striking and the hazards of an oral and written tradition might easily explain errors. As far as we know, the scribes of *IKN²* did not know of Alegret, either as a troubadour or as a *joglar*: it would hardly be surprising if they got wrong the name of someone they had never heard of.[22] These manuscripts are closely related and it is often supposed that they have a common source: an early scribal error may have resulted in a mis-copying of the 't' at the end of Alegret's name, and its substitution with an 'r'. Appel advanced the hypothesis that this line might be a reference to Alegret, the troubadour, whom Marcabru and Bernart de Ventadorn address. After a paragraph or so of speculation in the notes to his edition of the text, he prefers to leave the line blank because the manuscript readings are so inconclusive.[23]

Appel is clearly right that a sure reading of this line is not possible; it is nevertheless interesting to speculate on whether anything in the text of Raimbaut's poem might indicate that this Alegrat/Alegrar could be Alegret. The line in which the name occurs is itself interesting. The scribes of *AIN²* all seem to think that Alegrat/Alegrar is a monk and this may well indicate that he is an older man, of about the age Alegret might have been at the time of the poem's composition.[24] Also, the scribes of *AIN²* call Alegrat/Alegrar 'talkative', which fits the description of Alegret that Marcabru gives. Is there anything else in this poem that might suggest a connection between Alegrat/ Alegrar and Marcabru's Alegret?

Set against the rest of Raimbaut's corpus, the poem, in which the reference to Alegrat/Alegrar occurs, *Als durs* (xxxvii), is startlingly different. It is a bitter attack on the *lauzengiers* and the only poem in which Raimbaut gives vent to vituperation and Marcabrunesque moralizing. I have modified the last stanza of Pattison's edition.

I   Als durs, crus, cozens lauzengiers
      – Enojos, vilans, mals parliers –
      Darai un vers que m'ai pensat;*
      Que ja d'als no·i aura parlat,
      Qu'a pauc lo cor no m'esclata   5
      D'aisso qu'ieu ai vist a proat
      De lur malserva barata.

II   E dirai vos de lur mestiers
      Si cum selh qu'en es costumiers
      D'auzir e de sufrir lur glat;   10
      Si·m peza, mas non er laissat
      Qu'ieu ab mal dir no·ls combata;

E ja del plus no·m sapchon grat
Qar mos cors totz non los mata.

III   Lauzenjador fan encombriers   15
Als cortes et als dreituriers
E a cellas qu'an cor auzat
E quecx per aquel eis mercat
A l'autre cobre et aplata
Son verguonhos avol barat –   20
Aissi son de fer'escata!

IV   Per que·y falh totz bos cavaliers
Que·ls cre; q'us non l'es plazentiers
Mas per qu'en traga mielhs son at;
Qu'il pesson, ist malaürat,   25
Mas d'als non val una rata*
De que·l fara sa voluntat*
O·lh dira lauzenja grata.

V   D'autres n'i a que van estiers,
Que·s fa quecx cortes ufaniers;   30
Que per outracujar mot fat,
O cuj'aver mielhs guazanhat
Cel qu'a plus la lengua lata
En dir de partir l'amistat
De cels en cui Jois s'afata.   35

VI   Que·ls plus pros e·ls plus gualaubiers
Vei de lauzenjar prezentiers:
E pes me d'ome c'a amat:
Cum pot far amador irat.*
Mas ges (qui qu'en crit ni·n glata!)   40
Non amon tug cil qu'an baizat –
So sap sidons na Lobata.

VII   Tal cug'esser cortes entiers
Qu'es vilans dels quatre ladriers,
Et a·l cor dins mal ensenhat;   45
Plus que feutres sembla sendat
Ni cuers de bou escarlata
Non sabon mais que n'an trobat –
E quecx quo·s pot calafata.

VIII   Pos non aus mos durs deziriers   50
Dir, tan tem que·l dans fos dobliers,
Maldirai los en luec d'aurat;
E Dieus – car fara caritat –
Los maldiga e·ls abata
Sai, e pueys lai en Neiron prat   55
On recebran la liurata.*

IX   Alegrat, monges grans parliers,*
D'aquest vers ompli tos paniers
E porta tot ton col cargat
A·n Giraut, de cuy ai peccat,*   60

Raimbaut d'Aurenga

A Perpinhan part Laucata.
E di·l (per que m'aia comprat)
Qu'el cassa·s e'n desbarata.

x   Ben chant (qui que s'en debata)
    Dels lauzengiers qu'an Joi baissat   65
    Del suc entro la sabata.

I
I will give to the hard, cruel, biting slanderers – the infuriating, common, evil speakers – a verse which I have thought up, for nothing else will be spoken of in it because my heart almost bursts from what I have seen and proved of their evil dealing.

II
And I shall tell you of their occupations as one who is accustomed to hear and endure their yapping. It upsets me, but it will not stop me fighting them with curses, and let them not be grateful for more, for I do not kill them all.

III
Slanderers hinder courtly and upright men and those ladies who have bold hearts; and each one, through that very same bargain, covers and hides his shameful, wicked dealing from the other, of such a hateful race are they.

IV
Wherefore every good knight who believes them is at fault; for not one of them is pleasant to him except to get what he can out of him; for they think, these wretches, that he is worth no more than a mouse with which he will do as he pleases or flatter pleasantly [?].

V
There are others who behave differently, for each one becomes superficially courtly; and through extremely stupid presumption that man thinks he has the advantage who has the loosest tongue when it comes to saying things to break up the friendship of those in whom joy resides.

VI
For I see the most worthy and splendid man ready to slander and it worries me how a man who has loved can sadden lovers. But, whoever cries and argues about it, not all those who have made love are in love – his lady, lady Lobata, knows that.

VII
Such a man who is common on all four sides thinks he is completely courtly and inside his heart is churlish; no more than felt resembles silk or ox-hide good scarlet cloth, do they know any more than they have invented; and each one fills in the gaps as best he can.

VIII
Since I do not dare speak of my harsh desires, so much do I fear that the harm would be doubled, I shall curse them like a fool; and may God – for he will be kind – curse them and cast them down here, and then there, in the celestial field, where they will receive their reward.

IX
Alegrat, talkative monk, fill your baskets with this verse and carry it with your neck all heavily laden to Sir Giraut, who has wronged me, to Perpignan beyond Leuchate, and

131

tell him, so that he may redeem himself with me, that he is destroying himself and making a bad bargain.

X

I sing well, whoever may argue about it, of the slanderers who have brought down Joy from the crown of the head to the shoe.

It is surprising that Pattison does not group this poem with the poems he calls 'Marcabrunesque' or even mention its similarities to poems by Marcabru.[25] The style is so reminiscent of Marcabru that virtually every line, every formula and every sentiment has a parallel in Marcabru's work. This can perhaps best be tabulated thus:

1–2   Attacks *lauzengiers*. Compare Marcabru, II, IX, XI, XII[bis], XXIV, XXXII, XXXIV, XXXVIII, XL and XLI. In XXIV, the *lauzengiers* are called *mal parlier* (line 14).

3   Compare Marcabru, III, 8, 'Suy d'un vers far en cossirier', and XLI, 3–4.

5–7   Compare Marcabru XII[bis], 36, 'E non puesc mudar non gronda'.

8–9   Compare Marcabru, VII, 33, 'D'Amor[s] vos dirai com es', XVII, 1, XXXI, 16, XLIV, 33–4.

11–12   Compare Marcabru, XXXII, 91–3, 'D'aquest flagel / Marcabrus si coreilla / ses compaigno', and IX, 7–8.

18–21   Compare Marcabru, XI, 57, 'D'aqui nais l'avols barata', and for other examples of financial vocabulary used disparagingly about slanderers, husbands, and so on, II, IV, V, VII, IX, XII[bis], XIV, XVII, XIX, XX, XX[bis], XXII, XXIII, XXV, XXVI, XXX, XXXI, XXXIII, XXXVI, XXXVII, XXXIX, XL, XLI and XLIV. The most common words are *barat/barata* and *mercat*.

28   Compare Marcabru, XI, 60, 'Non sia lauzenja plata'.

29–30   Compare Marcabru, XXX, 40–2, 'Mas tals se fai cavalgaire / C'atrestal deuria faire / Los seis jorns de la setmana', and XXXII, 21–3, XI, 60–3.

31   Compare Marcabru, XIX, 32–3, 'Que per cuidar / cuich esser bar'.

33   Compare Marcabru, XXI, 19, 'Volpils lengua traversana'.

36–7   Compare Marcabru, XXXVI, 13–14, 'Proeza es forbandida / E son malvatz li meillor'.

42   Compare Marcabru, XXXI, 58, 'De si donz na Bonafo'.

46–7   Compare Marcabru, XI, 65–7, 'Alegretz folls, en qual guiza / Cujas far d'avol valen / Ni de gonella camiza?'

Raimbaut d'Aurenga

50–2   Compare Marcabru, XI, 9–10, 'Non aus so que m'atalanta / Dir d'una gen que·s fa cusca'.

51–2   Compare Marcabrunesque alliteration: Marcabru, IV, 31–2, 'Moillerat, li meillor del mon / Foratz mas chascus vos faitz drutz'.

53–4   Compare Marcabru, XXXIV, 15–16, 'Ist lauzengier, lenguas trencans / Cuy Dieus cofonda e azir'.

As can be seen, particular parallels may be drawn between lines 18–21, 28, 29–30, 46–7 and 50–2 and lines in Marcabru's *Bel m'es* (XI). Interestingly enough, the exceedingly rare rhyme -*ata* occurs in both poems.[26]

Raimbaut's address to Alegrat is hardly flattering. He calls him a talkative monk and as the poem is about slanderers this would seem to imply that Raimbaut thinks Alegrat is one of them. This hypothesis is confirmed by the following line ('D'aquest vers ompli tos paniers'), which clearly indicates that Raimbaut is sending Alegrat away with a flea in his ear, exactly as Marcabru had done with Alegret. Apart from the stylistic and formulaic similarities between *Als durs* and *Bel m'es*, it is noteworthy that Raimbaut's Alegrat/Alegrar strikingly resembles Marcabru's Alegret. For example, if it is accepted that Raimbaut is accusing Alegrat/Alegrar of being a slanderer, then he is also accusing him of being a *cortes unfaniers*, a man who pretends to be courtly but who is not; this is precisely how Marcabru describes Alegret:[27]

> Non sia lauzenja plata
> Cell qui sa maisnad'afama;
> Cest vest la blancha camiza
> E fai son seinhor sufren
> E ten si dons a sa guiza.
>
> Alegretz, folls, en qual guiza*
> Cujas far d'avol valen
> Ni de gonella camiza?
>
> Ans co·s pot? Levan cazen
> Qual gonella qual camiza.   (XI, 60–9)

Let the man who starves his household not be flattered superficially. This man [the flatterer] puts on the white shirt, makes his lord into a cuckold and holds his lady at his will.

Alegret, you fool, in what way do you think you can make a vile thing worthy or a shirt from a tunic?

But, how can that be? Whether getting up or falling down, a tunic is a tunic and a shirt a shirt.

Raimbaut says that the *lauzengier* will speak *lauzenja grata* (*IKN²* read *lauzenja plata*): Marcabru accuses Alegret of *lauzenja plata*. Raimbaut's slanderers can no more be worthy 'than felt resembles silk or ox-hide good scarlet cloth'; Marcabru's Alegret is not able to make his rough *gonella* seem like a *blancha camiza*.[28]

I propose the following hypothesis: the Alegret Marcabru addresses in *Bel m'es*, the troubadour Alegret, Bernart de Ventadorn's *joglar* and Raimbaut's Alegrat/Alegrar are all the same person. Raimbaut knew Alegret either through Bernart de Ventadorn or independently, and took a dislike to him. He knew *Bel m'es*, Marcabru's attack on Alegret, and set out to repeat the insult some ten or twenty years later, playing on the first poem and mimicking its author's style to perfection. This hypothesis is, of course, not provable. If, however, *Als durs* was composed under these circumstances, an initiated audience would have detected a great deal of irony at Alegrat/Alegrar's expense. If Raimbaut is not addressing Alegret in this poem, it is nevertheless clear that he is fulfilling a boast he makes elsewhere to sing well in every style (XVI, 1–8). He himself takes the trouble to point out in the *tornada* how well he sings about slanderers. As the poem is so obviously an imitation of Marcabru, this can be understood as a boast that he can 'outdo' the master of the moralizing poem.

Intertextual play in Raimbaut's poetry suggests not only that he knew other troubadours, but also that he actively strove in his poetry to show that he participated in the life of a community of poets who were aware of the tradition to which they belonged. There are other examples of intertextual play in Raimbaut's poetry. Roncaglia and di Girolamo demonstrate that Raimbaut is reacting to Bernart de Ventadorn's *Can vei* in his *Non chant* (XXVII), Milone makes a convincing case for seeing *Pos trobars plans* (XVI) as a deliberate parody of Jaufre Rudel and Raimbaut must have had Guilhem IX's *Farai un vers de dreit nien* in mind when he composed *Escotatz, mas no say que s'es* (XXIV).[29] Raimbaut is, of course, one of the great maverick figures of the troubadour tradition; however, the very fact that he spends so much of his time reacting to other poets and the conventions they uphold indicates his close links with them.

RAIMBAUT AND PARODY

The sheer volume of conventional courtly poetry, from the first troubadour onwards, shows that the courtly *canso* enjoyed considerable popularity; yet very few of Raimbaut's poems could be considered conventional love songs. He enjoys making a mockery of conventional *fin'amor*, and although it is his status as an aristocrat, and consequently as an amateur poet, that allows him to ironize so consistently at the expense of the 'courtly consensus', it is his unfailing sense of humour that disposes him to do this.[30]

In *Braiz, chans* (VIII), for example, Raimbaut deliberately misleads his audience and gives the impression it is hearing a conventional love poem:

> 1   Braiz, chans, quils, critz,
> Aug dels auzels pels plaissaditz. –

Raimbaut d'Aurenga

Oc! Mas no los enten ni deinh;
C'un'ira·m cenh
Lo cor, on dols m'a pres razitz 5
Per qe·n sofer.

II Si·m fos grazitz
Mos chantars, ni ben acuillitz
Per cella que m'a en desdeing,
D'aitan mi feing 10
Qu'en mains bons luocs for'enbrugitz
Mais que non er.

III Tristz e marritz
Es mos chantars aissi fenitz
Per totz temps tro q'ela·m deing 15
Pel sieu manteing;
Era mos bos, er es delitz!
Mas no·l sofer!

IV Jois m'es fugitz!
Un pauc mas tost mi fon faillitz! 20
S'anc mi volc, er m'a en desdeing.
Com no·m esteing
Can precs ni merces ni destritz
Re no i conquer?

V Mos cors me ditz 25
'Per qe soi per liei envilitz?'
'Car sap que nuill'autra non deing,
Per so·m n'estreing.'
Morrai, car mos cors enfollitz
Mas ges non quer. 30

VI Cum sui trahitz!
Bona dompn'ab talan voutitz,
Ab cor dur, a! nuill'als non deing,
Mesclat ab geing.
Volretz que torn flacs-endurzitz, 35
O que demer!

VII Trop sui arditz!
Dompna, mos sens eissabozitz
M'a faitz dir fols motz q'ieu non deing:
Contra mi reing. 40
Tant sui fors de mon sen issitz
Non sent qi·m fer.

VIII Mout es petitz,
Dompna, ·l tortz q'ieu vos ai servitz.
Per que vos m'avetz en desdeing? 45
Fatz n'esdeveing!
Pendutz fos aut per la cervitz
Qui a moiller!

Troubadours and irony

Humils, ses geing,
Dompna, ·l vostre sers fals-faillitz   50
Merce vos quer.

X Mas pretz, non sobrans', es tequitz:
Don en vos er.

I

I hear the calls, songs, cheeps and cries of the birds along the hedgerows – yes – but I do not listen to them or approve of them, for sorrow envelops my heart, where pain has taken root, wherefore I suffer.

II

If my singing were welcomed or well received by the lady who holds me in disdain, I flatter myself that it would be heard in many good places, more than it will be.

III

Sadly and woefully my singing is thus ended for ever, until she shows her approval of me through her support. It used to be good for me, now it is a fault since she does not permit it.

IV

Joy has fled me! It ended a little while ago! If ever she wanted me, now she holds me in disdain. Why do I not kill myself, when prayers, mercy and patient waiting attain nothing in all this?

V

My heart says to me 'Why am I reviled by her?' 'Because she knows I consider no other woman worthy of my love, because of which she values me little.' I shall die, for my heart, maddened, seeks nothing else.

VI

How betrayed I am! Oh, good lady with fickle desire and hard heart, ah!, I do not deceitfully consider any other thing worthy. You will want me to become soft and hard at the same time, or to be at fault.

VII

I am too bold! Lady, my confused mind makes me say words of which I do not approve. I act against my own interests: I am so out of my mind I do not realize who is striking me.

VIII

Lady, the wrong I have deserved of you is indeed small. Why do you disdain me? I am becoming stupid because of it. Any man who has a wife would be hung high by the neck.

IX

Lady, humbly, without deceit, your false, guilty serf begs mercy of you.

X

But worth, not pride, has grown; hence it will be in you.

Raimbaut begins by brushing away the joy of nature because of the great sorrow he has in his heart. His lady no longer favours him (stanzas II and III) and thus his singing is silenced: he despairs and is ready to die (stanzas IV and V). After a brief revolt against the tyranny of love and his lady (stanza VI), he submits to her again, attributing his temerity to madness (stanza VII). Thus far the poem might appear superficially to be a non-ironic love song; however, in the final stanza there is an admission which can only have been intended to surprise, and which modifies the implications of the main body of the poem. Raimbaut has been talking about his wife all along!

Is it possible that Raimbaut could be seriously addressing love poetry to his wife? Although recent scholarship has shown that the *domna* in the trouba-dour love lyric did not necessarily have to be married, it is fair to say that she usually was. Raimbaut himself implies as much in *Non chant* (XXVII), and Bernart Marti, Jaufre Rudel and Peire d'Alvernha make this quite clear.[31] The courtly lover usually woos another man's wife and to my knowledge there is no other example of a troubadour openly addressing love poetry to his own wife.[32] Raimbaut's admission that his song is addressed to his wife is startling and undermines the sincerity of the whole poem.

It is difficult to imagine how the song would have been performed. A superficial reading of the first seven stanzas gives the impression that Raimbaut has adopted the persona of a typical submissive courtly lover. Raimbaut, or the *joglar* performing the song, may have wanted to undermine this persona from the outset. This could have been achieved through tone of voice or gesture. However, there may also be some textual elements which a performer could have exploited to indicate irony to an initiated audience without exaggerating his tone of voice or using extravagant gestures: the surprise effect of the final lines would, of course, have been much greater if the performer played on textual ironies rather than indicating irony through physical means.[33]

The opening stanza, for example, may be ironic. It might appear conven-tional, but it is nevertheless somewhat unusual to have four monosyllabic synonyms strung together consecutively in an opening line. The effect of this can perhaps best be understood if Raimbaut's opening stanza is compared to the opening of a poem by Arnaut Daniel which may be modelled on it:[34]

> Doutz brais e critz,
> lais e cantars e voutas
> aug dels auzels q'en lur latin fant precs. (XII, 1–3)

I hear sweet calls, cries, airs and chirpings from the birds, who, in their own language, make supplications.

Arnaut has five synonyms for the bird songs and yet the effect is lyrical and sensual because he begins with an adjective, interposes conjunctions and varies the monosyllabic words with words of two syllables. Raimbaut, on the other hand, reels his synonyms off with breathtaking rapidity, taking up only four syllables and one short line. The resounding *Oc* at the beginning of line 3 is like a full stop, brushing aside, and irreverently dismissing, all this twitter-ing, which Raimbaut frankly admits he is indifferent to in any case. He is undermining the conventional nature opening, at the same time going one better than other poets.

The heaviest irony, however, could perhaps only be understood once the audience had realized that the poem is addressed to Raimbaut's wife. 'Why am I reviled by her?', asks the poet in stanza v. 'Because she knows I consider no other woman worthy of my love', comes the reply. Superficially, this would appear to be a common courtly *topos*: 'My only crime is loving my lady too much.' In an ordinary courtly context it would seem perfectly normal for a lover to consider no other lady worthy of his love and if Raimbaut were an ordinary *fin'amador* his indignation would be justified: the lady should cherish her admirer's fidelity, not despise him for it. Addressed to his wife, the words take on a new meaning. She despises him because he is in love with her, contrary to all the literary conventions of the day. The one thing that she does not expect, as his wife, is his fidelity. Raimbaut is admitting to the worst possible taste in wanting to be his own wife's lover (in all senses of the word).

It is abundantly clear that any persona Raimbaut adopts in a poem cannot necessarily be taken at face value. In *Braiz, chans* he adopts the persona of the submissive courtly lover, but this pose is undermined by the fact that he is singing (or claiming to sing) to his wife. In *Escotatz, mas no say que s'es* he admits to his *foudatz*:

> E soy fols cantayre cortes
> Tan c'om m'en apela ioglar. (xxiv, 33–4)

And I am such a foolish courtly singer that I am called a *joglar*.

Raimbaut, the aristocrat, is priding himself on his ability to behave like a *joglar*: he enjoys playing the fool and undermining the seriousness of virtually any subject.

RAIMBAUT'S UPSIDE-DOWN BOAST

Many of Raimbaut's poems are clearly humorous and have consequently been labelled *gaps*.[35] The critic to devote most attention in recent years to Raimbaut's work, Luigi Milone, considers Raimbaut's concept of the *gap* and his attitude towards *gabar* as the key to understanding, not only his poetry, but also his concept of *fin'amor*.

For Milone a fundamental opposition between *gabar* and *celar* runs throughout Raimbaut's thirty-nine poems. J. U. Fechner was the first to argue specifically for such an opposition in troubadour poetry. Taking his conclusions as a starting point, Erich Köhler argued that the *gap* should be seen as a counterpart to the courtly *canso*: the *fin'amador* must hide his feelings and above all make sure that the identity of his *domna* is kept a secret; the *gabador*, on the other hand, displays and vaunts his prowess, sexual and otherwise. Milone contends that Raimbaut equates *gabar* with the *trobar leu* or *trobar plan*, and *celar* with the *trobar clus* and *fin'amor*. He believes that Raimbaut

Raimbaut d'Aurenga

had an exceedingly negative view of *fin'amor*, equating it with deprivation, masochism and total frustration, all of which lead to *no poder* ('powerlessness' or 'impotence'). For Milone Raimbaut is trapped by the conventions of *fin'amor*: as an aristocrat he feels that his love can and should be consummated, but the conventions of *fin'amor*, which in Milone's view can be explained sociologically, dictate that it should not. Raimbaut mocks these conventions by composing *cansos enversas*, in which he indulges in *gabar envers*. In other words he boasts not of his sexual prowess, but of his sexual deprivation, showing up *fin'amor* for the sham it is. Thus in one song, *Lonc temps* (XXVIII), Raimbaut works the *amor de lonh* theme through to its logical conclusion and depicts himself as castrated. This indicates, for Milone, that Raimbaut suffered from a castration complex:

e nel segno della castrazione viene ora esibito – con gli inevitabili risvolti narcisistici – il masochismo dissimulato nella distanza d'amore: l'assunzione in prima persona, per narcisistico (aristocratico) eccesso di interiorizzazione, del processo esplicito in termini di grottesca e masochistica autoparodia – il doppio meccanismo inconscio della distanza: la paura della castrazione e il desiderio della castrazione.

If, for Milone, it is Raimbaut's social status that allows him to rebel against the tyranny of *fin'amor*, he nevertheless considers him to be deeply afflicted by the customs of his day and clearly implies that he is unable to break out of the prison they have imposed upon him. Behind Raimbaut's smile Milone senses a deeply troubled man suffering from a castration complex.[36]

At first glance, *Lonc temps* might seem to invite a psychoanalytic interpretation. Raimbaut boasts of being castrated and he would therefore seem to be an obvious candidate for a castration complex. However, there is a danger of being blinded (!) by the image of castration. Let us take a closer look at the text.

I   Lonc temps ai estat cubertz,
    Mas Dieus no vol qu'ieu oimais
    Puosca cobrir ma besoigna,
    Dont mi ven ira et esglais.
    Ez escoutatz, cavallier,   5
    S'a ren ai obs ni mestier

II D'aisso vos fatz ben totz certz:
    Qu'aicels don hom es plus gais
    Ai perdutz, don ai vergoigna;
    E non aus dir qui·ls me trais;   10
    E ai ben cor vertadier
    Car dic tant grand encombrier.

III Mas per so sui tant espertz
    De dir aisso que er plais
    Qu'ar voill leu gitar ses poigna*   15
    Totz los maritz de pantais
    E d'ira e de conssirier,
    Don moutz m'en fan semblant nier.

139

IV   Si·m fatz coindes e degertz
Si·m sui eu flacs e savais   20
Volpilz (garnitz e ses broigna);
E sui mizels e putnais,
Escars, vilan conduchier,
De totz lo plus croi guerrier.

V   Per quez es fols abubertz   25
Totz hom que ia ten a fais
S'ieu cortei – quar ja m'en loigna? –
Sa moiller, pois dans non nais
Ad el se son ben sobrier
Li mei mal sospir doblier.   30

VI   Car ia tot no fos desertz
D'aicels, per que·m pela·l cais,*
Tant ai d'als ont me peroigna
– D'autres avols decs on bais –
Per que domna ab cors entier   35
No·m deu prezar un dinier.

VII   E si mos chans m'es suferz
Eu chan, qu'enquers no m'en lais;
Pustel'hui sus en sa groigna
A totz marit si·s n'irais   40
S'ieu tant grant mon dol plenier
Voill cobrir ab alegrier.

VIII   A dompnas m'en soi profertz
E datz, per que m'en ven jais;
Si noc'ai poder que i joigna   45
En jazen, ades engrais
Solament del desirier
E del vezer, qu'als non quier.

IX   La comtessa a Monrosier
Volgra auzis mon gaug entier.

I

For a long time now I have kept my thoughts to myself, but God no longer wants me to hide my deficiency, because of which sorrow and fear afflict me. And listen, knights, if I am in need or lack anything.

II

Of this I make you entirely certain: that I have lost those things which make a man most happy, and I am ashamed of this. And I dare not say who took them from me. And my heart is indeed truthful for I reveal such a great embarrassment.

III

But, because of this, I am so quick to tell of that which I complained yesterday, for now I quickly and without delay wish to snatch all husbands from worry, sorrow and grief because of which many of them give me black looks.

Raimbaut d'Aurenga

IV

If I make myself kind and . . ., I am indeed flaccid and a base coward (armed and without a breastplate); and I am leprous and foul-smelling, a miser, a churlish host, by far the worst warrior of all.

V

Because of this a man is openly a fool if he worries when I court his wife – why does he try to distance her from me? – for no harm can come to him if my wretched sighs are even increased twofold.

VI

For even if I were not without these things, for which I pluck out my beard, I have many other things with which I can flatter myself – other vile vices to which I lower myself – whereby no lady with a whole body should think me worth a farthing.

VII

And if my singing is permitted to me, I sing, for I still do not give it up. May any husband have a pimple on his snout today if it annoys him that I should wish to cover up my immense and great grief with happiness.

VIII

I have offered and given myself to ladies, wherefore joy comes to me; if I never have the power to join myself to them in bed, I now grow fat only from desire and looking, for I do not seek anything else.

IX

I should like the countess at Monrosier to hear of my perfect joy.

Milone is, of course, right that Raimbaut is pushing *fin'amor* to its most absurd limits in a parody which is both 'railleuse' and 'grotesque'. To quote Leslie Topsfield, 'Raimbaut . . . pushes the theme of Joy in Desire to the limit of farce'.[37] Raimbaut is showing up the impossibility of the *amor de lonh* syndrome and the absurdity of pretending that a real man can live on (frustrated) desire alone.

However, in my view Milone's interpretation of this poem as proof that Raimbaut suffered from a castration complex is flawed by a fundamental false assumption. He assumes that the *eu* of the poem is Raimbaut, in other words that the voice of the subject of the poem and the voice of the poet are one and the same. He makes this quite clear when he refers to *Lonc temps* as an *autoparodia*;[38] in other words he believes that Raimbaut is presenting, in *Lonc temps*, a parody of the situation he finds himself in. Whilst a troubadour may compose 'personal poetry' and intend the 'I' of his poems to be identified with himself, he may also adopt a persona for dramatic reasons and it can never be *assumed* that there is a straightforward correlation between the *eu* of a troubadour poem and the poet. Moreover, it is clear that any persona adopted by Raimbaut in particular cannot necessarily be taken seriously. The parody here is of any man suffering from an *amor de lonh* and the *eu* of the poem is a fictitious character.

Elsewhere Raimbaut presents frustrated desire as comic:

141

Que sempre·m tornon l'oil blanc,
E·l cors, qu'est esglai mi presta,
Faill tro c'om la cara·m venta
Can mi soven, dompna genta,
Com era nostre jois verais
Tro lauzengiers crois e savais
Nos loigneron ab lor fals brais. (xv, 22–8)

For my eyes quickly turn white, and my heart, which brings this terror to me, fails to such an extent that I have to have my face fanned when I remember, gracious lady, how our joy was true until evil and wicked slanderers separated us with their false whining.

Qu'ie·n pert la color e·l sanc
Tal talent ai que·m desvesta
C'ab vos fos ses vestimenta
Aissi com etz la plus genta;
Que tan grans voluntatz m'en nais
Qu'en un jorn – tan ben c'om no·m pais –
En pert so que d'un mes engrais. (xv, 50–6)

For I lose my colour and blood, such a desire have I to undress so that I might be with you, unclothed, just as you are when you are at your most gracious; for such a great desire is born in me for this that, however well I am fed, I lose in a day all the fat I put on in a month.

He continually mocks the conventions of *fin'amor*, and makes it clear that his desire is, or has been, satisfied. He does adopt the persona of the frustrated lover, but it is often undermined by irony and humour.[39]

Milone misses much of the irony and underestimates the humour of *Lonc temps*. On one level the miserable, subservient courtly lover is presented as emasculated: as far as Raimbaut is concerned, he might as well be; his joy can only ever be a sham if he contents himself with desire and makes no attempt to satisfy it. Raimbaut puns in the *envoi* on the notion of *gaug entier*, which evokes the *domna ab cors entier* (line 35). *Gaug* is ironic because it could be understood on a physical or a spiritual plane. The lover's spiritual joy may be whole, but his physical joy can never be. The lady's body is whole, the lover's is not. He is *flacs* (line 20) both spiritually and physically and his *besoigna* is spiritual and physical. Given that Raimbaut opens his poem by punning on concepts of style and making a mockery of the *trobar clus*, the word *entier* may also be intended to evoke the controversy over *vers entiers*. The tone smacks distinctly of farce, whilst the overstated profession of sincerity (lines 11–12) suggests heavy irony. Evidence for Milone's anguished *autoparodia* is hard to find.

Moreover, the poem is open to an entirely different interpretation. The castrated lover-persona makes one point very forcefully: no husband should worry if he courts his wife; he is not capable of physically consummating a relationship; he is totally harmless and the ideal man to allow her to frequent. He only pretends to be *coindes*; underneath he is *flacs*, *savais* and *Volpilz*. The

Raimbaut d'Aurenga

notion of pretence is also present in stanzas I and II: for a long time he has
hidden his deficiency, in other words he has the appearance of a 'whole' man.
He is trying to reassure husbands that his motives are pure (lines 15–16, 35–6,
39–42), but if the puns, the farcical tone and the exaggerated profession of
sincerity all combine to indicate heavy irony, the parody of the courtly lover
may be quite different from the parody Milone has in mind. If it is ironic, the
boast of castration could be understood *per contrarium* as a boast of sexual
prowess. The persona boasts of castration to dupe husbands into thinking he
is harmless and his superficial appearance of happiness is, contrary to his
claims, authentic. The whole poem could be understood as an elaborate joke
at the expense of husbands who allow their wives to be courted by young men
who appear harmless. Perhaps the *gaug* of the last line is *entier* after all.[40]

CONCLUSION

Raimbaut's sense of humour and irreverent treatment of convention pervade
almost his entire corpus. He constantly undermines through irony the personae he adopts, laughing at the courtly circles he moves in and at the literary
world of which he is part. He may understand all the fears and trepidation of
the plight of the courtly lover, but in the song which perhaps represents the
culmination of his achievement as a poet, *Ar resplan la flors enversa* (XXXIX),
the persona he adopts clearly attains joy, united with his *domna* in fulfilled,
mutual love:

V   Anat ai cum cauz'enversa
Sercan rancx e vals e tertres,
Marritz cum selh que conglapis   35
Cocha e mazelh'e trenca:
Que no·m conquis chans ni siscles
Plus que folhs clercx conquer giscles.
Mas ar – Dieu lau – m'alberga Joys
Malgrat dels fals lauzengiers croys.   40

VI   Mos vers an – qu'aissi l'enverse,
Que no·l tenhon bosc ni tertre –
Lai on hom non sen conglapi,
Ni a freitz poder que y trenque.
A midons lo chant e·l siscle,   45
Clar, qu'el cor l'en intro·l giscle,
Selh que sap chanter ab joy
Que no tanh a chantador croy.

VII   Doussa dona, Amors e Joys
Nos ajosten malgrat dels croys.   50

V

I have gone about like a 'reversed' person, searching cliffs and valleys and hills,
saddened like one whom the frost torments, slays and cuts: for neither a song nor a
whistle triumphed over me any more than a rod conquers foolish clerks. But now,
praise be to God, Joy shelters me despite the false, evil slanderers.

VI

May my verse go – for thus do I reverse it, so that neither wood nor hill might hold it back – there where one does not feel the frost, and where the cold has no power to cut. May it be sung and whistled clearly to my lady, so that its shoots enter her heart, by a singer who can sing well with joy, for it does not befit a churlish singer.

VII

Sweet lady, may Joy and Love unite us despite the evil one.

To quote Topsfield, '*Ar resplan* is a triumphant song'.[41] It is the song of a man who has supreme confidence in his love, which in turn leads to confidence as a poet. Doubt and anguish are ultimately cast aside and joy is all.

Perhaps the last word should be left to Giraut de Borneil, who lamented on Raimbaut's death:

> Ar'es morta bella foudatz
>   E iocs de datz
>   E dos e dompneis oblidatz.   (LXI, 41–3)

Now beautiful folly and games of dice are dead, and generosity and courting forgotten.

For Giraut Raimbaut was the perfect lord, the perfect lover, and a perpetual joker.

6

Giraut de Borneil

Giraut de Borneil's surviving corpus is remarkable both for its diversity and for its size. The seventy-five poems which can be attributed to him with certainty include *vers*, *cansos*, *sirventes*, *planhs*, *tensos*, *pastorelas*, an *alba*, a *sirventes joglaresc*, a riddle poem and a group of poems Kolsen called *Sirventes-Kanzonen* because of the way they mix together moral themes with love poetry.[1] His is the largest corpus to have survived from the early years of the troubadour tradition and his popularity among the compilers of the *chansonniers* is well attested and unrivalled. Indeed, of the early troubadours Giraut is the most popular in the twelfth and thirteenth centuries.

Of course popularity and good poetry do not always go hand in hand. Dante praised Giraut as a *poeta rectitudinis*, but ultimately decided that he was overrated and that Arnaut Daniel was the better poet; modern scholars have tended to agree with Dante.[2] Giraut's lack of spontaneity and his scholarly approach to light-hearted subjects can often lead to flat and pedestrian poetry: he is thought of as a didactic poet, given to long digressions on moral themes and steeped in medieval rhetorical theory.[3]

It is not my intention to argue that Giraut de Borneil was a poet of the calibre of Marcabru, Bernart de Ventadorn or Arnaut Daniel. However, I do believe that Giraut has not entirely merited his reputation as a boring poet. By examining Giraut's use of irony, I hope to show that his sense of humour has perhaps been underestimated and that he can even be quite lively. He was an entertainer as well as a *poeta rectitudinis*, and it may have been the entertainment value of some of his songs that helped to earn him his reputation among his contemporaries.

Given the size and variety of Giraut's corpus, my study will necessarily be selective; I intend to focus on texts that jar somewhat with the daunting label Dante bestowed upon him for posterity. My approach is eclectic: his love poetry and his moralizing poetry will be studied separately, even though it is sometimes difficult to assign a poem to one category or the other, and where Giraut's irony concentrates consistently on one theme, I take a thematic approach.

Giraut has a constant tendency to moralize, but the vast majority of his songs are nevertheless essentially love poems. The corpus of his love poetry is as large as Bernart de Ventadorn's and although Giraut never achieves anything approaching Bernart's lyrical lightness of touch or intensity, the two poets are in many ways close in spirit, for both were professional entertainers. Unlike the aristocratic Raimbaut d'Aurenga, who could compose love poetry as he wished, Giraut and Bernart had to give their audiences what they wanted if they were to make a living. Furthermore, their art was theatrical as well as literary, and we have to imagine Giraut, or the *joglar*, performing his song, acting the part of the courtly lover in front of an audience.[4]

However, there are important differences as well as similarities between the love poetry of Giraut and Bernart. Bernart rarely laughs at the persona he has created: to do so would be to destroy the illusion he tried so hard to maintain, and would undermine the appeal of his poetry. Giraut, on the other hand, does not hesitate to present his lover-persona in a comic light:

> Vai t'en, que bon'anaras
> Al meu semblan,
> E pero membre·t del gan
> Don Mos Segurs
> Fetz avol bargajna,
> Que·l seus rics pretz sobeiras
> Es tornatz fragils e vas
> E d'avol parvenza,
> Per qu'es mort'e decazuda,
> Si·l cor flac en ferm no muda.
>
> Tot so del castiar las,
> Mais a d'un an,
> Mas al sieu leugier talan,
> No·m val aturs. (XXXI, 21–34)

Be gone, for luck will go with you, I think, but remember the glove with which my Segurs made a vile bargain, for her noble, superior reputation has become fragile and fickle and vile in its appearance, wherefore she is dead and decadent if she does not make her weak will firm.

I have been weary of reprimanding her about all this for more than a year, but perseverance gains me nothing in the face of her fickle desire.

Giraut is clearly insulting his lady here and any praise of her is consequently ironic. Her *rics pretz sobeiras* (line 26) is *fragils* and *vas* (line 27), and the *senhal* Segurs, meaning 'sure', 'certain', must also be understood ironically for we learn that she has a *cor flac* (line 30) and a *leugier talan* (line 33). Later in the poem Giraut again addresses the *joglar*:

> Torna saj, que non iras
> Un pas enan,
> Fe que·t dei, que per aitan

Giraut de Borneil

Son eu periurs
E fis, de gran lajna –
Quan que·n traines – certas.
Pus ves fina sui trefas,
Ia·l sejner d'Argenza
No·m dira que bona druda
Per dreg non aia perduda.

Ditz tu que non remanras
S'eu t'o coman?
Vai doncs, e si·t prec del chan
Que no·l peiurs. (41–54)

Come back here; you won't go a step further, by my faith, for if I let you go, I am false and yet true, certain of great sorrow, however much I might suffer for her. Since I am churlish towards a true lady, indeed the lord of Argenza shall never tell me that I have rightly lost a good lady.

Do you say that you will not stay if I command you to? Go then and I beg you not to falsify the song.

The syntax, punctuation and sense of lines 41–50 are not certain. Giraut appears to be saying in lines 44–6 that if the *joglar* takes the poem to his lady (*per aitan*, line 43), he will be a liar, because he will have insulted her, and yet true, because his insults are nevertheless truthful. The lord of Argenza, Raymond V of Toulouse, will presumably not tell him that he has rightly lost a good lady, first because she is not a good lady and secondly because Giraut is in the right, and therefore, by extension, his lady in the wrong. Giraut twice pretends here that the *joglar* is leaving against his will (lines 41–2 and 51–2). In other words, he tries to imply that all his insults were not really intended for his lady's ears and that the *joglar* should not take them to her. As Sharman points out, the situation is contrived and ironical.[5] The *joglar* is not really leaving against Giraut's will and Giraut's protestations are purely theatrical. If Giraut had really not intended his lady to hear his insults, why does he declare himself to be *fis* as well as *periurs* (line 44) and why does he ask his *joglar*, if he must go, not to alter anything in his song (lines 53–4)? Giraut ironically begs the *joglar* to stay in order to deny responsibility for the criticism of his lady, but he also uses this to create comedy. He is reversing the usual *topos* of sending a *joglar* off to a lady as quickly as possible and one can sense an indignant tone in lines 41–2 and 51–2, as if Giraut were physically trying to restrain the *joglar*. Of course the song would not have required two performers; one could have mimed the implicit scenario as effectively as two. However, if two performers were used, there is obvious scope for a great deal of boisterous stagecraft. Giraut is clearly prepared to use all kinds of devices to entertain his audience, including, although we can never be sure of how a song was actually performed, slapstick comedy.

Giraut's propensity to laugh at his lover-persona is not, however, the only difference between his love poetry and Bernart de Ventadorn's. With a few notable exceptions, when Bernart is critical of his *domna*, or of some aspect of the conventional poetic courtly world, this is a device to reaffirm his commitment and loyalty even more strongly and he admonishes himself for his foolishness.[6] Giraut, on the other hand, is often critical without taking his criticism back afterwards. As such criticism takes place within the framework of the courtly *canso*, it is not surprising that it is often expressed through irony, so that the courtly illusion can be maintained for one section of the audience. It also comes as no surprise, given that Giraut had a sound knowledge of rhetoric, and that he may even have been a teacher of rhetoric himself, that irony of this kind often takes the form of recognizable ironic figures and tropes.[7]

In *Ar auziretz*, for example, Giraut uses *ironia* when talking about love:

> A, tantas vetz
> M'a trag nesis parlars
> Joi d'entrels mans, per qu'esdevenc liars!
> E·l cors, pois en ren s'aficha
> Don s'alegra tan ni qan,
> Volri'eu chantes gaban.
> Qu'era, tro que s'esperec,
> Tenia·l dreg per envers,
> Tant er'en amar esmers! (VII, 10–18)

Alas, many times foolish words have snatched joy from between my hands, so that I have become white-haired! And my heart, since it aspires to a lady who makes it only a little happy, would like me to sing boastfully; for, until it woke just now, it considered right to be wrong, so perfect was it in love.

Sharman wonders whether *esmers* in line 18 is an unattested form of an unattested verb *esmerger*, 'to submerge', and in this she follows Kolsen, who translates 'versunken'.[8] However, there are no grounds for supposing the existence of such a verb in Occitan. Sharman's reluctance to translate *esmers* with its usual meaning, 'pur', 'parfait', is presumably because it would seem then to offer a *contresens*. Giraut has just listed a series of serious transgressions against the courtly code of behaviour. He is too talkative and given to boasting to such an extent that he gets everything back to front. All this happens because he is so *esmers* in love! The line makes perfect sense, however, if it is understood as *ironia*. Giraut is playing on the *topos* of love perfecting the *fin'amador*. Here love has quite the opposite effect on him and it induces him to uncourtly, churlish behaviour. By using the *topos* ironically here, Giraut manages to pander to a simplistic courtly audience and yet to criticize its *idée reçue* at one and the same time. The literal meaning of *esmers* remains valid for one section of the audience, but the intended meaning conveyed to the initiated is its opposite.

Elsewhere Giraut uses *ironia* to overstep the mark of what is acceptable in courtly behaviour and this too amounts to criticism of courtly conventions and ultimately of his *domna*. In *Can creis*, for example, he claims too insistently that he is not complaining about his lady:

Giraut de Borneil

E cuiatz c'aiso sia clams
Ni que m'e rancur? Non fas ges!
Tota ma rancur'es: 'Merces!'
Si be·s passa·l ditz los garanz,
  Non sui clamanz.   (XXVII, 23–7)

And do you think that thus I complain and that I am bitter about this? Not at all! All my rancour amounts to a cry of 'Mercy!' Even if my words go beyond the pale, I am not complaining.

These lines might profitably be compared to a similar protestation by Bernart de Ventadorn:

Eu·m sui cel qu'e re no tira,
si tot ma domna·m sostrai,
ja de re no·m clamarai;
car es tan pur'e tan fina
  que ja no creirai
si de so tort li quer plai,
que merces no l'en prenha.   (XVIII, 15–21)

I am the one that nothing irritates; even if my lady reviles me, I will complain of nothing; for she is so pure and true that I will never believe, if I complained of her wrong doing, that she would not have mercy in this.

Bernart's humble tone is not undermined, as he explains that he is not complaining because he knows his lady to be faultless. Whilst this may be an astute piece of moral blackmail, it is not ironic. Giraut's tone, on the other hand, is insolent. He repeats that he is not complaining, but the repetition is, if anything, too insistent because of the verbal echo between *clams* and *clamanz* and between *rancur* and *rancur'*, because of the virtual juxtaposition of *rancur'* and *Merces*, and because of the pointed way in which he admits he knows his words go beyond the pale. He thus skilfully uses typical signals to irony here: he overstates his case, at the same time bringing together contradictory elements. The result is an indignant rejection of the courtly convention that a lover should not complain, no matter how his lady treats him. 'Non sui clamanz' should be understood, *per ironiam*, as its opposite.

Giraut's use of *ironia* when transgressing courtly conventions is not always so indignant or critical. Sometimes it merely serves to add a humorous, erotic sparkle to an otherwise serious love poem:

E si saubes can ni cora
N'aurai luec c'als prex m'eslais,
Tot l'afan sofrir'en patz,
  E sapchatz
C'ab menz m'en tengr'a pagatz
Que vos non cuidariatz.   (XXXIX, 35–40)

And if I knew when and how I will have the chance to entreat her ardently, I would suffer all the sorrow in peace, and know this: I would be satisfied with less than you would think.

Troubadours and irony

The urgency of the verb *eslaisar*, and the presence of the overstated profession of sincerity *sapchatz*, which is frequently a verbal signal to irony in the troubadour lyric, make unlikely Giraut's claim that he would be satisfied with a lot less than one might think. Lines 39–40 are probably a way of communicating, through irony, the urgency and extent of his desire.

Ironia is not the only ironic trope Giraut uses in his love poetry. He seems to be fond of using *antiphrasis*, although in some cases he rather labours the point:

> E s'ieu ia ves emperador
> Ni vas rey vauc, si·m vol grazir
> Tot aysi com al sieu trachor
> Qui no·l sap ni no·l plot gandir
>   Ni mantener ostage,
> Mi luenh'en us estrayns regnatz;
> C'aissi serai iusticiatz
>   E fis de gran damnatge
> Si·l sieus gens cors blancx e prezatz
> M'es estrainhs ni m'estai iratz.   (XXXVII, 61–70)

And if I go towards an emperor or a king, and he wishes to welcome me as he would a traitor, whom he cannot and does not wish to protect or have as a guest, he exiles me to a foreign land; and thus will I be condemned and sure of great harm if her pure, noble and worthy person is hostile or angry towards me.

The word *grazir* in line 62 must, of course, imply a pleasant welcome. Here Giraut makes it clear that the welcome he is describing is unpleasant, (lines 63–7). *Grazir* may therefore imply its opposite here. However, Giraut states so clearly that this is the case that the subtlety of his *antiphrasis* is completely lost.

Elsewhere Giraut's use of *antiphrasis* is far more effective, creating an ambiguity which enhances the import of the stanza in which it occurs:

> E per ma guereira cui am,
> Car es una de las meillors,
> Cove, si noca·m son amatz,
> Qe per l'aventura·m trebail
> E m'en fegnha coindes e letz?   (XIX, 9–13)

And because of my enemy whom I love, for she is one of the best, is it fitting, if I am not loved, that just in case [she could love me] I should torment myself and pretend to be cheerful and happy?

By calling his lady his enemy, and then immediately saying he loves her, Giraut is bringing together opposites in a dramatic fashion. On one level *guereira* must imply its opposite, but on another it underlines the fact that the lady is cruel to Giraut and that his love is not requited (line 11). Images of fighting and warfare are also, of course, common sexual metaphors, and the use of the word *guereira* may well add erotic overtones to the stanza which may be picked up in line 12 by the word *aventura*.

Giraut de Borneil

Giraut's use of *antiphrasis* is equally subtle in *Iois e chanz*:

> Mas qui que·s laing
> Qu'il ias'e·s baing
> E iense sas colors,
> E lui cresca dolors
> Qu'es en latz et espres,
> Jes Amors mais no·ill pes!
> No m'es vis ben egaill
> C'om desir e badaill
> E viva consiros
>   E qu'ella chan
> D'autrui dolsas chansos.   (XLVI, 104–14)

But if a man complains that she rests and bathes and paints her face while his pain grows, because he is tethered and on fire, let him not care for love any more! For it seems to me hardly fair that a man should desire and sigh and live on, careworn, while she sings another's sweet songs.

Giraut is extremely critical of his lady here. Both *jazer* and *se banhar* (line 105) can have sexual connotations; make-up (line 106) is a sure sign of decadence. Giraut is accusing his lady of debauchery and wantonness, harsh criticism indeed for a courtly lover to level against his loved one, and nowhere does he retract this accusation. In the last line of this stanza Giraut talks of 'another's sweet songs'; *dolsas*, however, can only be understood as ironic and consequently as *antiphrasis*. The songs may indeed be sweet to the lady and to her new lover, but to Giraut they can only be bitter.

Giraut also proves to be adept at using different types of *significatio*. In *Era si·m fos*, for example, he employs *significatio per consequentiam*, by means of which one states something which implies another by association:

> Qe? – Vira
> Talan;
> Qu'enianan
>   Van
> Tric'e galiaire
> Gentil de bon aire! –
> No·m voillatz retraire
>   D'enian
> Vas cellas qe galiaran!   (XXIX, 30–8)

What? – She changes her mind because the treacherous and false go about cheating the noble and well-born! – Don't talk to me about cheating women being deceived!

Giraut indulges here in an imaginary dialogue. These lines offer two propositions: first, that his lady is fickle because of other people's treachery and, secondly, that only treacherous women allow themselves to fall prey to other people's treachery. The only logical conclusion is that Giraut's lady is treacherous; however, as this is only intimated, and remains unstated, these lines are ironic. If it is accepted that Giraut is attacking his lady in this stanza, then it

151

is also worth noting that the 'noble and well-born' people mentioned in line 35 are also being criticized through irony and that the words *Gentil de bon aire* must be understood as *ironia* and as false praise.

Significatio also occurs in *Non puesc sofrir*:

> Non puesc sofrir c'a la dolor
> De la den la lengua non vir
> E·l cor a la novela flor,
> Lancan vei los ramels florir
> E·ill chant son pel boscatge
> Dels auzeletz enamoratz. (XXXVII, 1–6)

I cannot stop my tongue touching the tooth that hurts, nor my heart being touched by the new flower, when I see the branches in blossom and the songs of the lovesick birds are in the wood.

Significatio per similitudinem occurs when 'we cite some analogue and do not amplify it, but by its means intimate what we are thinking' (*ad Herennium* IV. 54.67). This is precisely what Giraut does here. The unstated, ironic meaning of these lines is that the poet's apparently pleasant feelings about the joys of spring are in fact as relentlessly painful as toothache. As Sharman comments, 'in making this comparison is Giraut not being deliberately ironical?'[9] However, there may be further irony here. The notion of the aching tooth attracting the tongue was probably proverbial,[10] but these lines may have been intended to evoke particularly Marcabru's use of the image in a context which makes it clear that the aching tooth represents, in a rather scabrous manner, lust:

> Puois qu'ieu vei qu'ella non crei castiador,
> Anz de totz malvatz pren patz, cals l'a groissor,*
> A la den torna soven la leng'on sent la dolor. (XXIV, 16–18)

Since I see that she does not believe the one who reproaches her, rather she satisfies herself with all the wicked ones, whichever one has the biggest, the tongue often returns to the tooth that aches.

Giraut uses the same rhyme here as Marcabru (*-or*) and it is tempting to see the opening lines of *Non puesc* as an intertextual reference to Marcabru's poem and, consequently, as also implying lust. Needless to say, if this is the case, the irony in these lines is intensified.

Giraut's use of rhetorical irony in his love songs indicates a rejection of courtly conventions and a distance between the persona he has adopted and his own identity as a person and as a poet. Moreover, the fact that ironic figures and tropes are so easily recognizable in his work is an apt reflection of the scholarly background that has been attributed to him. In moralizing poetry rhetorical irony leads to the kind of acidic vituperation that is to be found in Marcabru's work; in love poetry it certainly makes the tone critical, but it also indicates humour.

Giraut de Borneil

It is worth dwelling briefly on Giraut's use of ironic sexual metaphors, as they underline the fact that he is far from being just the *poeta rectitudinis* Dante labelled him and that in fact his sense of humour is often quite mischievous. In *Ajtal cansoneta*, for example, Giraut alludes, in a seemingly straightforward manner, to the importance of fantasy:

> Si noqua s'es castellana
> Mais l'am que tal que·m laisses,
> E ia res de que·m cuges
> A coita no·m paregues,
> Be·s deu hom d'aisso servir,
>   Voler e jauzir
>   Ans que·s n'abays.   (XXXII, 36–42)

Even if she is not a chatelaine, I love her more than one of that rank who might leave me, and if nothing of what I imagine appears real to me when I need it, it is this [fantasy] that a man must use and desire and enjoy, before it goes down.

The evocation of fantasies is probably a courtly commonplace. Consider, for example, the following lines by Bernart de Ventadorn:

> Qui ve sas belas faissos
> ab que m'a vas se atraih
> pot be saber atrazaih
> que sos cors es bels e bos
> e blancs sotz la vestidura
> (eu non o dic mas per cuda)
> que la neus, can ilh es nuda,
> par vas lei brun'et escura.   (VIII, 33–40)

Whoever sees her beautiful features, with which she has attracted me, can indeed know certainly that her body is beautiful and good and white beneath her clothing – I only say this through imagination – for snow seems brown and dark compared to her when she is naked.

Giraut, however, does not describe his fantasy like Bernart. He says that a man must use and enjoy his fantasy before it 'goes down'. The words *Voler* and *jauzir* (line 41) clearly have erotic overtones. It would also seem likely that the expression *a coita* evokes the sexual act,[11] thus alerting the audience to the fact that 'going down' here is not simply a metaphor for despair. It is significant that Giraut should use the verb *abaisar* to describe the fading away of his fantasy, for verbs denoting rising and falling lend themselves very well to sexual innuendo. Giraut's fantasy is probably sexual and, like all sexual metaphors, *abays* is ironic, for the lines are open to a completely innocent reading. The implication is that satisfaction in fantasy is all the satisfaction that can be expected from a courtly *domna* and there can be little doubt that Giraut is being humorous here.

Troubadours and irony

In *La flors el vergan*, Giraut again uses the semantic field of rising and falling for sexual innuendo. Again the effect is ironic and comic:

> Mas ara si·m sona
> M'amia fellona
> Sera·l bes poiatz.
> Doncs a que
> No·m poiara be
> Si·m sona ni m'acuoill gen?
> No·i a gran refraignemen?   (XXVIII, 54–60)

But now, if my wicked lady addresses me, the 'good thing' will rise. So, to what heights will she not inspire me if she addresses me and welcomes me kindly? Is there not great relief in this?

Bes, used as a noun in line 56, is ambivalent. It could mean 'goodness', but it could equally well mean 'the good thing'. The repetition of the verb *poiar* emphasizes the idea of 'rising' and this, together with the use of the word *refraignemen*, 'consolation' or 'relief', means, as Sharman points out, that there is probably a bawdy pun intended here.[12]

All Giraut's sexual metaphors and references to sex are in fact characterized by a bawdy wink at his audience that jars somewhat with his reputation as a *poeta rectitudinis*. One can even sense, occasionally, an element of macho boasting in Giraut's tone:

> Qu'ieu c'ai pres
> En mant loc trebaill,
> De man mol lieg man dur iaser,
> Lais, ab alques de bon saber,
> Ma rancur'e·m vauc conortan.   (XXII, 27–31)

And I, who have had hardship on many occasions, and many a hard night in a soft bed, give up, with a little pleasure, my complaining and take comfort.

The juxtaposition of *mol lieg* and *dur iaser* almost certainly leads to sexual innuendo here, and it would seem that Giraut is boasting of his sexual prowess.

Given Giraut's reputation as a moralist, it is striking that his use of ironic sexual metaphors, and his allusions to sex in general, differ greatly from allusions to sex in moralizing poetry. Though he undoubtedly derives humour from ironic sexual metaphors, Marcabru alludes crudely to sex first and foremost in order to give his censure greater force. Giraut's moralizing poetry contains no bawdy allusions that I can detect; he only ever refers to sex in his love poetry. The difference between the two poets' use of ironic sexual metaphors can perhaps best be illustrated by a poem where Giraut may be using images borrowed directly from Marcabru.

The first four stanzas of *Razon e luec* (XX) apparently contain no ironic sexual allusions. Giraut begins by declaring that he is abandoning moralizing poetry for love poetry (stanza 1); he goes on to preach the virtues of restraint (stanza II) and to express his deference and loyalty to his lady in conventional courtly terms by using a feudal metaphor (stanza III). In stanza IV he evokes the courtly *topos* of improving the quality of his song through love. Then the mood of the poem changes:

V   Qu'aissi s'apluec
Tot bellamen
S'amors al cor, que·m bruelh'e·m nais,
Ab que m'a fag iauzen languir.
Qu'al partir de Sanhtonge,   65
  Cum per essaj,
– No sai si·m notz quar o diraj –
Qu'al comensar
En cugei eu plus leu passar,
Mas pueis, per la fe que dey vos,   70
M'es si camjat, que del laissar
No suj ni serai poderos;
  Per qu'ieu egalh,
  Si noqua·us par,
Los fols e·ls savis amoros.   75

VI   Qu'ar*d* cum del fuec
Que s'escompren,
Don nays la flam'e puja·l fais
E creis tan qu'om no·l pot sofrir,
Que d'aissi non ha monge   80
  Tro en Velaj
Ves son bon abat ta veraj!
  Que, ses trichar,
Tan finamen e de cor clar
Non l'am? Per que la sospeissos   85
Me fai partir e delonhar
De manhs vilas clams enojos;
  E si·m nualh,
  Quan dei aussar,
Camjat m'a·l nom de Bonafos!   90

VII   Mai s'anc amicx per esperar
Fon bautz ni jauzens ni ioios,
  Sobre-Totz, i*a-lh*
  Deg ben cujar
Qu'enquer aura·i nom Bonafos!*   95

V

For thus did rain beautifully into my heart, where it shoots and grows, her love, with which she made me languish joyfully, for when I left Saintonge, as if it were a test (I know not if my saying this will harm me), at first I thought I could easily do without it, but then by my faith, I changed so much that it is not within my power to give it up, nor will it ever be; for this reason I say that foolish and wise lovers are equal, although it might not seem so to you.

VI

For I burn like the fire that consumes itself, from whence the flame is born and the burden rises, and it grows to such an extent that it cannot be tolerated, for from here to Velay there is no monk truer to his good abbot! For do I not love her so truly and with a pure heart? For this reason hope makes me leave and distance myself from many vile and churlish complaints; and if I fare worse, when I ought to fare better, she has changed for me the name of Bonafos!

VII

But if ever a lover was happy, jubilant or joyful through hoping, Sobre-Totz, I ought indeed to believe that she will again have the name Bonafos!

At the beginning of stanza v, Giraut explains how his lady's love made him 'languish joyfully' to such an extent that when he first left her, he thought that he could take the separation in his stride.[13] Then he realized that he was unable to do this and he admits implicitly that however wise he or another lover might seem, he is in fact foolish. In stanza VI the atmosphere becomes distinctly erotic. Burning is an image of lust for both Marcabru and Raimbaut d'Aurenga, and here Giraut emphasizes its intensity by using the verb *escomprendre* (line 77).[14] *Puja·l fais* (line 78) may also have erotic overtones: Marcabru says that a *fols fais* inflicts those who are in love and Jaufre Rudel says that he is *descargatz de fol fais* when he finally achieves satisfaction in love.[15] Giraut is consumed with lust when he is separated from his lady and it is perhaps significant that he uses the verb *aussar* ('to rise', line 89) to denote his 'faring better'.

At the end of the stanza Giraut uses the *senhal* Bonafos. Sharman follows Kolsen in seeing Bonafos as a *senhal* which Giraut applies to himself.[16] However, the composition of the *senhal* would seem to suggest that it ought only to be applied to a woman, for the most obvious derivation is *bona* from *bon*, *fos* from *esser*, and *bona* is clearly a feminine form. If Bonafos is a *senhal* referring to a woman, then it can only denote Giraut's lady and line 90 must therefore mean literally 'she has changed for me the name of Bonafos', in other words her behaviour no longer allows Giraut to call her Bonafos.

Moreover, the *senhal* also occurs, denoting a woman, in a poem by Marcabru:

> Aquest intr'en la cozina
> Coitar lo fuoc al tizo
> E beu lo fum de la tina
> De si donz na Bonafo.　　　　　　　(XXXI, 55–8)

That man goes into the kitchen to blow on the fire in the embers, and he drinks the perfume from the fountain of his lady Bonafo.

Pollina suggests that Bonafo in Marcabru's poem means 'she was good' or 'good fountain' and that it is a disparaging nickname which contributes to the satire of the poem.[17] There is no reason to suppose that Bonafos in Giraut's poem has a different derivation from Bonafo in Marcabru's, especially since the *senhal* is otherwise unattested in twelfth-century troubadour poetry.[18]

Furthermore, the striking use of the fire/lust metaphor by both poets in the same stanza in which the *senhal* occurs would seem to suggest a close connection between Giraut's and Marcabru's use of the *senhal*. However, if Giraut is imitating Marcabru here, his intentions are quite different. Marcabru uses the *senhal* ironically and he is clearly condemning lust in his poem. Giraut does not condemn lust, he merely describes his own feelings; moreover, it is clear from lines 88–9 that Giraut thinks that something ought to be done about satisfying his lust and that the nickname Bonafos is connected to this. Perhaps the final *-s* of Bonafos in Giraut's poem is significant, for whereas Bonafo in Marcabru's literally means 'she was good', Bonafos could translate 'would she were good'. One possible interpretation is that Giraut's lady used to deserve the name Bonafos when she returned his love, but that now that this is no longer the case, he can no longer give her this name. He hopes, however, that she will one day allow him to call her Bonafos again, in other words that she will again look kindly upon him, and he encapsulates all his longing in the *senhal* Bonafos. This interpretation concords perfectly with the information given in stanza v about Giraut's separation from his lady. Whereas Marcabru's use of the *senhal* is satirical as well as humorous, Giraut's is simply humorous. The name Bonafos may, in Giraut's poem, denote his lady's kindness, but given the images of lust that precede it, it is probably also intended to evoke his own frustrated desire. Of course, if such an interpretation is accepted, the stanza is heavily laden with irony.

One further enigma remains. What is the significance of the image of the monk and the abbot in lines 80–2? Coming immediately after the striking images of lust, is it not surprising that Giraut should evoke bonds between religious men to express his feelings towards his lady? If the lines are taken literally, Giraut is comparing his lust to the feelings a monk has towards his abbot, a somewhat outrageous aspersion. There may, however, be another explanation. Given that Giraut may have taken the *senhal* Bonafos from Marcabru's work, it is also possible that the *monge/abat* image also has a source in Marcabru's poems, for he too talks of the abbot:

> Az una part es partida
> Ma fin'amistatz plevida;
> Son joc revit, s·l m'envida.
> Auzels, per ta conoisensa,
> So·l diguatz
> Qu'en un glatz
> Lev'e jatz
> Desiratz:*
> Er l'abatz
> An sasatz*
> Que n'ajam lezensa.   (XXVI, 45–55)

My pledged, noble love has gone off somewhere else; I revive his game, if he invites me to do it. Bird, with your wisdom, tell him this: the desired one rises and falls in an instant; now may the abbot go away satisfied, as we have the leisure for it.

As I have attempted to show, Marcabru uses the word *abatz* here as a metaphor for the penis, with satirical intentions.[19] If Giraut is imitating him in *Razon e luec*, lines 80–2 take on a completely different, ironic meaning, for *abat* in line 82 would then be an exceedingly mischievous pun and the image of lusty monks would considerably reinforce the images of Giraut's burning lust.

There is a steady progression in *Razon e luec* from pure, restrained *fin'amor* to an admission on Giraut's part that he is consumed by physical desire. His allusions to this progress from the erotic to the comic and bawdy: his sexual metaphors indicate a marked lack of respect for his lady. Giraut in no way refers to sex in order to moralize and his intentions are thus entirely different from Marcabru's.

GIRAUT'S IRONY AND THE INTERTEXT

It has been implicit in my discussion of Giraut's poetry so far that he considered his work to be part of a tradition. His prominent position in Peire d'Alvernha's satire, his reputation as the *maestre dels trobadors* and his constant concern with style all point to the fact that Giraut knew and was in frequent touch with other troubadours.[20] Given the sense of humour he displays in his love poetry, it would be surprising not to find ironic intertextual play in his work.

In *Ajtal cansoneta*, for example, Giraut may be parodying Jaufre Rudel:

> Trop m'es m'amigua lonhdana,
> Ves que·l deziriers m'es pres,
> E no sai quossi·m crezes,
> Que nostr'amors s'avengues.
> Peccatz la·m fetz encobir
> Qu'er m'en a morir,
> Qu'oras que·m lays. (xxxII, 8–14)

The lady-friend whom I desire so closely is too distant from me, and I do not know how I could believe that our love might be made real. Sin made me desire her so that now I must die whenever she leaves me.

As Sharman points out, this stanza is reminiscent of Jaufre Rudel's poetry in more ways than one.[21] Obviously Giraut imitates the theme of Jaufre's *amors de terra lonhdana* (III, 8), but compare also line 12 with Jaufre's III, 24–5:

> e cre que volers m'enguana
> si cobezeza la·m tol,

and lines 13–14 with Jaufre's II, 23:

> alres no·i a mais del murir.

The contrast between Giraut's distant love and 'close' desire is heightened by the emphasis given to the words *lonhdana* and *pres* as rhyme words. Giraut

Giraut de Borneil

thus undermines any pleasant connotations that distant love might have. He takes the pain of separation to ridiculous extremes, stating quite clearly that he dies every time he leaves his beloved; he says that his love will never be requited. The appeal of Jaufre Rudel's poetry is derived from the way he conveys the excitement of moving towards a distant love. Here Giraut implies that Jaufre's *amor de lonh* can only lead to frustration. He thus reverses Jaufre's theme and the result is an ironic parody.

Jaufre Rudel must have been dead by the time Giraut composed *Ajtal cansoneta*. Elsewhere, however, Giraut criticizes and pokes fun at his contemporaries. The following stanza, for example, may be directed at Peire d'Alvernha:

> S'es chantars ben entendutz
> E s'ofris pretz e valor,
> Per qu'es lag de trobador,
> Des que sos chans er saubutz,
> Qu'el eix en sia lauzaire?
> Que ben pareys al retraire
> Si·l n'eschai blasmes o laus. (LXV, 1–7)

If singing is properly understood and promises fine reputation and worth, why is it wrong for a troubadour to praise his own song as soon as it is known? Because it will be apparent in the performance whether it should be praised or blamed.

It is strikingly reminiscent of Bernart Marti's attack on Peire in *D'entier vers*:

> So dis, qu'om si conogues,
> e qui aisso gardaria
> ia no·s sobrelauzaria,
> que sobrelaus follesc es
> e pareys be si pros es
> ia el mezeis non o dia. (V, 61–6)

He [God] says this, that one should know oneself, and he who observes this would not praise himself too much, for praising oneself too much is folly, and if someone is worthy, this is apparent without one saying so oneself.

There may be grounds, then, for seeing the first stanza of *S'es chantars* as a retort to Peire d'Alvernha's *Sobre·l vieill trobar* and as closely linked to Bernart's *D'entier vers*. If so, it is ironic, because any criticism of Peire is implicit: what appears to be a statement of a general moralizing nature in fact has a very specific target.[22]

In other poems Giraut may well be taking issue with Bertran de Born's bellicose ideas, for example:

> Qe ren el mon non vei
> Qe joi ni solatz vailla;
> Qe guerra ni batailla
> Ni nauza ni tenzos
> Non es mas trics als pros. [XL, 12–16]

159

For I see nothing in the world worth as much as joy and pleasant company; for war and battle, turmoil and strife are no more than deception to men of worth.

Bertran's ideas on war are well known:

> Patz no·m fai conort,
> Ab gerra m'acort
> Q'ieu non teing ni crei
> Negun'autra lei. (XVIII, 21–4)

I find no comfort in peace; I am at my best in war, for I neither follow nor believe any other law.

If Giraut is referring to Bertran in *Qui chantar sol*, he is being ironic, for his words appear to have a general application, when, in fact, they are directed specifically against Bertran. The likelihood of this being the case is increased by lines later in the poem where Giraut again appears to be reacting specifically to Bertran:

> Son ges trop dereiatz
> En dir so qe non dei?
> Ben pot esser, mais vei,
> Si mos branz nonca tailla
> Ni non latz ma ventailla,
> Q'a mas bonas chanzos
> Si taing ben guizardos. (42–8)

Have I stepped too far out of line by saying what I should not? This may well be, but I do see, even if my sword never cleaves and although I never lace my visor, that my fine song deserves a reward.

As Sharman points out, these lines are probably a direct response to lines from a poem by Bertran:[23]

> A Peiraguors, pres del muraill,
> Tan qu·i puesc'om gitar ab maill,
> Venrai armatz sobre Baiart,
> E se·i trop Peitavin pifart
> Veiran de mon bran com tailla,
> Que sus pel cap li farai bart
> Del servel mesclat ab mailla. (XVI, 43–9)

To Périgueux, close enough to the walls for men to throw mallets at them, will I come armed, riding Baiart, and if I find any guzzling Poitevins, they will see how my sword cleaves, for upon his head I will make a mixture of brain and chain mail.

It is easy to see why Giraut did not take kindly to Bertran, for the two men were worlds apart, one admitting his love of letters and learning, the other thirsting for the cry of battle, one a professional troubadour and the other a nobleman.

The troubadour with whom Giraut de Borneil clearly had the closest links was Raimbaut d'Aurenga. He names him specifically nine times in four poems, using the *senhal* Linhaure, and he composed a moving lament on his death.[24] Raimbaut's sense of humour was anarchic and ironic, and so it is hardly surprising that whenever Giraut alludes to him, with the obvious exception of the *planh*, there are comic overtones.

In *Ar auziretz*, for example, Giraut probably mocks Raimbaut's propensity for exaggerating:

> E cuiatz setz
> M'enuei, ni deiunars,
> Ni·m tenga dan? Non fai! Que·l douz pensars
> M'aduri'ab una micha
> San e let al cap de l'an! –
> Fools, c'as dig? Pauc t'en creiran
> De so c'anc vers non parec! –
> Si fara ben, se l'enquers,
> Mos Lignaures, lai part Lers!   (vii, 64–72)

And do you think that thirst or fasting can disturb me or harm me? No, it cannot! For sweet thoughts of her could keep me healthy and happy until the end of the year on just a crumb! – You fool, what have you said? They will hardly believe you when you say something that can never appear true. – My Lignaure will, if I ask him to, over there beyond Lers.

However, Giraut is laughing with Raimbaut here, rather than at him, for he himself is showing off and boasting. In *Ges de sobrevoler*, Giraut may again be referring to Raimbaut's tendency to exaggerate and joke:

> E pero veiatz en l'escuoill
> Linnaura vers de trobador,
> E no·m n'aiatz per gabador
> Si tant rics motz mi passa·l cais!
>   C'aitant m'atrais
> Mos Socha de son bel saber,
>   Per qu'ieu esper
> Que s'ab mo ver dire bobanz,
> C'a defendre·m n'aiut rasos.   (xxv, 55–63)

But behold a verse in the manner of Linnaura, and do not consider me boastful if such a rich word passes my lips! For my Vine-Leaf has so attracted me with her fine words that I hope that if I boast when I speak the truth, my theme will defend me.

Paterson thinks that *rics motz* may refer to Raimbaut's manner of composing, and Sharman comments:[25]

Giraut seems to be referring to a recognized type or school of poetry, of which Raimbaut was the principal representative . . . *rics motz* (58) is then a pun, both implying that Giraut is boasting and, at the same time, defining the 'style of Linnaura'.

The pun implies, of course, not only that Giraut is boasting, but also that Raimbaut is given to boasting: the link between being a *gabador* and using *rics motz* is quite explicit and would seem to imply that *rics* could have the same meaning as its modern English equivalent, 'exaggerated'. *Rics motz* is ironic, then, designating both Raimbaut's 'noble' or 'splendid' style, and his outrageous boasting.

It is well known that Raimbaut and Giraut composed *Era·m platz* (LIX) together. Less attention is usually paid to another song the two poets may have composed together, *Ailas!* (V):

I   Ailas, co muer! – Qe as, amis? –
     Eu son trais! –
     Per cal razon? –
     Car anc iorn mis m'entention
     En leis qe·m fes lo bel parven. –   5
     Et as per so ton cor dolen? –
     Si ai. –
     As aissi doncs ton cor en lai? –
     Oi eu, plus fort. –
     Iest doncs aissi pres de la mort? –   10
     Oi eu, plus qe no vos sai dir. –
     Per qe·t laissas aissi morir? –

II   Car soi truep vergoignos e fis. –
     Non l'as re quis? –
     Ieu? Per Dieu, non! –   15
     E per qe menas tal tenson,
     Tro aias sauput son talen? –
     Segnier, fai mi tal espaven. –
     Qe·l fai? –
     S'amors qe me ten en esmai. –   20
     Be n'as gran tort.
     Cujas te q'ela t'o aport? –
     Ieu, no, mas no m'aus enardir. –
     Trop poiras tu ton dan suffrir. –

III Segnier, e cals cosseils n'er pres? –   25
     Bos e cortes. –
     Er lo·m digatz! –
     Tu venras denant lei viatz
     Et enqerras la de s'amor. –
     E si s'o ten a desonor? –   30
     No·t cal! –
     E s'ela·m respon lag ni mal? –
     Sias suffrenz;
     Qe totztemps bos suffrire venz. –
     E si·s n'apercep lo gelos? –   35
     Adoncs n'obraretz plus gingnos. –

IV Nos? – Hoc ben! – Sol q'il o volgues! –
     Er. – Qe? – Si·m cres. –
     Crezutz siatz! –
     Ben ti sera tos iois doblatz,   40
     Sol lo digtz no·t fassa paor. –
     Segnier, tan senti la dolor

Mortal,
Per q'es ops c'o partam egal. –
Ar doncs tos senz   45
Te vailla, e tos ardimenz! –
Oc, e ma bona sospeissos. –
Garda ti qe gent t'i razos. –

v   Raisonar no·m sabrai ia ben. –
     Digas, per qe? –   50
     Per leis gardar. –
     Non sabras doncs ab leis parlar?
     Iest aissi del tot esperdutz? –
     Oc, cant li son denant vengutz . . . –
     T'espertz? –   55
     Oi eu, qe non son de ren certz. –
     Aital fan tug
     Sil qe son per amor perdug. –
     Oc, mas ieu forzarai mon cor. –
     Ara, non o tornz en demor! –   60

vi   Ben m'a adug
     Amors a so qe sabon tug:
     Qe mal viu qi deziran mor,
     Per q'ieu non sai plaigner mon cor. –

vii Vas ton desdug   65
     Vai, amics, anz c'o sapchon tug,
     Per qe non perdas ton tesor;
     Qe levet pert hom son demor!

I

Alas, I am dying! – What is wrong, my friend? – I am betrayed! – For what reason? –
Because I once placed my hope in a lady who gave me a fair look. – And because of this
your heart grieves? – Yes, it does. – Is your heart then over there [with her]? – Yes, it is,
more than ever. – Are you then close to death because of this? – Yes, I am, more than I
can say. – Why do you let yourself die in this way?

II

Because I am too ashamed and true. – Have you asked her for anything? – I? By God,
no! – Then why do you make such a racket [or 'compose this *tenso* with me'] before
you know what she desires? – My lord, it frightens me so. – What does? – Her love,
which troubles me constantly. – You are greatly mistaken in this. Do you think that
she will make the first move? – No, I don't, but I dare not make so bold. – You could be
too long-suffering. –

III

My lord, and what way can be found? – A good and courtly way. – Tell me now! – You
will come before her at once and ask her for her love. – And if she considers this
dishonourable? – Don't let that worry you! – And if she replies harshly or cruelly? –
Suffer patiently; for true patience always triumphs. – And if the jealous one notices
this? – Then you will have to work with more cunning. –

IV

We? – Yes, indeed! – As long as she wants it so! – Now . . . – What? – If you trust me. –
You will be trusted! – Your joy will indeed be doubled, as long as speaking does not

frighten you. – My lord, I can feel the mortal pain to such an extent that we must share it equally. – So, now may your wisdom and your boldness help you! – Yes, and my good hope. – Make sure you speak to her sweetly. –

V

I will not know how to speak well at all. – Tell me, why not? – Because of looking at her. – Will you not then know how to speak with her? Are you thus completely without hope? – Yes, when I am confronted with her . . . – Do you despair? – Yes, I do, for I am certain of nothing. – All those who are lost because of love behave in this way. – Yes, but I will exert force on my heart. – Don't delay now. –

VI

Love has taught me what all men know: that a man who dies of desire lives badly, wherefore I cannot pity my heart. –

VII

Go to your pleasure, my friend, before they all know about it, so that you don't lose your treasure; for one easily loses one's pleasure.

Kolsen, Panvini, Nicholson and Sharman all argue that this is a real *tenso* with a friend and they identify this friend as Raimbaut d'Aurenga.[26] It is noteworthy that Giraut addresses his interlocutor here as *Segnier* (lines 18, 25, 42), as he does Raimbaut d'Aurenga in *Era·m platz*, and that whereas this *Segnier* addresses Giraut with the familiar second person form (lines 1, 6, 8, and so on), Giraut uses the polite form, *vos* (lines 11, 27). The two protagonists clearly come from different social classes, just as Giraut and Raimbaut did in real life. Further evidence for identifying the *Segnier* of *Ailas* with Raimbaut comes in manuscript V. *Ailas* is not, in this manuscript, grouped with Giraut's songs, but with Raimbaut's. Although it is not attributed to Raimbaut, it follows six poems which are correctly attributed to him.[27]

The mocking, tongue-in-cheek tone adopted by the *Segnier* in *Ailas* certainly supports the hypothesis that he is none other than Raimbaut d'Aurenga. The persona Giraut adopts is that of the meek and humble courtly lover, bemoaning his fate and desperately seeking advice as to how to consummate his love. In the first stanza he complains, using a conventional courtly *topos*, that he is dying of love. His interlocutor at first politely enquires what is wrong, but when he learns why Giraut is 'dying', he is incredulous (line 6), as if he cannot understand why Giraut is making so much fuss, and finally dismissive and mocking (line 10).

In the second stanza, Giraut's interlocutor makes him look stupid. How can he lament so when he does not even know what the lady feels about him? The discussion has developed into one between naïve, if not comic, emotion and plain common sense. The mocking tone in Giraut's interlocutor's voice is emphasized by the pun on *tenson* in line 16. The word can designate both the type of poem which they are in the act of composing and 'a racket' (*LR, V*, 345), so that the line could either mean 'why do you compose this *tenso* with me?' or 'why do you make such a racket?' In either case lines 16–17 are ironic, implying either that Giraut has no grounds for feeling unhappy, or that he should not be composing this poem, thus undermining his plaintive tone in the first stanza.

At the beginning of stanza III the rhythm and pace of the exchange quicken as Giraut begs his interlocutor for advice, but the breathless expectancy of Giraut's 'Er lo·m digatz!' (line 27) is completely deflated by his interlocutor's reply, which states the obvious so flatly that it can only be tongue-in-cheek. Giraut's persona is now becoming slightly ridiculous, for he takes his interlocutor's advice perfectly seriously (line 30). His interlocutor emphasizes this ridicule with his next piece of advice, 'Sias suffrenz', as this is probably an intentional pun. Giraut will wait patiently, he will also suffer, he may even be deceived.[28]

The comic tone continues in stanza IV. As Sharman points out, there is probably a pun intended on *o volgues/o faire*, 'to want it/to do it',[29] and in lines 45–6 Giraut's interlocutor is clearly being ironic. Giraut has shown little *senz* and even less *ardimenz*! In stanza V, Giraut's interlocutor manages to convey, through irony, just what a pathetic creature he thinks Giraut is. 'Iest aissi del tot esperdutz?', could mean either 'Are you so totally in love?' or 'Are you so totally beyond hope?' Literally, of course, the context requires the first meaning. The ironic meaning is not, however, difficult to discern.

Giraut binds up the end of the poem with the beginning by returning, in the first *tornada*, to the commonplace of dying of love. However, he may well be undermining his own persona now, for the bringing together of the opposites *viu/mor* (line 63) may well indicate irony and thus undermine the opening of the poem as well as making the *tornada* comic. Giraut's interlocutor may also end on a comic note as he advises his friend to go to his pleasure quickly 'before they all know about it'. He may be implying that everyone will know of Giraut's love because, contrary to courtly convention, he makes such a noise about it, or because he himself intends to tell them.

To realize the full force of the comedy in *Ailas*, a performance has to be imagined. Giraut and, if he is the interlocutor, Raimbaut, are playing rôles. The rôles reflect, more or less, their own personalities and station in life, but the whole piece is nevertheless theatrical and Giraut's persona must therefore be seen as a caricature of the fawning and obsequious courtly lover at his most ridiculous. All his words are ironic because, whatever their literal meaning may be, they are also intended to mock the very voice that speaks them. Moreover, the parody may be specific as well as general. As Sharman points out, *Ailas* is particularly reminiscent of Peire Rogier's *Ges non puesc* (VI):[30]

> VI   Ailas! – Que plangz? – Ia tem murir. –
> Que as? – Am. – E trop? – Ieu hoc, tan
> que·n muer. – Mors? – Oc. – Non potz guerir? –
> Ieu no. – E cum? – Tan suy iratz. –
> De que? – De lieys, don suy aissos. –   45
> Sofre. – No·m val. – Clama·l merces. –
> Si·m fatz. – No·y as pro? – Pauc. – No·t pes,
> si·n tras mal. – No? – Qu'o fas de liey.

VII Cosselh n'ai. – Qual? – Vuelh m'en partir. –
No far! – Si faray. – Quers ton dan. –   50
Que·n puesc als? – Non vols t'en ben jauzir? –
Oc, mout. – Crei mi. – Era diguatz. –
Sias humils, francs, larcx e pros. –
Si·m fai mal? – Sufr'en patz. – Suy pres? –
Tu oc, s'amars vols; mas si·m cres,   55
aissi·t poiras jauzir de liey.

VI

Alas! – Of what do you complain? – I'm afraid of dying. – What's wrong? – I'm in love.
– Are you too much in love? – Yes, so much so that I am dying of it. – Are you dying? –
Yes. – Can you not be cured? – No. – Why? – I am so saddened. – What by? – By the
lady who makes me anxious. – Be patient. – I gain nothing from this. – Beg her for
mercy. – I do so. – Does this not help? – Hardly. – Do not grieve if it is painful for you.
– No? – Do this for her.

VII

I have a way. – What way? – I want to leave. – Don't! – Yes, I will. – You want to suffer
then. – What else can I do? – Do you really want to have joy in this matter? – Yes, I
really do. – Trust me. – Tell me now. – Be humble, honest, generous and worthy. –
And if I suffer? – Suffer in peace. – Am I a prisoner? – Yes, you are, if you want love;
but trust me and thus you will have joy with her.

Parallels between lines 41–3, 49–52 and 54 of Peire's poem and lines 1–3, 25–7
and 33–4 of Giraut and his friend's are particularly striking. Kolsen and
Nicholson both see these poems as closely connected: they clearly think that
both poems are serious and also suggest that Peire and Raimbaut may have
composed these two stanzas of *Ges non puesc* together.[31] Sharman, on the
other hand, assumes both poems are 'almost certainly humorous in intention,
parodying the situation of the courtly lover, too afraid to tell his lady of his
love'.[32] I cannot, however, agree with her that Peire's two stanzas are almost
certainly humorous. Peire uses the dialogue form elsewhere (poems IV and
VII); as his dialogues are inserted into first-person poems, they would appear
to be internal dialogues, whereas the different social ranks of the voices in
Ailas make internal dialogue unlikely. Moreover, nowhere in Peire's poetry
does one of the voices undermine the seriousness of the other. A more
plausible hypothesis is that Giraut and his friend, probably Raimbaut d'Aurenga, are specifically parodying Peire Rogier, a troubadour both must have
known personally, and who was probably solely responsible for the two
stanzas of *Ges non puesc* which are in dialogue form.

Ironic intertextual play in Giraut's poems indicates that he was as much a
part of the *Dialektik des Trobar* as Marcabru, Bernart Marti, Raimbaut
d'Aurenga, Bernart de Ventadorn and Peire d'Alvernha. I have not so far
discussed, however, the most important indicator of the fact that Giraut had
frequent contact with other troubadours and very much felt himself to be a
poet belonging to a tradition: Giraut's comments on style.

166

Giraut de Borneil

Giraut de Borneil's poetry has been the focal point of all discussions of style in the troubadour lyric. This is because there are numerous instances where he uses words pertaining to style such as *clus, cobertz, entrebescar, leu, levet,* and *escur,* and because he composed the *tenso Era·m platz* with Raimbaut d'Aurenga, which is ostensibly about whether an 'easy' style is preferable to the *trobar clus.*

Kolsen, Jeanroy and Panvini all believed that Giraut gave up the *clus* style in order to compose in the *trobar leu,* and there is perhaps an implicit value judgement in their work that the *trobar leu* is the worthier of the two styles.[33] Mölk also argues that Giraut moved away from the *trobar clus* towards the 'easy' style, basing his arguments on what appear to be shifts in Giraut's ideas:[34] here Giraut praises the *clus* style (XXIV, XXX), there he appears to defend the *leu* style against the *trobar clus* (VIII, XXXIII, XXXVII, XLVIII, LIX, LXV). In fact there are no grounds for supposing a progression from the *trobar clus* to the *trobar leu* in Giraut's work.[35] Moreover, one might well ask, with Paterson, 'if Giraut changed from one style to another, why is it so difficult to tell them apart in his poems?'[36] Giraut probably composed in the *trobar leu* and the *trobar clus* concurrently throughout his career, if indeed he thought in terms of such rigid distinctions at all.

Various theories have been formulated as to what the *trobar clus* and *trobar leu* actually were. However, it is likely that the terms meant one thing to one troubadour and something else to another.[37] Köhler developed ideas first put forward by Salverda de Grave, according to which Giraut's choice of style depended on his mood, but as any statement concerning a poet's state of mind may be a *topos,* such an argument is tenuous.[38] Paterson suggests that Giraut's concepts of the *trobar clus* and *trobar leu* were influenced by the medieval arts of poetry and that his ideas on style are particularly close to those of Geoffrey of Vinsauf, who was writing slightly after Giraut's lifetime. She concludes:[39]

he sees the *trobar leu* as easy to sing and understand, light and entertaining, apparently carefree, smooth and polished, with obscurity planed away; and while he describes it in deliberately pejorative terms to forestall criticism, he still regards it as a high level of style. To justify his change from *clus* to *leu* he draws on rhetorical arguments: the level should be suited to the audience, and gravity of thought and craft should be combined with clarity, apparent ease, and lightness of touch.

Giraut's importance in any discussion of style in troubadour poetry is indisputable. However, his comments on style, and particularly on the *trobar leu,* may not always be as straightforward as they first appear. Sharman has argued that Giraut was often ironical about the 'easy' style.[40] If this is the case, it need not necessarily affect the way we view Giraut's ideas about the composition of different types of poetry; but it does modify the way Giraut's attitude to his audiences and to the reception of his poetry should be viewed.

The most obvious place to start any study of Giraut's attitude to style is with his *tenso* with Raimbaut d'Aurenga, *Era·m platz* (LIX), and numerous scholars have pored over this poem looking for definitions of the two styles in question.[41] I shall forego a detailed commentary on this text, as it has recently been the object of admirable analyses by Ruth Sharman and Sarah Kay. Both suggest that neither poet is serious in his defence of the style he purports to advocate. Kay further argues that in *Era·m platz* each poet adopts the style he apparently rejects and she discerns a web of intertextual allusions to each poet's own work in his stanzas of the poem.[42] Elements of parody, comedy and contradiction of this kind concord perfectly with Raimbaut's tongue-in-cheek attitude whenever he talks about style. What of Giraut? If he is ironic in his defence of the *trobar leu* here, what is his purpose? Is his intention to imply that the *trobar leu* is inferior to the *trobar clus*?

Giraut does not actually define the *trobar leu* in *Era·m platz*. His main concern is with getting the broadest possible public acclaim, which Raimbaut apparently despises. This in itself is explained easily enough. Raimbaut, as a great lord, can afford to please himself and compose any way he chooses, disregarding the popularity of the end result. In order to make a living, Giraut, as a professional troubadour, depends on his public liking his poetry. Whereas Raimbaut seeks the approval of a discriminating few (lines 18–21), Giraut wants everyone to like his poetry (lines 25–8), including the *fatz* (line 18) Raimbaut so clearly despises: he makes this quite clear, for his poetry must be known by 'one and all' ('tal e cal', line 27). However, the terms Giraut uses to describe his poetry are pejorative. *Venansal* means 'low', 'menial', and *levet* means 'easy', but with patronizing overtones, perhaps giving the sense 'facile':[43]

> 'Senher Linhaure, no·m coreill
> Si quex se trob'a son talan;
> Mas me eis vueill iutgar d'aitan
> Qu'es mais amatz
> Chans e prezatz,
> Qui·l fai levet e venansal;
> E vos no m'o tornetz a mal.'   (8–14)

My lord Linhaure, I do not complain if everyone composes as he thinks fit; but I myself like to think that a song is better loved and valued when it is made easy and ordinary, and do not take me wrong in this.

Paterson argues that Giraut is deliberately adopting here 'an apologetic, pejorative tone to forestall criticism',[44] but the irony that pervades his whole defence of the *trobar leu* suggests that the poem may be more complex. If Giraut's defence of the *trobar leu* is intended to be burlesque, he must, on one level at least, have intended the adjectives *levet* and *venansal* to be taken at face value. Moreover, the apparently paradoxical proposition that what is *levet* and *venansal* should be *mais prezatz* points to heavy irony in this stanza. Giraut is surely criticizing those who are stupid enough to value what is *venansal*.

Giraut de Borneil

I propose the following hypothesis. Giraut composed concurrently in both the *clus* and *leu* styles, depending on the audience or the patron he was trying to please. He often gave in to public demand for easier poetry, but he retained his belief that the allusive style was the more worthwhile. He despised people who sought facile pleasure in easy poetry, but, because he was obliged, as a professional troubadour, to give them what they wanted, he was only able to criticize them ironically, in such a way that they could remain under the impression that he was giving in to their demands wholeheartedly. If this hypothesis is to be substantiated, it is necessary to look in detail at all the instances where Giraut apparently defends the *leu* style against the *trobar clus*. Does he really abandon the *trobar clus* for the *trobar leu*, or does he mock an audience he feels is unwilling to make an effort to understand the complexities of what he is trying to convey?

There is evidence, apart from in *Era·m platz*, that Giraut despised audiences who preferred *leu* poetry. In *Era si·m fos*, for example, he is ostensibly proud of his 'delicate' little song:

> Era si·m fos en grat tengut
> Preir'eu sens glut
> Un chantaret prim e menut;
> Qu'el mon non ha
> Doctor qi tan prim ni plus pla
> Lo prezes,
> Ni miels l'afines. (XXIX, 1–7)

Now, if I were appreciated, I would capture, without any lime, a delicately and finely worked little song; for there is no learned man in the world who could capture it more delicately or smoothly, nor perfect it so well.

The adjective *plan* can mean 'plain', 'uni', 'simple', 'clair', 'pur' and 'imbécile' (*PD*) and may consequently have pejorative overtones. The adverb *pla* ('smoothly') probably implies 'clearly', 'plainly' here, and this would seem to suggest that Giraut is alluding to the 'easy' style.[45] This is perhaps made clearer in the second part of the stanza, but in such a way that Giraut's pride may be undermined:

> E qi·m creses
> Q'aissi chantes,
> Polira,
> Forbira,
> Mon chan
> Ses afan
> Gran;
> Mais a lor veiaire,
> Qar no·n sabon gaire,
> Fail, car non l'esclaire
> D'aitan
> Qe l'entendesson neus l'enfan. (8–19)

169

And if anyone believed me that I sang in this way, I would polish and adorn my song without great trouble; but in their opinion, because they know nothing, I am at fault, because I do not make it clear enough for even a child to understand.

Giraut has said that no one could make a song more delicate or easy (lines 4–6), and yet people still complain that his songs are not clear enough. They want him to compose in a style that is so 'clear' that *even* a child would understand. Giraut is clearly mocking this audience and their demand for simpler and simpler poetry: 'they know nothing' (line 16), they have no more intelligence than children, generally thought to be stupid by the troubadours.[46] The ironic force of the use of the conditional in lines 2 and 10 is perhaps clearer when this has been recognized: even with all the effort he puts into making his song *prim*, *menut*, and *pla*, Giraut implies, he is still not appreciated because of his audience's desire for totally undemanding poetry.

In *Leu chansonet'e vil*, Giraut appears to be giving in with good grace to the demand for easy poetry:

> Leu chansonet'e vil
> M'auria obs a far
> Qe pogues enviar
> En Alvergn'al Dalfi,
> Pero, s'el dreit cami
> Pogues n'Eblon trobar,
> Be·l poiria mandar
> Q'eu dic q'en l'escurzir
> Non es l'afanz
> Mas en l'obr'esclarzir.   (XLVIII, 1–10)

I ought to compose a light and sprightly [or commonplace] little song which I could send to the Dauphin in the Auvergne, but if on the way it could find Sir Eble, I could indeed send word to him that the difficulty lies not in darkening the work, but in making it clear.

Paterson argues that in this poem 'Giraut uses the decidedly pejorative epithet *vil* to shock his listeners into thinking about his new style'. Sharman, on the other hand, thinks 'Giraut may be using the word *Leu* in an ironical sense . . . [he] is probably punning on the two meanings of *vil*, "quick" and also "low, menial"'.[47] Giraut's use of the word *vil* here is reminiscent of his use of the words *levet* and *venansal* in *Era·m platz*. Moreover, *leu* too can have pejorative overtones, giving the sense 'too easy', 'fickle', or even 'frivolous'.[48] The ambiguity of both these epithets, *leu* and *vil*, would seem to imply that Giraut is being ironical here, pretending to give one section of his audience what it wants, whilst at the same time mocking this for another, initiated and more discriminating section. Lines 8–10 indicate that Giraut does indeed think that the *trobar leu* is a high level of style, but on the other hand the word *afan* implies that although it is difficult to 'clarify' a poem, it is not at all an enjoyable process. The following stanza confirms that Giraut is being ironical about the easy style here:

Giraut de Borneil

E qi de fort fozil
Non vol coutel tocar,
Ja no·il cuid affilar
En un mol sembeli;
Qar ies aiga de vi
Non fei Dieus al manjar,
Anz s'en volc eisauzar
E fei esdevenir
    D'aiga q'er'anz
Pois vin per meils grazir.   (11–20)

And whoever does not wish to place his knife on a hard whetstone should not imagine that he can sharpen it on a soft sable; for God did not make water from wine for our nourishment, rather he wanted to exalt himself and he then made the water that existed before become wine, in order to give greater pleasure.

Paradoxically Giraut introduces these images, which are far from clear, into a song which he has said ought to be easy. What do they mean?

Given that the opening stanza is about 'clear' and 'dark' poetry, Giraut is probably continuing this theme. The *fort fozil* might then represent 'dark' poetry, because of its connotations of hardness, and the *mol sembeli* 'clear' poetry because of its connotations of smoothness and almost sensual pleasure. The image of the soft sable is probably also intended to pick up the image of frivolity, present in the very first line of the poem through the word *Leu*. Moreover, *coutel* as an image of the tools required for the composition of poetry is not without precedent in the troubadour lyric:[49]

> Qu'ieu tenc l'us e·l pan e·l coutel
> de que·m platz apanar las gens
> que d'est mestier s'an levat *un* pairon.
> (Peire d'Alvernha, XI, 7–9)

If this interpretation of Giraut's imagery in lines 11–14 is accepted, he is implying that the *clus* style is more worthy than the *leu* style because a poet can only 'sharpen his knife', in other words prove his craft, in the former. The use of the verb *cuidar* in line 13 is probably a signal to irony, for through it Giraut manages to insinuate that the poet who attempts to show his skill in the easy style does not really succeed in doing so, but only imagines he does.

The image of water and wine in lines 15–20 probably also continues the theme of 'clear' and 'dark' poetry. Water is clear; it is a necessity, like eating, but mundane. Wine, on the other hand, is dark, but gives real pleasure. In other words, Giraut is again intimating that the *clus* style is more satisfying than the easy style. If Giraut is attacking the *trobar leu* in lines 11–20, the images of easy pleasure and banality pick up the irony of *Leu* and *vil* in the opening lines. There is also an ironic opposition between his stated intention, to compose an easy song, and what he actually does, for the second stanza is allusive and definitely in the 'dark' style. It is even possible, given this ironic

171

context, that the diminutive form *chansoneta* also has pejorative overtones, giving the sense 'a trivial little song'.[50]

There are other instances where Giraut appears to mock the *trobar leu* through an opposition between his statement of intent and the style he actually adopts. This seems to be the case in *Tot suavet*:

> Tot suavet e de pas,
>   Rjen iugan,
> Vau un chantaret planan
>   De ditz escurs,
> C'us non i remajna.
> C'aixi leu, si s'era plas,
> Poiri'entre·ls Catalas
>   Passar en Proenza;
> Que chanzos leu entenduda
> Lai val e lai s'esvertuda. (XXXI, 1–10)

Slowly, agreeably, laughing and joking, I go along, planing away the dark words from a little song so that not one remains in it, for thus, if it is smooth, it could quickly pass among the Catalans through to Provence; for there a song that is easily understood is considered worthy and makes its mark.

The adjective *suavet* and the present participles *Rjen iugan* set up an expectation of a pleasant, light-hearted, cheerful and limpid song. The clipped sounds, short words, diminutives and short lines all suggest 'fineness and delicacy'.[51] It is therefore paradoxical that this song develops elements which are decidedly burlesque, as Giraut attempts to restrain his *joglar*, and it is somewhat surprising that Giraut insults his lady in no uncertain terms.[52] The way in which the song develops would seem to suggest that the opening lines are ironic. Whilst *Rjen* and *iugan* might indeed describe the mood of the song, the comedy produced by Giraut trying to prevent his *joglar* from running off with a song full of insults is not exactly the type of laughing and joking he has led his audience to expect. Similarly, although *suavet* describes the form and sound of the song, it certainly does not describe the content. There may even be two further strands of irony in this opening stanza. First, it is possible that *escurs* sometimes meant 'angry'.[53] If *ditz escurs* (line 4) here is understood to mean 'angry words', then the proposition in lines 3–4 is ironic, for the song is full of angry words. Secondly, Giraut sends his song to Provence, where an 'easy' song is appreciated (lines 6–10). This is usually taken to be an allusion to the fact that Alfonso II of Aragon, also Count of Provence from 1166, preferred the *leu* style to the *trobar clus*.[54] However, as this poem was probably composed in the lifetime of Raimbaut d'Aurenga,[55] and as Raimbaut also lived in Provence, Giraut could just as easily be alluding ironically to the well-known fact that Raimbaut did not like *chanzos leu entenduda*. In *Tot suavet* Giraut is making a mockery of the expectations of an audience that prefers *leu* poetry, and he may even be making an ironic reference to the literary preferences of his friend and patron, Raimbaut d'Aurenga. He is certainly not making an unqualified statement in support of the *trobar leu* as some have thought.[56]

There also seems to be an ironic opposition between Giraut's stated intentions concerning style and what he actually does in *De bels digz*. Here he claims that he will compose a song which is easy to understand:

> Trop volgra mais donar
> Mos gais sonetz ioyos
> Ab bels ditz et entiers
> Entendables e plas
> Que trop escurs ni sobrestorias. (LXVI, 9–13)

I would very much like to give people my gay, joyful little tunes, with fine, whole words, easy to understand and smooth, rather than with words that are too dark or over-elaborate.

As Sharman points out, 'ironically "De bels digz" typifies the very style Giraut says he is abandoning'.[57] Giraut uses in this song metaphors which are allusive, if not obscure:

> Qu'ades m'es pretz mos chans,
> Laissa·m! No·m plaj mazans
> Senes razonadors!
> Tant es lo mescaps sors,
> No faj a razonar.
> Be·m puesc meravilhar
> Que sols nada·l peissos!
> En totz bos autz mestiers
> M'aib aissel rovilhas
> A ben triar los brezilhatz dels sas. (43–52)

For now my song is of value to me, it leaves me! I do not like applause without rational people! This evil has risen to such an extent that it is beyond reason. I can indeed marvel that the fish swims alone. In all fine and exalted activities, this blight helps me to tell the whole from the broken without mistakes.

He points out, at the end of the poem, that he considers his song to be essentially a moralizing song:

> No·m fauc de mans lor ays
> A be-mas taynar,
> Quan ieu vuelh sermonar.
> C'auia, quar sermonans
> Mi bat, selh non-fezans:
> Qu'ieu no vuelh refeitors
> Ni reglas de colors;
> Quar ja per sopleyar
> S'ab fin cor ferm e clar,
> Ni per trops capairos
> No sera·l frair entiers
> Nj verais ni certas,
> Si·l dreit no siec e no·l guida la mas. (79–91)

I am not willing to put off their pain until early tomorrow morning, when I want to preach. Since I fight with moralizing words, let the faithless one hear this: I do not want to see deceitful monasteries or orders; for never through kneeling, unless it is with a firm and pure heart, nor through wearing many habits, will a brother be whole or true or sure, if he does not follow the right path and is not guided by the rule.

If there is no direct correlation between moralizing and the *clus* style, it is true that poets who compose in the *trobar clus* also often have moral preoccupations.[58] Here Giraut clearly intends to moralize, and this undermines his stated intention to compose 'easy' *gais sonetz ioyos*. Note, in the two stanzas I have quoted, the verbal echo between words like *razonadors* and *razonar* (lines 45 and 47), and *sermonar* and *sermonans* (lines 81 and 82), suggesting the *clus* technique of word-weaving (*entrebescar*), and note also the elliptical syntax. There seems to be little doubt that Giraut's initial claim to be composing a song which is 'Entendables e plas' is ironic. Moreover, this song dates from the later part of Giraut's career.[59] It is thus proof that Giraut never gave up the *clus* style in order to compose exclusively in the *trobar leu*.

Giraut also shows his distaste for the *trobar leu* through parody. Sharman comments:[60]

in *Ajtal cansoneta* (xxxii) he says ironically that he cannot compose a simple little love song because he is thinking of something else: he cannot focus his attention on something that is no more than *plana*. Often what may seem to be a straightforward love song can in fact be interpreted as a parody: *A penas*, *Ajtal cansoneta*, *Ailas* (v) and perhaps also *Aquest terminis* (xv).

All these poems have been taken to be clear indications that Giraut felt totally committed to composing in the easy style.[61] If, however, they are parodies they undermine any commitment Giraut might ostensibly make.

Even when Giraut appears to say specifically that he is abandoning the allusive style for clearer poetry, there may be more to his words than meets the eye. Consider, for example, the two *tornadas* of *Non puesc sofrir*:

> E vos entendetz e veiatz,
> Qui sabetz mon lengatge,
> Qoras que fezes motz serratz,
> S'era no·ls ay ben esclairatz.
>
> E sui m'en per so esforsatz
> Qu'entendatz quals chansos eu fatz.   (xxxvii, 71–6)

And if ever I composed words which were tightly locked together, you who know my language must now hear and see whether I have made them clear enough.

And I have made an effort so that you might understand the sort of songs I compose.

On one level Giraut's song is certainly clear. However, it is not without figurative speech. The opening stanza, for example, is ironic, as has been indicated:[62]

> Non puesc sofrir c'a la dolor
> De la den la lengua non vir

Giraut de Borneil

E·l cor a la novela flor,
Lancan vei los ramels florir
E·ill chant son pel boscatge
Dels auzeletz enamoratz.   (1–6)

Further irony occurs later in the poem:[63]

E s'ieu ia ves emperador
Ni vas rey vauc, si·m vol grazir
Tot aysi com al sieu trachor
Qui no·l sap ni no·l pot gandir.   (61–4)

Giraut makes extensive use of metaphors in this poem:

Qu'ieu no m'esfors d'autre labor
Mas de chantar e d'esiauzir;
C'una nueit soniava'en pascor
Tal somge que·m fetz esbaudir,
D'un esparvier ramatge
Que m'era sus el ponh pausatz,
Et si·m semblav'adomesgatz,
Anc non vi tan salvatge,
Mas pueis fo maniers e privatz
E de bons ietz apreiszonatz.   (11–20)

And I do not exert myself, other than to sing and to be joyful; for one spring night I had a dream of the kind that gave me great joy, about an as yet untamed sparrowhawk, which had come to rest on my hand; and although it seemed to me to have been tamed, I never saw such a wild one, but then it was trained and friendly and tethered by fine thongs.

Qu'ieu ai vist acomensar tor
D'una sola peir'al bastir
E cada pauc pugar aussor
Tro c'om la podia garnir.   (51–5)

For I have seen the building of a tower begun with just one stone, and its rising until it was ready to be garrisoned.

There can be little doubt that this poem is composed of a web of figurative meanings even though the syntax is straightforward, the style is apparently limpid and the rhyme scheme and rhyme words are not uncommon. Giraut's *tornadas* may well, then, be tinged with irony, as Sharman has pointed out.[64] The interesting thing about this poem is that although there are often two levels of meaning, Giraut's use of figurative language is not obscure. The ironic comparison in lines 1–6 and the incongruity of the word *grazir* (line 62) are obvious. The metaphor of the *esparvier* is relatively common, and that of the tower not difficult to recuperate. Giraut has made an effort to 'clarify' his poetry, but only to a certain extent. He will offer his audience clear-sounding words, simple rhymes and limpid syntax, but they must still make some effort to penetrate to deeper levels of meaning, even though these are not far from the surface.

Nowhere is Giraut's support of the *leu* style totally convincing. In *Ben deu*, for example, he again uses the possibly pejorative adjective *levet* to describe it:

> Ben deu en bona cort dir
> Bon sonet qi·l fai,
> Per q'ieu retrairai
> Un levet, et qi l'apren,
> Parra d'ome non-chalen;
> C'aissi con si no·m chalia,
> Faz lieugiers sonetz,
> Per qe·l plus greus sembla sia
> Leus e bos a faire. (XLIX, 1–9)

A man who composes a good tune ought to perform it in a good court, wherefore I will sing an easy one, and whoever learns it will think it the song of an easy-going man; for, as if I did not care, I compose light tunes, so that even the most difficult seems to be easy and pleasant to compose.

The repetition of the notion of *nonchaler* (lines 5–6), implying that really Giraut is indifferent to his song, undermines all the positive adjectives Giraut uses to describe it. Moreover, most of these are ambivalent. *Levet* can be pejorative, *leus* can mean 'too easy' or 'frivolous', and *lieugier* can mean 'fickle' as well as 'light'.[65] The accumulation of pejorative words (*levet, nonchalen, no·m chalia*) and ambiguous adjectives (*lieugiers, Leus*) would seem to suggest that Giraut is once again being ironical about the 'easy' style.

Giraut's defence of the *clus* style, on the other hand, does not appear to be lacking in sincerity, as for example in *La flors el vergan* (XXVIII):

> II   Dreitz es doncs q'ieu chan
> C'ab precs que per man.
> Mas eras diran
> Que si m'esforses
> Cum levet chantes   20
> Mieils ester'assatz.
> E non es vertatz;
> Que sens e cartatz
> Adui pretz e dona,
> Si cum l'ochaisona   25
> Nonsens eslaissatz.
>   Mas ben cre
> Que ies chantars se
> Non val al comenssamen
> Tant cum puois, qand hom l'enten.   30
>
> III   E doncs a qe·m van
> Totz iorns chastian,
> Que puois plaigneran,
> Si ia ioi cobres,
> Car no·n serai pres   35

Car s'ieu ioing ni latz
Menutz motz serratz
Puois en sui lauzatz
Quan ma razos bona
Par ni s'abandona;   40
C'om ben enseignatz
    Si be·i ve,
Ni mon dreich capte,
Non vol, al mieu escien,
C'a totz chant comunalman.   45

II

It is right then that I should sing, whether by request or on command. But now they will say that if I made an effort to sing in an easy way, this would be much better, and this is not true! For meaning and richness bestow and bring reputation just as unbridled nonsense destroys it. But I indeed believe that singing is not worth as much at the beginning as it is later when one understands it.

III

And so why do they continue to criticize me all the time, since they will complain, if ever I possessed joy, that I will not be close to it. For if I join and lace together tightly locked words, I am then praised when my fine theme appears and yields itself up; for a well-educated man, if he sees correctly in this matter, and supports my case, does not want me, in my opinion, to sing to everyone at the same time.

Kolsen and Mölk both think that Giraut refers to a specific *om ben enseignatz* here and that this is Raimbaut d'Aurenga.[66] It is, however, more likely that, by calling them 'well-educated', Giraut is flattering those in his audience who prefer the allusive style of poetry. He is consequently implying, through irony, that detractors of this style are lacking in taste and culture. Giraut is proud here of his skill in the allusive style: his *razos* is *bona* (line 39), he knows that his rich and many-faceted poem will bring him a fine reputation (lines 23–6). He does not deliberately exclude any members of his audience, but he makes it quite clear that it is up to the listener to delve for the deeper meaning of his 'tightly locked words'.[67] Only when close attention has been paid to his poem will Giraut's meaning 'yield itself up' and only then will his skill be truly recognized. The easy style is again described here with the pejorative epithet *levet*. The ideas expressed in these stanzas thus reflect those expressed through irony in *Era·m platz* and *Era si·m fos*. In these songs Giraut shows that he despises an audience which prefers easy, superficial poetry, requiring no effort whatsoever on the part of the listener. In *La flors el vergan* he expresses his preference for a discerning audience, willing to make an effort to appreciate hidden and deeper meanings.

Elsewhere the pride which Giraut takes in the composition of allusive poetry is equally evident and, as Sharman argues, 'Giraut was undoubtedly most at home in reflective poetry.'[68] When he composed in the 'easy' style he did so reluctantly, because he had, as a professional performer, to give his audience what it wanted. He may have considered the *trobar leu* to be a high level of style inasmuch as it was difficult to compose in it, but he clearly

177

considered it inferior to the allusive style and despised people who preferred the facile pleasure it afforded to the richer and more rewarding experience of more difficult poetry. Whenever he did compose in the *trobar leu*, he managed to convey his disdain for the style and for its public through irony, thus on one level giving a part of his audience what it wanted, and on another laughing at it with another section of his audience. Giraut's views on style are thus far closer to Raimbaut d'Aurenga's than their opposing positions in *Era·m platz* might suggest: in reality they probably saw eye to eye and the *tenso* was conceived, in all likelihood, to entertain an audience that appreciated a literary joke. Looking back with hindsight on the controversy about easy and allusive poetry in the troubadour tradition, we may find it ironic that Giraut, who probably had a low opinion of the *trobar leu*, should be held responsible by certain modern scholars for having 'invented' it.

IRONY IN GIRAUT'S MORALIZING POETRY

Giraut's reputation as a *poeta rectitudinis*, his obvious knowledge of rhetoric, and his effective use of irony in his love songs and when discussing style, might lead one to expect a good deal of biting irony in his moralizing poetry, but this is not the case. For Marcabru irony and moralizing go hand in hand. What better way to criticize and express one's disgust? Giraut's moralizing contrasts sharply with Marcabru's: where Marcabru is ironic and at his most vituperative, Giraut is direct and his tone flat; where Marcabru is incisively laconic and to the point, Giraut is expository and his tone discursive. Before attempting an explanation of why Giraut generally chose not to use irony, which he was capable of handling quite deftly elsewhere, in his moralizing poems, where it might in some ways have been more appropriate, I should like to examine briefly the instances in his moralizing poetry where I believe Giraut *is* ironic.

When Giraut is ironic in a *sirventes*, his irony is usually fairly obvious, as in the following example from *Per solatz*:

> Ar es pres de raubar
> E d'ebrancar berbitz.
> Cavalliers si'aunitz
> Que·s met en doneiar
> Pois qe tocha dels mans moutons belanz
> Ni que rauba gleisas ne viandanz.   (LXXIV, 25–30)

Now renown is won by robbery and stealing sheep from the flock. Shame on a knight who courts ladies after touching a bleating sheep and robbing churches or pilgrims.

Giraut's proposition that 'renown is won by robbery and stealing' is ironic because of the incongruous use of the word *pres* (*pretz*), which usually implies a good reputation. Had he contented himself with this initial proposition, his irony might have verged on the vituperative; however, Giraut's discursive nature takes over and he goes on to explain his irony (lines 27–30), thus attenuating the effect.

In *Si per mon Sobre-totz non fos*, Giraut again lacks the bite of vituperation:

> Q'er apell'om pros los peiors,
> E sobra cel que pieitz s'irais,
> E cel que mais adui,
> Cum qe·is pot, de l'autrui,
> Sera plus enveiatz,
> De qe·m teing per forsatz
> C'om d'avol plait savai
> Cuoilla bon pretz verai,
> Don degr'esser blamatz.　　　　(LXXV, 21–9)

For now the worst men are called worthy and the most choleric superior, and the man who takes as much as he can from others is more in demand, wherefore I feel constrained when I see a man of bad faith getting a fine, true reputation for something for which he ought to be criticized.

Pros (line 21), *sobra* (line 22), *enveiatz* (line 25) and *bon pretz verai* (line 28) are all used ironically here, but Giraut repeats the 'world upside-down' *topos* in such a heavy-handed manner throughout the stanza that the result is prosaic, if not pedestrian.

Giraut only seems to achieve the concision required for truly biting irony in his moralizing poetry when he is talking about the Third Crusade:

> E Dieus aienz
> Ogan nostre captal
> E·l nos enanz
> Tan que Sarracin fer
> Sofran perdas e danz,
> Tro veingn'al descazer.
> Et hom non deu temer
> Mal per Dieu gazaignar
> Ni non fai a doptar
> Lo comensars,
> Que Gascons e Navars,
> Si lor aond'avers,
> Aduira·l bos espers
> E Dieus ira denan
> Los nostres chapdelan!　　　　(L, 76–90)

And henceforth may our victory please God and may he bring it closer for us, so that the cruel Saracens might suffer losses and injuries until they are defeated. And one should not fear evil when one is seeking salvation, nor is setting out to be feared, for fine hope will bring the Gascons and men of Navarre, as long as there is plenty of money in it for them, and God will go out in front, protecting our men.

As Sharman notes of lines 86–8, 'the inference is ironical'.[69] The *bos espers* that brings the Gascons and Navarrese on the Crusade ought to be spiritual (lines 82–3), but Giraut implies that their only hope is for material gain, and that if the prospects of making some money on the Crusade seem slight, they will stay at home. *Bos espers* is ironic here, as is the inference that the motives of the men of Gascony and Navarre are purely venal.

It is the venal motives of certain crusaders that inspire Giraut to irony elsewhere. In the crusading song *Ben es dreitz*, Giraut criticizes the rich in no uncertain terms:

> Qu'er a envitz,
> Tan vau trebaillatz e temens,
> Non puesc suffrir que non comens
> Un fol chantar
> Ab que cuiava remenbrar
> Los avols ricx de valor blos,
> Per qu'es faillitz conduitz e dos.   (LXX, 42–8)

For now, because I am invited to do so, I am so deeply troubled and fearful, that I cannot stop myself beginning a foolish song with which I thought to recall the vile rich who are devoid of worth and because of whom feasting and gifts have declined.

This outspoken vituperation perhaps makes irony earlier in the poem clearer:

> Car cel qui·lls defraitz e·ls fronitz
> E·ls mal noiritz
> Acueill e·ls fai viure valens,
> Ben sembla que·ls ricx penedens
> Vueilla logar,
> Si·l cors e l'obra ven e par,
> Trop mieills que·ls forfaitz sofraitos,
> Car mais val lor confessios.   (17–24)

For it indeed seems to me that he who welcomes the infirm, the crippled and the starving, and makes them live well should indeed wish to reward rich penitents more than the guilty poor, provided that their heart is in it and that this is apparent, for their confession is worth more.

On one level Giraut is alluding to the Christian idea that poverty can be a virtue and that it is harder for a rich man than for a pauper to achieve salvation, because his sins are bound to be greater.[70] The last line of the stanza is, however, ambiguous. Giraut may well be implying that God particularly cherishes the repentance of a rich man because he has more to repent, but the emphasis could equally well be on the magnitude of the sins of the rich, and the line could therefore be read as an ironic jibe. Moreover, if *valer* is taken in a different sense, the line might even be translated 'for their confession earns them more'.

Further irony at the expense of greedy rich men spoiling the Crusade's chances of success occurs later in the poem:

Giraut de Borneil

Doncx puesc ieu segur afiar
C'uei non son son tan belas meissos
Com d'aver pretz entrels baros!　　　　　　　　(70–2)

So, I can vouchsafe that there is no fair harvest like the winning of fine reputation among the rich!

These lines should be compared to the criticism of the *avols ricx* earlier in the poem (quoted above), and to the first *tornada*:

> Laissem estar las avols gens;
> 　C'aissi·s fai far,
> Que trop es greu d'els a parlar,
> E pensem dels Turqx erguyllos
> Com lur avols leys caia ios!　　　　　　　　(85–9)

Let us leave the vile ones, for thus it is fitting, as it is too painful to speak of them, and let's think of the proud Turks and of how to cast down their vile religion!

In the light of these lines, lines 70–2 can only be understood as *ironia* and biting false praise. Moreover, the ambiguity of the word *pretz* may add venom to Giraut's sting here. Its most obvious meaning in the context is 'fine reputation', but *pretz* can also mean 'money', or 'wealth' (*PSW*, VI, 525–7). Giraut may therefore be implying that all the barons are interested in is increasing their wealth. If this is the case, he is 'binding up' the end of the poem with the beginning by reintroducing the theme of venality.

Apart from these examples, Giraut's moralizing poetry seems to be singularly lacking in irony. One possible explanation of this is that Giraut never cast himself in the rôle of a preacher: he is rarely vituperative and lacks the preacher's zeal that leads to some of Marcabru's most inspired poetry. Giraut sees himself as a man of letters or as a court poet; he has a constant tendency to moralize, but he does so in a somewhat detached manner. Although irony can indicate detachment, it in fact often implies a very definite point of view which the ironist believes in fervently. Giraut is ironic in his love songs and when he talks about style because he feels involved and committed; his moralizing texts, however, often appear to be the ruminations of a man of letters who feels somewhat removed from the world. The possible exception to this is Giraut's clear commitment to the Third Crusade, and here we find irony.

CONCLUSION

Giraut de Borneil's use of irony could be compared unfavourably to that of Marcabru, Raimbaut d'Aurenga or Bernart Marti. His poetry lacks Marcabru's satirical bite, Raimbaut's anarchic sense of humour or the personal touch of Bernart Marti. Like Peire d'Alvernha, Giraut is also clearly not a natural ironist, but a poet who can use irony when appropriate. His use of irony supports the view that he was well versed in rhetoric, shows he was a part of the *Dialektik des Trobar*, and throws interesting new light on what we know of his attitude towards style. It also highlights an important element of his poetry that has perhaps been somewhat obscured by his reputation as a *poeta rectitudinis*: Giraut de Borneil had a sense of humour.[71] Giraut was an entertainer and irony was a device he often used to this end. Perhaps his reputation as the *maestre dels trobadors* reflects his skill as an entertainer as much as his skill as a poet.

Conclusion

Nobody now believes in the idealized image of the timid, lovesick and sincere troubadour wearing his heart on his sleeve as he composed songs about his haughty lady; this is an image some troubadours sought to create in order to enhance the effect of their songs. But this image obviously struck a chord with the first modern critics of troubadour poetry and courtly literature in general, for it dominated their critical writing; in the wake of Romanticism, nineteenth-century philologists, textual critics and literary critics alike imposed a model on the medieval texts they pored over with such enthusiasm, a model finally baptized *amour courtois* by Gaston Paris in an article on Chrétien de Troyes, published in 1888. Although some of the premises that have continued to underlie medieval literary studies ever since then have been questioned in recent years, students of medieval literature are still, on the whole, confronted with critical assumptions that have their origin, not in the Middle Ages, but in nineteenth-century France and Germany. The modern idealizing image of the troubadour lyric as plaintive love poetry does not give an adequate picture of the tradition and it has obscured, not only the great variety, but also the humour and vitality, of the corpus. Moreover, if we accept that the modern reception of troubadour poetry has tended to play down its humour and irony, then we need also to re-examine the troubadours' reception in the Middle Ages in other courtly and non-courtly genres, both in Occitan and in other languages. That later courtly culture was profoundly influenced by the troubadours is beyond doubt, but recent critical work on the courtly romance, whilst highlighting the importance of irony in the genre, has also tended to assume that writers like Chrétien de Troyes drew on a tradition of lyric poetry that offered a straightforward model of courtliness, one which was less a courtly consensus, open to question, than a courtly imposition with only a few, marginal dissenters. This is clearly not the case: humour, irony and playfulness are inherent in courtly culture from the outset.

Thus, ironic intertextual play is an important feature of the troubadour tradition. The recent work of Jörn Gruber and Maria-Luisa Meneghetti demonstrates that troubadour poets knew each other's work well, engaged in poetic rivalry and exchange, and felt themselves to be part of a tradition, of a *Dialektik des Trobar*. Sensitivity to irony helps us to sharpen our perception of this, for intertextuality in troubadour poetry frequently involves irony as part of a playful and questioning dialectic. The study of ironic intertextual

Conclusion

play also reminds us that to argue that medieval poetry is purely formalistic is reductive, for poets often use *topoi*, or take a conventional stance, ironically. In doing so they are both reflecting a tradition and playing with it, affirming it and denying it, absorbing it and transforming it: the early troubadours were individualists who felt themselves to be part of a community of poets with which they shared a sense of sophistication and self-awareness.

An analysis of an individual troubadour's irony helps us to sharpen our view of his *eloquentia*. Irony was an essential element of Marcabru's *eloquentia* and the ironic techniques he uses are often close to those described in the Latin rhetorical manuals; his irony often seems to imply a detailed knowledge of rhetoric. Though neither can compare to Marcabru as an ironist, it is also possible that Peire d'Alvernha and Giraut de Borneil were influenced in their use of irony by the manuals. Raimbaut d'Aurenga, as a noble, is unlikely to have had a formal rhetorical training and if he did know the techniques described in the manuals, he does not appear to use them in his poetry; his irony reflects rather an anarchic and capricious sense of humour, which in turn is reflected in his individualistic attitude to style. Of the troubadours studied, Bernart Marti uses irony in the most interesting manner, for through irony he questions and undermines the apparent meaning of his text without suggesting what might replace it; his *eloquentia* is subtle and sophisticated.

In some instances an awareness of irony helps us to revise our view not only of individual poems, but also of a troubadour's work as a whole. It is easy to imagine why Marcabru enjoyed such influence and popularity once it has been realized that his poetry is pervaded by irony. Although his most characteristic procedure is virulent moralizing and the insulting of his audience, his songs are extremely entertaining and he strives constantly to combine his moralizing with devices, often ironic, that are intended to amuse and thereby to retain his audience's undivided attention. Bernart Marti is less concerned with his audience than Marcabru; his irony shows that he was preoccupied with self-knowledge and he emerges as a marginal, introspective poet. Giraut de Borneil, on the other hand, is far from marginal. The huge corpus of his surviving poetry makes him one of the central figures of the tradition, yet despite his unrivalled reputation among his contemporaries, modern scholars have found him dry, humourless and pedestrian. The irony in his work indicates that his sense of humour has been underestimated, that his attitude to style is less cut-and-dried than has been thought and that much of his poetry must have been entertaining when performed.

One of the limitations of this book is that irony cannot be reduced to linguistic prescriptions. It reflects a way of thinking and it often depends, when it occurs in the spoken language, on delivery and gesture. The troubadours' songs were intended for oral delivery, for a dramatic performance to music before an audience, and some of their irony is doubtless lost on us, but I hope that I have drawn attention to the pervasive existence of textual irony in their work. Sometimes the troubadours wished to move their audience; frequently they wanted to make them laugh. The humour of the troubadour lyric has often been neglected and if I have at times concentrated on sexual innuendo, obscenity, or some of the less 'elevated' aspects of the poetry, my purpose was to suggest that these poets were addressing a public whose sense of humour was not, in some respects, different from that of a modern audience. The troubadours' public might have enjoyed the cathartic effect of a refined courtly *canso*, but it also enjoyed laughing at the more vulgar aspects of life.

Many of the troubadours studied in this book are also mentioned in Peire d'Alvernha's satire *Cantarai d'aqestz trobadors*: Peire Rogier, Giraut de Borneil, Bernart de Ventadorn, Raimbaut d'Aurenga, possibly Bernart Marti, and, of course, Peire d'Alvernha himself. If, as has often been suggested, they were all present at the poem's first performance, one can indeed imagine them *tot iogan rizen*:

> Lo vers fo faitz als enflabotz
> a Puioch-vert, tot iogan rizen.   (XII, 85–6)

The troubadours' irony is a reflection of their playful and lively spirits; I hope I have succeeded in conveying this.

Appendix

Notes to texts, translations and re-editions will be arranged by troubadour and then following the numbering of the poems in the edition usually referred to. After the poem and line numbers I give the page(s) on which the lines in question are discussed.

BERNART MARTI

I re-edit all the poems and passages which I quote. The poems are preserved in the MSS as follows:

Number and *incipit* of poem		PC	MSS and folio or page number
I	*Amar dei*	63.1	*E* 110
II	*A senhor*	63.2	*C* 325 v°, *E* 112
III	*Bel m'es*	63.3	*E* 110
IV	*Companho, per companhia*	63.5	*E* 111
V	*D'entier vers far*	63.6	*C* 326 r°
VI	*Farai un vers*	63.7	*C* 325 v°
VII	*Quan l'erb'es*	63.8	*C* 326 r°, *E* 112
VIII	*Qant la plueia*	63.7a	*a* 457
IX	*Lancan lo douz temps*	104.2	*a* 456

All variants and emendations to the MSS will be noted except that the consonant *v*, written in all MSS *u*, is transcribed by me *v*.

I (pp. 80–5)

Corrections to the MS: 1 deg, 10 duna, 14 enguna, 24 mas la nuiailla dieus labais, 59 e *missing*, terrena.

1   The correction to the MS is required by the rhyme scheme but represents no change in meaning.

10   I adopt Hoepffner's correction, which restores the scansion whilst only changing one letter; not all the lines in this song have regular syllable counts (see note to line 17), but lines as short as three syllables are unlikely to be irregular. Hoepffner translates 'alors je me donne l'air d'être heureux en amour' and

186

Beggiato 'dunque corteggio una vana apparenza'. Beggiato thus understands *dompnei* as a verb and compares the collocation *color en peintura* to Marcabru's use of the word *peintura* to designate illusion (ix, 10, and xxx, 88–92). However, lines 9–10 make better sense if *color* is understood as a verb and *dompnei* as a noun, which gives the literal translation 'so I paint courting as a picture'. As both *colorar* and *peintura* can imply illusion and deception, 'I pretend to pay court' renders the spirit, if not the letter, of these lines. On *colorar*, see *PS W*, i, 283–4, which also gives *dir color*, 'to tell lies'; compare Giraut de Borneil, lxv, 84–5, where *reglas de colors* must mean 'deceitful orders'. On *peintura* indicating illusion, see *L R*, iv, 477, and Roncaglia *'Aujatz de chan'*, p. 34. There may, nevertheless, be other levels of meaning in lines 9–10. Elsewhere Bernart calls himself Bernart Martin *lo pintor* (iv, 38) and Goddard, 'Early troubadours', p. 74, suggests that this refers to his profession, indicating that he was a paid cleric of roughly the same rank and status as Marcabru and Cercamon. Bernart may well have been a *pintor* and lines 9–10 may thus be an allusion to this, but they can also be interpreted as a reworking of the classical painter/poet metaphor. If *dompnei* is understood as the means of paying court as well as the act, in other words the poem itself and the act of composition, Bernart could well be alluding here to the rhetorical 'colouring' of words with different layers of meaning. Another possible translation of lines 9–10, albeit extremely liberal, might then be 'I colour my poem as a painting'. Note that only two lines later a word plucked straight from troubadour stylistic terminology occurs, *plan.*

13 *Rancura*, a legal term: see *L R*, v, 40, and *PS W*, vii, 25–6.
14 The correction to the M S is required by the rhyme scheme.
17 Hypermetric in the M S. Hoepffner corrects *delir* to *d'est* and Beggiato to *delh*, a form which appears to be unattested. Neither emendation is satisfactory and in the light of Marshall's recent work ('Versification'), which suggests that irregularity of this kind was relatively common, particularly amongst earlier troubadours, I retain the M S reading.
20 *Forfaitura*, 'crime', or, more specifically, 'the breaking of an oath': see *PS W*, iii, 544–5; a legal metaphor.
21 *Plaidei* from *plaideiar*, another legal term, 'to contest a case'.
24 Previous editors correct this line. Hoepffner reads 'mas la nivailla dieus la bais', which he emends to 'Mas, si·m vailla Dieus! la bais', commenting that 'la correction . . . me paraît sûre' (p. 41). Beggiato correctly reads 'mas la nuiailla dieus labais', which he emends to 'mas la·m vailla Dieus, la bais', but without commenting in the notes. The M S reading 'la nuiailla' is an understandable scribal error for 'la·m vailla', given that the number of minims is the same. I understand *mas* as a conjunction indicating opposition between the first and second halves of the stanza: 'I do not reproach her . . . on the contrary I kiss her'.
25 *Gardan*, a present participle indicating continuous action; *de mal plena* must refer to the lady.
26 *Destremena* from *destermenar*, 'mettre fin à', 'détruire': see *P D* and *PS W*, ii, 168–9. There may also be a pun on the legal expression *menar un plait*, 'mener un procès': see *PS W*, v, 190, and vi, 336.
31 I follow Hoepffner in understanding *quers* as a form of *cuers*, 'leather', 'hide'.
36 Hoepffner (erroneously) reads *cant* and Beggiato (correctly) *cuns*. On *veillums<veillor*, see Hoepffner, 'Le troubadour', p. 140, *PS W*, viii, 618, and compare Marcabru, ii, 4, where *frescum<frescor*, Bernart de Venzac, v, 4 and 53, where *frescum<frescor* and *altum<autor*, and *Girart de Roussillon*, 1347,

where *ferum*<*feror*. I have found no other examples of *langorar* in Occitan, but compare OF *langorer*, 'être faible, languissant': see Godefroy, IV, 715, and *TL*, V, 142–3. The line remains somewhat obscure.

46   *Eslei*, 'justification' (?), *PSW*, III, 232–3. Possibly another legal term.

58   Hypometric in the MS. Hoepffner corrects to 'ric'es de mezura' and Beggiato to 'ric'e de mezura', but *ricx* in the MS is clearly masculine and thus refers to the poet. I preserve the MS reading even though it may be erroneous.

59   The rhyme scheme requires a word ending in *-ana* at the rhyme. I adopt Hoepffner's correction, which preserves the original meaning. The line is also hypometric and needs the insertion of the conjunction *e* for the syntax of the whole stanza to make sense; lines 58–9 obviously remain problematic. Beggiato corrects line 59 to 'e d'onor certana', commenting that *certana* is 'less improbable' from a palaeographic point of view and concords better with the sense of the text (p. 64).

II, 25–36 (p. 91)

Base and orthography *E*. There are no substantive variants in these stanzas.

Variants: 25 C forquet, 26 C sil, denan, 27 C a, can, 28 C deyssa, 31 C cujatz, 32 C avez, 33 C elh o, 34 C quel, 36 C dreg bayssar.

IV (pp. 92–96)

Corrections to the MS: 15 mentir, 34 vau, 53 escarida, 56 estec.

9   *Chantador* here is vocative: see Cingolani, '*Chantador*', p. 178.

15   I correct the case of the noun to make it concord with the adjective.

23   *Trichador*, singular oblique. Hoepffner understands it as another vocative and Beggiato makes it the subject of the sentence, which would appear, however, to be *amor* (line 10). *Saillia* (line 22) from *salhir*, 'faire sortir' (*PD*).

26   The caesura falls in an unusual place, but this would seem to be the only way to make sense of lines 26–8 as they are preserved in the MS. Hoepffner corrects to 'mas pel trichament ceria'; Beggiato edits as I do.

34   Like previous editors, I emend *vau* to *vai*, as a third person form seems more likely here.

36–8   Difficult lines. Hoepffner translates 'ainsi il ferait la légèreté selon le conseil de Bernart Martin le Peintre', followed by de Riquer, *Los trovadores*, I, 246, and Payen, 'Bernart', p. 38. Beggiato comments that he has no difficulty in understanding 'Bernart Martin' as the subject (p. 99) and translates 'però, secondo senno, farrebe la cosa più facile Bernart Marti il pittore'. I agree with Hoepffner that the name is clearly oblique and must be genitive, but the syntax does not allow it to refer to *conseill*; it can consequently only refer to *leuior*.

53   The correction restores the rhyme scheme.

56   The preterite form of the MS is implausible, hence the correction.

V, 55–6 (pp. 91–2)

No corrections to the MS.

59–60 Compare Matthew 23:12 and see Mölk, *Trobar clus*, p. 114.

Appendix / Bernart

VI, 1–6 (p. 91)

No corrections to the MS.

1–3   Strictly speaking, the rhyme sound should be -*elh*. Previous editors correct, somewhat pedantically.

VII (pp. 85–8)

Base and orthography: *E*. Stanzas VII–X are in *E* only, thus *C* has a much less interesting version of the text. On this point, see also the note to line 21.

Variants: 1 *C* lerbaes, 2 *E* el, *C* rossinhols brayle crida, 4 *C* florit, 5 *C* adoncx, temps, 6 *C* quan hom las ranas aus, 7 *C* per lo marcx e per lo riu, 9 *C* cossirier, 10 *C* vuelh, 12 *C* quanc pus nasquey, 15 *C* nay una cauzida, 16 *C* desturbier, 18 *C* yeu, 20 *C* suy, 21 *C* ses falhir sous iur eus pliu, 22 *C* a, rissida, 24 *C* e nom pretz sillam, 26 *C* sant, 27 *C* quom non, 29 *C* sillam, cossentida, 30 *C* dont, 31 *C* quieu la bays nudo vestida, 33 *C* emperaire, 34 *C* vayre, 35 *C* belh, *E* maizina, 36 *C* Blanchae grayl, 37 *E* coratage, 38 *C* doussae fresquae, 39 *C* cum flor de may, 41 *C* suy de re guabaire, 42 *C* quassatz, 46 *E* que mon ver, 58 *E* mesatger, 63 *E* enlestrebesquieu, 64 *E* Nalnes.

19   Two syllables short in both MSS. Hoepffner comments (p. 54) that 'on pourrait compléter le vers en lisant: *leis ai don* . . .' Beggiato edits 'l'ai fe . . .' It is impossible to ascertain with any degree of certainty what the missing syllables were, but it would seem likely that one was *ai*, as the past participle *iurat* (line 18) has no auxiliary.

21   Contains the only substantive variants. If the reading of *C* is preferred, Bernart is addressing his audience and attempting to convince it of his sincerity. If, however, *E* is adopted, he is reporting the fact that he tries to convince his lady of his sincerity. If my interpretation of the poem is accepted, the reading of *E* is by far the more interesting. As the last stanzas are missing in *C*, the tone of the whole poem is different, in effect far more conventional.

31   Note the elisions required for the line to scan. *E* does not indicate them; compare *C* and see also line 36.

46   The line is one syllable too long in the MSS. Hoepffner and Beggiato simply suppress *mi*, but if *que* is a scribal error for *e*, which it could quite easily be, and if *e* is then seen to elide with *garnida* of the previous line, *mi* can be retained. For examples of this kind of elision in Occitan, see Marshall, 'Versification', pp. 51–2.

57   Eblon has been variously identified as Eble III, Viscount of Ventadorn (Roncaglia, 'Due postille', pp. 74–5; Hoepffner, 'Le troubadour', p. 109), and as Ebles de Saigna, the troubadour of whom Peire d'Alvernha sings in his satire (Beggiato, *Il trovatore*, pp. 34–5). Roncaglia's identification rests on the fact that Eble III's wife was called Marguarida, but as de Riquer points out (*Los trovadores*, I, 144), it is almost certainly a place name here and it is listed as such in Wiacek, *Lexique*, p. 131. It is possible that Bernart alludes to Ebles de Saigna here, but in his detailed discussion of the problem Pirot concludes that there is no firm evidence to prove this (see 'Le troubadour', p. 659). Giraut de Borneil may also allude to Ebles (see XLVIII, 6).

58   The rhyme scheme requires the correction.

63   The rhyme scheme requires the correction. Previous editors see the two names as *senhals*. Roncaglia, 'Due postille', p. 75, and Beggiato, *Il trovatore*, pp. 36–7, suggest that they designate Giraut de Borneil and Raimbaut d'Aurenga, but

such conjecture is not susceptible to proof. Naimes is Charlemagne's wisest counsellor in *La Chanson de Roland* and this may be the source of the *senhal*. Estrebesquiu must be derived from the verb *entrebescar*, which often evokes allusive poetry. Aimes might well therefore be a fitting *senhal* for Giraut, and Estrebesquiu for Raimbaut.

64   The correction seems plausible in the light of the previous lines. One possible interpretation is that Bernart is announcing to Ebles that he has carried out a plan to bring two friends together after a dispute, but the lines remain obscure.

VIII, 8–14 (p. 90)

No corrections to the MS.

13   Previous editors correct. I understand *l* as an object pronoun used redundantly, as in French 'il l'avait, le livre?'

IX, 15–21 (p. 90)

No corrections to the MS.

IX, 43–6 (p. 83)

Corrections to the MS: 46 blau.

46   The correction is required by the rhyme scheme.

GIRAUT DE BORNEIL

All references and quotations use Sharman's edition.

V (pp. 162–6)

22   Literally 'bring this [her love] to you'.
25   Sharman translates 'My lord, what advice can you give me?' (*Cansos*, p. 64), but the verb is clearly not a second person form. See *PS W*, I, 335, *prendre conselh*, 'trouver moyen'.
39   Literally 'May you be obeyed', *siatz* being subjunctive. Sharman translates lines 38–39 'She will. – How? – If you'll trust me . . .', and so on (p. 64). However, *er* cannot mean 'she will' here, as 'will' in Sharman's translation is an auxiliary, and for this meaning the future of *voler* would be required, in other words 'she will want it so'. Also there is no evidence that *que* can mean 'comment'.

VII, 10–18 (p. 148)

18   Levy lists *esmerger* with a query in *PS W*, III, 240, but it is not listed in *PD* and so Levy must have decided that the verb did not exist. In his discussion of these lines he concludes that the usual meaning of *esmers* is more likely here anyway.

XX, 61–95 (pp. 155–8)

61   Levy does not list *aploure*, but compare OF *apleuvoir*, Godefroy, I, 342, 'tomber du ciel en pluie', and Arnaut Daniel, x, 13.

93 Sobre-Totz, a *senhal* for either Aimar V of Limoges or Alfonso II of Aragon: see Sharman, *Cansos*, pp. 7–8.

95 Sharman edits 'Qu'enquer aurai nom Bonafos', but this rests on the assumption that Bonafos designates Giraut, hence my alteration to her text. Alternatively, one could correct *aurai* to *aura*; the *tornada* is clearly corrupt, as in line 93 both MSS *CSg* read 'sobre totz ieu' and MS *a* reads 'sobre totz en', whereas the rhyme scheme requires a word ending in *-alh*.

XXXI, 41–54 (pp. 146–7)

50 The *non* is expletive.

XLVIII, 1–10 (p. 170)

6 *N'Eblon*: possibly the troubadour Ebles de Saignes or the troubadour Eble d'Ussel: see Pirot, 'Le troubadour', p. 659.

LXVI, 9–13 (p. 173)

13 On *sobrestorias*<*estoriar*, 'to depict?', see *PSW*, III, 332 and VII, 723, and Paterson, *Troubadours*, pp. 95–6, who translates 'over-embellished'. Compare Salverda de Grave, *Observations*, p. 72, who emends to *sobrestojan* and translates 'obscur'.

LXVI, 79–91 (pp. 173–4)

87 I follow Sharman's translation (*Cansos*, p. 432), but despite her note (p. 434), the construction *si ab*, 'unless it is' (*s'ab*, line 87), is not satisfactory.

LXXIV, 25–30 (p. 178)

26 *Ebrancar* is not listed in *PSW*, *PD*, *LR* or *REW*; compare, however, Godefroy, III, 345, OF *ebrancher*, 'aliéner une partie d'un fief'. These lines may also be a reply to Bertran de Born, XV, 43–9.

GUILHEM IX

All quotations and references use Pasero's edition.

I, 1–3 (pp. 19, 29)

1 Pasero edits 'Companho, farai un vers [qu'er] covinen', interpolating *qu'er* for the missing syllable. He gives a detailed discussion of the other possible interpolations, *tot-* or *des-* (p. 20), but the simplest solution is to leave the line hypometric: see Marshall, 'Versification', pp. 56–7.

VI, 57–60 (pp. 21–2)

57 *Tauler*: Pasero, p. 184, argues for a double meaning, 'gaming table' or 'piece of cloth', but Bond, 'Philological comments', p. 356, argues that there is no

Appendix / Marcabru

evidence for *tauler* designating an article of clothing before the thirteenth century.

59 Pasero edits 'e·l dui foron cairat nualler', which is in none of the MSS. They read *C carauallier*, *D* missing, *E caramaillier*, *N cairat valer*. Pasero understands *cairat nualler* as 'un ironico ossimoro "buoni, ma senza valore"' (p. 185), but *nualler* is not attested elsewhere and it is perhaps unwise to correct an MS reading to create a hapax. *Valer* (*N*) is also a hapax, but according to Bond, 'Philological comments', p. 357, it 'is easily traced to *val* "value" or to *valer* "to be of value"; *valer* would mean "of value, useful" (like the common *valedor*)'.

MARCABRU

Fourteen of Marcabru's poems have been re-edited individually since the publication of Dejeanne's edition in 1909. I shall refer to these re-editions, but use Dejeanne's numbering of the texts. Otherwise I refer to and quote from Dejeanne's edition. The re-editions are as follows (full references in the bibliography):

Poem	Re-edition
I	Pirot, '*A la fontana*'
II	Ricketts, '*A l'alena*'
III	Roncaglia, '*Al departir*'
VI	Roncaglia, 'La tenzone'
IX	Roncaglia, '*Aujatz de chan*'
XIV	Paterson, *Troubadours*, pp. 43–7
XV	Roncaglia, '*Cortesamen*'
XVI	Roncaglia, 'Il *gap* di Marcabruno'
XIX	Ricketts, '*Doas cuidas ai*'
XXII	Roncaglia, 'I due sirventesi'
XXIII	Roncaglia, 'I due sirventesi'
XXXII	Ricketts, '*Lo vers comenssa*'
XXXIII	Roncaglia, '*Lo vers comens*'
XXXV	Hathaway and Ricketts, 'Le *vers del lavador*'

II, 1–15 (pp. 69–70)

12 *Pel*, 'scrotum', *PSW*, VI, 188. I take *bussa* to be a scribal error for *busca*, 'kindling wood', *PSW*, I, 174–5; Ricketts translates 'buisson', but gives no note.

13 *Guasta-pa*, 'bread-wasters'; eating bread is a metaphor for illicit sex in Marcabru's poetry, hence my translation. Compare XX, 37, and XVI, 16–18.

14 *Li don*, 'the ladies', by analogy with *midons* and *sidons*; alternatively 'the gifts'.

II, 16–25 (pp. 40–1)

20 *Broc*, 'stick': see Bertoni, 'Due note', p. 645; Ricketts, '*A l'alena*', p. 113, and compare Bernart de Venzac, IV², 32, where Simonelli translates *broc* as 'giavellotto'. Thiolier-Méjean prefers to translate *broc* as 'pitcher', following Levy in *PD*, but she offers no explanation (*Poésies satiriques*, p. 277).

23 *Revolum*, 'winding', hence 'subtle': see Lewent, 'Beiträge', p. 315, and *PSW*, VII, 329.

24   *Guazalhan*: see *L R*, III, 449; *P S W*, IV, 91–2, and the comments of Lewent, 'Beiträge', p. 315, and Nelson, 'Animal imagery', p. 52. Marcabru may use the verb *enguassalhar* in poem XIV: see Paterson, *Troubadours*, p. 46.

III, 33–6 (pp. 60–1)

33–4   These lines are punctuated as individual questions in Roncaglia's edition of the poem.

IV, 1–12 (pp. 66–7)

3   On the reflexive construction with *om* and the meaning of *engaill*, see Gaunt and Harvey, 'Text and context', pp. 66–7.

9   *Regaing*, 'second harvest': see Gaunt and Harvey, 'Text and context', p. 67.

IV, 19–30 (p. 44)

22   Dejeanne edits line 22 'Dizo mil essais encogan'. The M S S give *A I K Deso, N De zo, a Dizo*. I adopt the reading of *A I K* and also alter Dejeanne's punctuation, following Paterson, *Troubadours*, p. 8.

IV, 31–42 (pp. 41–2)

34   *Acaminar* is not listed in *R E W* or *P S W*, but see the examples of *encaminar* and O F *acheminer* in *L R*, I, 302, and Godefroy, VIII, 23, which suggest that the word may have military overtones.

35   I accept Dejeanne's correction to this line: see Gaunt and Harvey, 'Text and context', p. 69. The M S S read *A astrobauditz, I N acropanditz, K acropandiz, a afrobanditz*.

37   *Pretz, dan* and *barat* can have a variety of meanings. On *pretz*, see *P S W*, VI, 525–7. On *dan*, see *P S W*, II, 5–7. On *barat*, see *P S W* I, 126, and compare Marcabru, XLI, 19–22. On the collocation *aver lo pretz de*, see *P S W*, VI, 526.

V, 31–6 (p. 54)

31   Could also be translated 'I censure nothingness', in other words 'I censure folly/illusion'; compare Guilhem, IV, 1.

36   *Meire*, 'harvester', *P S W*, V, 156. Marcabru may be alluding to the parable of the seed falling on stony ground. Compare Matthew 13, where casting seed is a metaphor for preaching.

VIII 26–30 (p. 55)

26   I adopt the correction (presumably Jeanroy's) suggested in the variants to Dejeanne's edition. As Lewent's translation of this stanza suggests, *bravas* (feminine) must refer only to the *moillers* and *braidiu* (masculine) only to the *drut* and the *marit* ('Beiträge', p. 323).

XI, 60–9 (p. 133)

65   Dejeanne has *quiza*. A misprint?

xv (p. 73–9)

2 Dejeanne's text reads 'un vers si l'es qui l'escout'ar', but see Roncaglia, 'Cortesamen', pp. 956–97, for the construction used here.

31–6 *Lieis* and *ill* could conceivably refer to a lady, but as there is an opposition in this stanza between *amor* and *amar*, it would seem more likely that they refer to *amor*.

xvi, 31–6 (p. 53)

31 Roncaglia suggests that *estoc breto* may have a 'particularo senso figurato' ('Il gap', p. 65). He cites the *Donatz proensals*, 836, *bretoneiar = loqui inpetuose*, 'to gabble' (?), but it is hard to see what figurative sense he is suggesting. The context suggests that *estoc breto* is a weapon. See also Ashdown, *Armour*, p. 67, where an *estoc* is described as a two-handed stabbing sword designed for thrusting!

xvi, 37–45 (pp. 55–6)

37 Paterson, *Troubadours*, p. 22, translates *broill* 'thicket' and Roncaglia, 'Il gap', p. 62, 'parco', but *broill* may have a more specific meaning. See du Cange, I, 1312–13, where *brolium* is defined as 'nemus silva aut saltus in quo ferarum venatio exercetur'. Compare Godefroy, I, 740, O F *broillet*, 'petit bois', and the *Donatz proensals*, 2074, *brolhz = locus plenus arboribus*. The conjunction of the word with an image of hunting may suggest that Marcabru uses it with the specific meaning of 'wooded hunting ground'.

xvii, 25–36 (p. 47)

32 Dejeanne edits 'Atal paratz lo coissi', translating 'vous préparez de telle sorte le coussin', which is hardly possible.

36 *Badoï<badoc/badiu*, 'ignorant', 'stupid' (?): see *PSW*, I, 119.

xxiii (pp. 48–51)

21–4 *Se falhir az alcuna ren* is discussed by Levy, but his interpretation is based upon a dubious reading according to Roncaglia (see 'I due sirventesi', p. 178), who suggests *me faill<Latin me fallo* or *fallor*, 'to be disappointed'. *Falhir* can nevertheless mean 'to cease', 'to lack', 'to refuse', or 'to be at fault' (*PSW*, III, 401–3), and these lines are consequently ambiguous.

xxiv, 16–18 (pp. 56 and 152)

17 Dejeanne edits 'cals la groissor' and translates 'de même la langue tourne souvent vers la grosseur qui rend la dent douleureuse'. I adopt Lewent's suggested emendation, which does not correct the MS reading ('Beiträge', p. 429).

xxv, 67–77 (pp. 57–8)

68 Following *E*, Dejeanne edits 'Az una flor', taking *Az* as an otherwise unattested form of *aver*, and translating 'elle a une fleur'. I adopt the reading of *C*.

Appendix / Marcabru

69   *Pauzada*<*pauzar*, 'to prostitute oneself': see Roncaglia, 'Per un'edizione', p. 49, and compare *PS W*, VI, 155.

XXVI, 45–55 (pp. 57–8 and 157)

50–5   Dejeanne's punctuation differs from mine; he translates 'il se couche et se lève dans un glaçon [il est froid comme glace]; l'abbée sera assez désiré (retenu) (?) pourvu que nous ayons tout loisir'. Lewent, 'Beiträge', p. 433, and Roncaglia, 'Per un'edizione', p. 50, both suggest corrections in order to make sense of the stanza, but this may not be necessary. I make only a slight modification to Dejeanne's version of line 54; he renders the MS reading 'ans asatz', I give 'an sasatz'. According to Roncaglia, 'Per un'edizione', p. 50, *en un glatz* is an adverbial expression indicating 'simultaneità instantanea'.

XXXIII, 1–6 (pp. 65–6)

6   *Vais*<*vaisa*, 'noisetier'; *brondilh*<*brondilhar*, 'to bear leaf': see Roncaglia, '*Al departir*', pp. 35–6.

XXXIV, 29–49 (pp. 61–2)

39   Dejeanne retains the MS reading *post*. The correction is required if the word is to be read as a form of *poder*.

XXXVI, 1–12 (p. 66)

5   The last word in the line in all the MSS is *aizida* (*A E I Ka*), retained by Dejeanne. It is possible that the rhyme scheme requires a correction to a word ending in -*ina*, but it is equally possible that 'inaccurate' rhyming was a feature of the original. On this kind of 'imperfect' rhyme, see Marshall, 'Versification', particularly pp. 45–7. This is not the only place where the rhyme scheme of this poem appears corrupt and there may be a stanza missing between stanzas II and III: see Frank, *Répertoire*, I, 78, § 403, 5.

XXXVII, 7–12 (p. 79)

11   *Per esmanssa*, 'deliberately': see Lewent, 'Beiträge', p. 441. See Paterson, *Troubadours*, p. 10, for a different interpretation.

XXXVII, 49–54 (pp. 42–3)

52   *Amoreiar* is not listed in *PS W* or *R E W. L R*, I, 63, gives 'rendre amoureux' and quotes this as the only example. Compare, however, OF *s'amourer*, 's'amour-acher' (Godefroy, I, 279), and Gascon *amourache*, 'aimer à la légère', (*FE W*, I, 90). The context requires *amoreia* to be in opposition to love, hence 'infatuated'.

53   *Costans* could be related to *costar*, 'to be of value', or to the Latin *constans*, 'constant': see Appel, 'Zu Marcabru', p. 442, note 2, and Roncaglia, '*Al*

departir', pp. 18–20. However, *costans* usually meant 'reliable': see *L R*, VI, 22, and *P S W*, I, 339.

XXXVIII, 1–21 (pp. 67–8)

19   Dejeanne reads *aquist*, following *A I K*, but *Ea* offer *aquest*, a better reading.

XXXVIII, 29–30 (p. 56)

29   *Briola*: Levy, *P S W*, I, 166, does not understand, but suggests that the word is a form of *bricola*, 'machine de guerre'; he is followed by Lewent, 'Beiträge', p. 444. Dejeanne translates 'et celui-là retire du meilleur la brassée', which is based on MS *R*; he is followed by Topsfield, *Troubadours*, p. 77. The MSS read *A bruoilla*, *C maiola*, *Ea briola*, *I K broilla* and *R brassola*. As a word ending in -*ola* is required for the rhyme, and as *A E I K Ra* agree that the word should begin with *br*-, only *briola* and *brassola* are possible. The scribes of *A I K* clearly had the impression that the word was related to *broill*: compare XVI, 37, and see above, p. 194. Like *broill*, *briola* may also mean a wooded hunting ground: see Du Cange, I, 1313, 'Nicephorus in eadem coena me interrogavit. Si vos perivolia, id est briolia, vel si in perivoliis onagros vel caetera animalia haberetis. Cui cum vos briolia, et in brioliis animalia, exceptis onagris habere affirmarem, ducam te, inquit in nostrum perivoliam.' *Perivolius*, 'an enclosed hunting ground': see Du Cange, V, 393.

XXXVIII, 32–5 (p. 43)

32   Dejeanne punctuates with a semi-colon at the end of this line.

XLII, 15–23 (p. 45)

20   *Enleconir* is otherwise unattested. I follow Levy's suggested meaning: see *P S W*, III, 8.

PEIRE D'ALVERNHA

Unless otherwise indicated, the edition used is del Monte's.

II (pp. 99–106)

I have re-edited the poem. It is preserved in two MSS: *C* 178 v° and *E* 51 r°. It is poem VII in Zenker's edition and P C 323.3. Both MSS have errors, namely *C* in lines 23, 34, 41, 42 and 43 and *E* in lines 14, 20, 27, 28, 30, 31, 38, 40, 50 and 51. On the whole *C* offers the best version. Base and orthography: *C*.

Variants: 1 *C* descebrar, *C* pays, 3 *E* fais, 4 *E* mirais, 6 *E* com soi, 7 *E* dei, 8 *E* con plus puesc ades nom, 9 *E* vas, soi, 10 *E* calieis, gequis, 11 *E* metrais, 12 *partly missing in C*, *missing in E*, 14 *E* dousana, 15 *E* metrais em fai dessaillir, 16 *E* queill tric, 17 *E* anei, 18 *E* francx, 19 *E* mieils, iais, 20 *E* ni plus pretz amatz verais, 22 *E* eill gens, *C* cortezae, 23 *C* selhs, 24 *E* tan, delonia, 25 *E* fui, 27 *E* ameraus, roais, 28 *E* forsa, brais, 29 *E* trassaillir, 30 *E* doussa et alamia conia, 31 *E* si mesca esamentir, 32 *E* mensonia, 33 *E* Dezer hueimais, 34 *E* pos, *C* amar, 35 *E* queram sen, assais, 36 *E* blanx, bais, 38 *E* comia, 39 *E* quen paor,

40 *E* e noles obs, 41 *E* Er an ses cors els fals ris, *C* cor, 42 *C* tot ais cum, *E* com labelis, 43 *C* grup, *E* me gurp de lieis em lais, 44 *E* veira, 45 *E* al partir, 46 *E* maven, 47 *E* per els sis nair, 48 *C* fora en, *E* men fora, 49 *E* nestreup, 50 *E* aman ioi iauvir, 51 *E* fai som no loi calonia.

8   *Puesc*, first person indicative. *Ponia*<*ponher* 'to sting', 'to stimulate', first person subjunctive. *Ponher* can be used metaphorically to mean 'to urge': see *P S W*, VI, 453, and *L R*, IV, 597; hence my translation 'to censure'.

12   Zenker leaves the line blank. Del Monte interpolates: 'ben fazen e *trop m'afrays*'.

16   *Tric*, 'delay' or 'cheating' if a noun; alternatively it could be the third person subjunctive of *tricar*: see *E*'s reading, 'quan que·ill tric'. The ambiguity is probably intentional. I understand the syntax of this line differently from del Monte, taking *mas* to mean 'more'. 'L'er vergonia' must refer back to the *quar ... quar* construction of lines 11–14 and this is not possible if *mas* is taken as a conjunction. For *mas* as a graphy or scribal error for *mais* 'more', compare variants to Bertran de Born, VII, 67 and XXIV, 31.

23   *C* gives *selhs* (plural oblique), but if the pronoun is the subject, *E* must be correct.

28   On the construction *si no·m fos*, compare *P S W*, III, 211, '*esser* + *Inf.* "zu sein"; *m'es* + *Inf.* "ich muss"'. Compare line 47.

31   Both del Monte and Zenker correct here.

41   *C*'s reading *am* can be retained providing that the reading *cors* is taken from *E*. There is probably intentional ambiguity here: *cors*, 'heart', but also 'haste'.

42   Zenker adopts *E*'s reading here; del Monte corrects. *E* makes perfect sense and as the line is one syllable too short in *C*, taking *aisi* from *E* is the most economical solution. On this point, see also Lecoy, '*Peire*', pp. 388–9.

49   *Estrieu* is not identifiable but the *senhal* may well designate the same person as Raimbaut d'Aurenga's Estreup (poem X), particularly since Pattison dates this poem 1162.

IV (pp. 114–19)

4–5   See my commentary (p. 116) on the meaning of these lines.

36   Del Monte's text reads 'Ab sol qu'ilh – ayso no m'esfer', which he translates 'purchè essa non si curi-mi, questo, non allontana'. To justify this emendation and translation he refers to *P S W*, III, 216, but Levy queries his own example of *esferar*, 'to distance', and keeps the query in *P D*. Levy's example is from Giraut de Borneil, cited here from Sharman's edition:

<blockquote>
Qu'ieu vei a las granz poestatz
Laissar solatz e bruda,
C'un'ampla recrezuda
Perpren
Qe tol Ioven
E l'encauz'e l'esfera.   (XLII, 36–41)
</blockquote>

As Levy himself points out, the meaning of *esferar* here could equally well be the usual 'effaroucher' and this is how Sharman translates. Del Monte's text is not in any M S, the variants being as follows: *C missing (del Monte's base)*, *E* ab sol quenaiso non esfer, *R* am sol quilh ayso nom sofer, *T* ab sol qeil aso (*Zenker reads* aiso) no suefre (*Zenker* sufre), *V* acel que aizo non esfer, *m* ab sol qelaisso

Appendix / Peire

non esfer. If *esfer* is understood to be the third person singular present subjunctive of *esferar*, the line makes perfect sense. I adopt the reading of *E*. Lecoy, '*Peire*', p. 389, also rejects del Monte's text.

V, 61–70 (p. 98)

70 Del Monte corrects *aquelh*, a masculine form and the reading in the only MS (C), to *aquilh*, a feminine form, saying in a note that Peire must refer to love. Zenker notes the correct MS reading (poem 11 in his edition), but corrects to *a cela*. Coulet, 'Zenker', p. 374, suggests retaining the MS reading and argues that Peire is referring to God. Whilst this is possible, it is more likely that Peire is alluding to a patron or another troubadour he admired, possibly Marcabru.

XI, 1–4 (p. 99)

I refer to Paterson's edition in *Troubadours*, pp. 60–5.

XII, 19–24 (pp. 119–20)

22 Del Monte has *nanal*, which is probably a misprint. *ADIK* read *manal*.

XIII (pp. 106–10)

I have re-edited the text. It is preserved in three MSS: *E* 52 v°, *T* 152 r° and *m*. The readings of *m*, parts of which are illegible, are taken from Monteverdi, 'Peire d'Alvernia', pp. 136–7. The poem is number x in Zenker's edition and PC 323.7. Base and orthography: *E*, except for lines 38–42, which are almost totally missing due to the removal of an initial.

Variants: 1 *T* canla rosa, *m* qant la rosa, 2 *T* gent termini sennan sa, *m* genz t'minis se nanssa, 3 *m* faz, 4 *T* em belansa, *m* enballanssa, 5 *T* pels doutz cant del rosignol, *m* dolz cant de rossignol, 6 *T* cauc cantar la nuot, *m* qant aug cantar la nuoch, 7 *T* pels vergiers e pels plans, *m* pels vergiers e ples plais, 8 *Tm* cristians, *E* faillitz, *T* fallis, 9 *T* carmas tauz nos fan, *m* car masmuz nos fan sobranssa, 10 *T* ducx non segn, *m* ducs non cein centura, 11 *T* meltz de vos fieran, *m* meills, delanssa, 12 *T* lenperador me duogll, *m* mi, 13 *T* car moutas gen, *m* qe moutas genz fai . . . (*illegible*), 14 *T* tal en plura cuna giais, *m* tals . . . (*illegible*) plora qe naiais, 15 *T* coragies ses claris, *m* corages, 16 *T* naves, *m* avez, esperanssa, 17 *T* paien gient, *m* paianz genz, 18 *T* cavalcatz senes, *m* cavalchaz senes dotanssa, 19 *T* premier prenetz, *m* prenrez lo badol, 20 *m* anaz, *T* adretura, 21 *E* fieran, *T* dretz a monroc faran, *m* dreit a maroc (*rest of line missing*), 22 *T* cel cel gioi del segle, *m* Eel qel ioi del segle, 23 *T* ceson pretz desenansa, *m* qe son prez desenanssa, 24 *T* figlhes davol cratura, *m* fills, creatura, 25 *T* per ce fai avol mostransa, *m* per qes avols demostranssa, 26 *T* ni per tan nom abasal col, *m* tant, baissal, 27 *T* car, *m* cagittatz, 28 *T* esta, etrals sauvais, *m* ester, entres, 29 *T* mabellis, *m* per mi non dic tant ma . . . (*illegible*), 30 *T* can vei mout, *m* . . . (*illegible*) vei mot gran alegranssa, 31 *E* amors vol calonias dura, *T* amors vol canlongias dura, *m* . . . (*illegible*) voill calienes dura, 32 *T* no pot hom aver fiansa, *m* enon pot a . . . (*illegible*) ssa, 33 *E* cel, armar, *T* sicar nalarma novol, *m* sel car . . . (*illegible*) nonovol, 34 *T* car vei qe, *m* . . . (*illegible*) qel cors non acura, 35 *T* ma de segnor ce, *m* mas de so io . . . (*illegible*) grais, 36 *Tm* Cantadors, fenis, 37 *T* aprendes la comensasa, *m* . . . (*illegible*) la comenssansa, 38 *T* grant dretura, *E* -ura missing, *m* Marchabr . . . (*illegible*) gran dreitura, 39 *E* missing, *T* seblansa, *m* trobet daitretal . . . (*illegible*) nssa, 40 *E* missing except gon lo tug, *T* e tengolo tut por, *m* E tengnenlo tuit, 41 *E missing, m* . . . (*illegible*) nois sa natura, 42 *E missing except* oill mem, *T* enolmebre, *m missing*.

8 Lacks two syllables (possibly one if *crestians* is scanned as three). Del Monte's interpolation, 'Reis per Christ ja*mais no·*ns faillis', alters the meaning of the line. I leave the line hypometric, as this might well be deliberate: see Marshall's comments on irregular syllable counts ('Versification', p. 45). *Faillis* (*m*) is required by the rhyme scheme.

21 The line could also mean 'they would compose songs as far away as Morocco'.

31 Del Monte's text reads 'amors vol c'a longias dura' and he translates 'l'amore esige che duri a lungo'. *Amors* is clearly the subject (compare Topsfield, *Troubadours*, p. 179), but what does the line mean? Given that the first two lines of the stanza form a syntactic unit, one possibility is that *calonias* (*E*) is a noun and the object of *vol*. *Calonja*, 'dispute', 'refus': see *L R*, II, 295, which gives this example; *calonjar*, 'disputer'; O F *chalonge* has the same sense as its Occitan cognate (Godefroy, II, 40, see also *R E W*, § 1527). I have corrected *E*; the scribe presumably thought *dura* was a verb and the *s* a reflexive pronoun, but this is not possible, as the *voler que* construction would require a subjunctive.

32 It is possible that *T* offers a better reading than *E* here. A new clause must begin in line 32 and 'no pot hom . . .' might therefore be preferable to 'e no pot . . .'

33 Del Monte's text reads 'si·l', which is in none of the MSS. *E* may have this sense if *cel* is taken as a graphy for *si·l*. Compare line 18, where *cenes* is a graphy for *senes*, and see *PS W*, VII, 642–9, for examples of *se* or *ses* for *si*. My reading is taken from *m*, which gives the same sense as *E*. The correction of *E*'s *armar* would seem uncontroversial.

41 Del Monte edits *conoissa*, a form of *conoisser* I have not found attested elsewhere.

42 According to del Monte, *membre* has to be subjunctive; however, it may also be indicative: see Topsfield, *Troubadours*, p. 266, note 8. The conjunction *e* at the beginning of the line depends solely on *T*'s testimony, as the readings of both the other MSS are lost. I suggest inserting the letter *q* to make the syntax of the stanza clearer.

XIV (pp. 110–14)

20 *Verguonhos*, 'modest', 'restrained', but it may also mean 'careful with money' (*PS W*, VIII, 674, Deux MSS, 42 v 30):

> Trop larguejar teni per gran folor,
> E totz om prims es savis e guiscos,
> Humils, suaus, e tostemps vergonjos.

34 'Be-tailed' was a common nickname for Englishmen: see Zenker *Peire*, p. 843, and Godefroy, II, 167.

35 There may be a pun intended here. Apart from 'sneeze', O F *esternu* can mean 'à peu près comme on dit volée, dans le sens d'état, situation: "Je ne vis jamais homme de si hault esternu"' (Godefroy, II, 610, from Louis XI, *Nouv.* XXIX). All examples of this usage are late, but the meaning would fit the context perfectly. Zenker understands the word in this way, citing an example from Deschamps and commenting: 'von Peire offenbar mit ironischem Beigeschmack gebraucht' (p. 844).

XV, 57–64 (p. 98)

58   Del Monte emends here; I follow Paterson, *Troubadours*, p. 76, note 1, in adopting the reading in *z*. She derives *acomtos* from Latin *como*, 'to deck', 'to adorn', which is frequently used in a rhetorical context, and cites Occitan *acomtir*, 's'orner', 'se parer' (*PD*), to support her translation 'embellishments'.

XXI (p. 118)

I cite the text from Appel's edition in his *Bernart von Ventadorn*, where it is poem II. Del Monte does not edit it.

RAIMBAUT D'AURENGA

All quotations and references use Pattison's edition.

III, 9–16 (p. 126)

10–11   Pattison translates 'I can't help revealing my passion' (p. 75), but *sufrir* + *de* with this sense is not attested in *PSW* (VII, 749–51).

15   Pattison edits 'ans m'ai trop suffert', translating 'but rather I have abstained all too much' (p. 75). However, the *m* of his text is not in any MS. Pattison justifies this correction by saying that the line as it stands in the MSS 'offers a contradiction to what has gone before' (p. 77), but if *ans* is taken to mean 'before', the whole stanza can be understood as based upon an opposition between the poet's present and previous situations.

VIII (pp. 134–8)

36   Context makes it clear that *demer* is present subjunctive, but the verb of which it must therefore be a form, *demerar*, is apparently otherwise unattested. Levy gives *demeren*, 'coupable' (*PSW*, II, 80, and *PD*), and Godefroy, II, 499, OF *demerir*, 'démériter'. As Pattison concludes, 'we must postulate a verb *demerar* on the same root' (p. 96).

44   On *servir*, 'to deserve', see *PSW*, VII, 624. Pattison punctuates with a comma after 'servitz' and a full point after 'desdeing' (line 45).

XVII, 23–7 (p. 123)

25–6   Pattison's text is only in *R*. *CDM* have *cubert uer* for line 25 (*IKN²* missing), but lines 25–6 are inverted, which is inadmissible because of the rhyme scheme. If the reading of *CDM* is preferred to *R*'s (with the lines restored to their correct position), these lines certainly imply the *trobar clus*: see Köhler, *Trobadorlyrik*, pp. 143–4, and Paterson, *Troubadours*, pp. 166–8.

XXVIII (pp. 139–43)

15   Pattison's text reads 'Car voill . . .', but all MSS (*IKd*) read *quar*, hence *qu'ar*, 'for now', which is more logical, given the perfect tense in the previous line.

19   *Degertz* is problematic. The context requires it to mean something similar to *coindes*.

23–4   I follow Pattison's text and translation even though they are unsatisfactory. All MSS read *conclucher* in line 23 and *tot* and *guerrer* or *guerer* in line 24. The text is clearly corrupt in the MSS, as it deviates from the rhyme scheme, but Pattison's text fails to resolve the problems, as the case of the rhyme words in his text is incorrect. I am unable to arrive at a better solution.

32   Pattison edits 'per qu'om pela·l cais', which is not in any MSS. All MSS read *quem*.

XXXVII (pp. 128–34)

3   Pattison follows *ACD*, 'dirai un vers'. *IKN²a* read *darai*, which is the reading preferred by Appel, 'Raimbaut', p. 399, and Roth, 'Local', p. 461.

7   *Malserva* is not listed by Levy. I follow Appel's suggestion ('Raimbaut', p. 399) that Raimbaut invented the word. Compare Peire Vidal, XXII, 20.

13   Pattison suggests that *del plus* is 'an expression like the French "du reste", here used to pad out the line and adding little or nothing to the meaning' (p. 192). I translate literally, taking the sense to be that the *lauzengiers* should be grateful that Raimbaut does not kill them all.

25–8   Pattison's text in these lines reads:

> Qu'il pesson, ist malaürat!
> Pus d'als non val una rata
> Des que·l fara so voluntat
> O·lh dira lauzenja grata.

I have altered several elements. *Pus* is taken from *CDa*; *AIKN²* read *mas*. *Pus* makes sense providing that Pattison's correction *des* is retained in line 27: all MSS (*ACDIKN²a*) read *de*. Furthermore, *so voluntat* (line 27) would appear to be a misprint; not only is *so* an unacceptable form, but according to Appel, 'Raimbaut', p. 395, all MSS read *sa*. Even if *sa* is restored, the text still seems corrupt, for the subject of *fara* ought to be *ist malaürat* (line 25), and the reading *lor* might consequently be expected. I suggest that the lines might be read as I present them. The sense seems to be that the *lauzengier* discards the good knight as soon as he has done his will and told him some *lauzenja grata*, 'pleasant flattery' or 'pleasant gossip'. *IKN²* read *lauzenja plata*; compare Marcabru, XI, 60.

39   I have changed Pattison's punctuation.

41   As Roth, 'Local', p. 464, suggests, there is probably intentional ambiguity here. *Baizat*, 'kissed' or 'lowered'.

55   Nero's Meadow was the place where St Peter passed judgement on the souls of the dead.

56   Pattison's text reads 'On recebran deliurata', which is not in any MS. He translates 'where they will receive their due'. *A* reads *laliurata*, *Ca* read *denauata*, and *IKN²* *de nuata*. In *PD* Levy gives 'récompense (?)' as the meaning of *liurata*; see also *PSW*, IV, 412. Compare *OF livree*, 'livraison', 'a pound's worth', which can be used figuratively, giving the sense 'reward': see Godefroy, V, 7.

57   Pattison takes the reading of *a* here against all the other MSS. I follow *A*. For a discussion of the problems raised by this line, see pp. 128–9.

60   Pattison's text reads 'Girart', which is only in *a* (*AIKN² giraut*, *C guiraut*, *D* missing). Could this be an allusion to Giraut de Borneil?
Pattison gives a second *envoi*:

Joglar, s'eu ja cautz sabata,
Qi no·us ve pauc a cavalgat,
Ni sap per qe se debata. (67–9)

Joglar, if ever I wear shoes again, the one who does not see you has ridden little, nor does he know why he argues.

The meaning is obscure. I do not include this *envoi* in my text since it occurs in *a* only and my discussion of the poem concerns aspects of the text that only occur in other MSS.

XXXIX, 33–50 (pp. 143–4)

36 Pattison translates *mazelh'* 'tortures', but the meaning is stronger: see *PS W*, v, 150.

Notes

1 On Socrates, see Muecke, *Irony*, p. 14; on *ironia* in the Middle Ages, see Knox, '*Ironia*', *passim*, and on Erasmus, see *ibid.*, p. 115; on Balzac, see his 'Avant-propos de la *Comédie humaine*', p. 12 in volume 1 of the Pléiade edition.

2 For example, Batts, 'Hartmann's *humanitas*', p. 39, quoted by Green, *Irony*, p. 14.

3 Haidu, *Aesthetic Distance*; Green, *Irony*, p. 391.

4 Green, *Irony*, pp. 103–7; Muecke, *Irony and the Ironic*, p. 5.

5 For Green's comments, see *Irony*, pp. 104–5. Compare Kay's comments on personality, 'Rhetoric', p. 111.

6 I am thinking principally of scholars such as Guiette, Dragonetti and Zumthor. The work of these scholars is based upon the poetry of the *trouvères*, but they have a tendency to extend their conclusions to all medieval lyric poetry.

7 Paterson, *Troubadours*; Kay, 'Rhetoric' and 'La notion de personnalité'; Gruber, *Dialektik*.

8 A poet affirms a text by acknowledging a debt to it, he negates it by transforming and rewriting it, and he surpasses it through both activities. Gruber's conception of intertextuality is in many ways close to Julia Kristeva's, Kristeva being the first critic to use the term 'intertextuality' (see her *Révolution*, pp. 337–40, and *Semiotiké*, p. 146). As Kristeva argues, every text is informed by the reading of other texts which it absorbs and transforms.

9 Maria Luisa Meneghetti's fascinating book, *Il pubblico*, has an important chapter on intertextuality in the troubadour lyric seen from the perspective of reception (pp. 99–165). She comes to similar conclusions to Gruber whose work she was unable to consult before going to press.

10 On Lejeune's dating of the text, poem XII in del Monte's edition, see 'Le troubadour lombard', p. 319. My corpus therefore consists of Guilhem IX of Aquitaine (1071–1126), Jaufre Rudel (. . . 1125–48 . . .), Marcabru (. . . 1130–49 . . .), Cercamon (. . . 1137–49 . . .), Alegret (. . . 1145 . . .), Bernart Marti (mid-twelfth century), Peire de Valeria (mid-twelfth century), Peire Rogier (third quarter of the twelfth century), Grimoart (third quarter of the twelfth century), Peire de la Cavarana (third quarter of the twelfth century), Peire d'Alvernha (. . . 1149–68 . . .), Raimbaut d'Aurenga (. . . 1147–73), Bernart de Ventadorn (. . . 1147–70 . . .), Giraut de Borneil (. . . 1162–99). I take the datings of these troubadours' careers from de Riquer, *Los trovadores*; members of the third generation of troubadours not mentioned in Peire's satire are Marcoat, Torcafol, Berenguier de Palazol, Guilhem de Berguedà, Gaucelm Faidit, Rigaut de Berbezilh. Bernart Marti is included in my corpus, first because he may have been a contemporary of Marcabru's and secondly because it is likely that he is the Bernart de Saissac mentioned in

Peire's satire: see Roncaglia, 'Due postille', pp. 72–5, and Lejeune 'La "galerie littéraire"', pp. 271–2.

I. IRONY: MEDIEVAL AND MODERN

1 Hunt, 'Irony', p. 98, dates the earliest example of *yronie* in French 1370. *Las flors del gay saber* (c. 1323) is the earliest Occitan text to use the word *yronia* (III, 258).
2 On rhetoric in schools, see Curtius, *European Literature*, pp. 42–3 and 48–57; on the influence of rhetoric on vernacular writers, see Green, '*Alieniloquium*', p. 120; Haidu, *Aesthetic Distance*, pp. 13–14, and Paterson, *Troubadours*, pp. 5–6. For a fascinating account of the interaction between the early troubadours and Latin culture in general, see Goddard, 'Early troubadours', *passim*.
3 For detailed accounts of rhetorical tradition and the teaching of rhetoric in the Middle Ages, I refer readers to scholars such as Curtius, Faral, and particularly Murphy; for more thorough accounts of the history of *ironia* and related tropes in the Middle Ages, the studies of Haidu, Campbell, Green and particularly Knox are indispensable.
4 Where an edition exists with a parallel English translation, this will be quoted; otherwise the original will be quoted with a translation.
5 On Quintilian and Cicero in the Middle Ages, see particularly Murphy, *Rhetoric*, pp. 107–30; on Quintilian as a writer only deemed fit for intellectuals in the Middle Ages, see Mollard, 'Diffusion', *passim*; on 'curriculum' authors in the Middle Ages, see Curtius, *European Literature*, pp. 48–54. Kelly demonstrates how some twelfth-century treatises were basic textbooks: see 'Scope and treatment', *passim*.
6 Quintilian defines a trope as 'the artistic change of a word or phrase from its proper meaning to another' (VIII.6.1). I shall refer to Donatus wherever possible as he was by far the most widely read author of my corpus. For a comprehensive catalogue and description of all tropes and their traditions throughout the Middle Ages, see Krewitt, *Metapher*, *passim*, and on *allegoria* and its species in particular pp. 93–4. Some of my translations echo the wording of Tannenhaus's translation of Bede.
7 See Isidore, *Etymologiae* I, 37.22; Bede, *De schematibus* II.2.12; Julian, *De vitiis*, pp. 74–9; Gervase, *Ars poetica*, pp. 155, 149 and 141–2; Quintilian *Institutio* VIII.6.54–7 and IX.2.65 and 92; Hugh, *De grammatica*, lines 2266–90.
8 Kelly, *Medieval Imagination*, p. 24.
9 *Irony*, p. 4; see also '*Alieniloquium*', p. 124.
10 Green does not mention Capella's definition, which does use the word *aliud* (p. 259). It is, however, no more than a passing reference.
11 Haidu, *Aesthetic Distance*, p. 18, thinks Pompeius' treatise is a transcription of classroom lectures. Holtz, 'Tradition', p. 50, shows how Pompeius is 'animé par des préoccupations pédagogiques'.
12 For other definitions, see Bede, *De schematibus* II.2.12; Hugh, *De grammatica*, line 2270, Gervase, *Ars poetica*, p. 155, Julian *De vitiis*, p. 80. See also Quintilian, *Institutio* VIII.6.54.
13 Knox, '*Ironia*', pp. 296–7.
14 'Faint praise', pp. 139–40.
15 See particularly Julian, *De vitiis*, pp. 80–3, and the examples of *ironia* given by Donatus, *Ars grammatica* III.6, Gervase, *Ars poetica*, p. 155, Hugh, *De grammatica*, line 2270; see also the gloss to Bede, *De schematibus* XII.2.12, and Bernard of Utrecht's *Commentum in Theodolum*, 99–106.
16 Translation from Benton, 'Clio and Venus', p. 37.
17 Gallo's translation, *Poetria Nova*, p. 37.

18 The first three examples I discuss are taken from Knox's thesis.
19 Peter's poem is number XII and Paul's number XIII in Neff's edition of Paul's poems. I quote stanza III of Paul's poem.
20 Godman, *Poetry*, pp. 9–10.
21 '*Ironia*', p. 40.
22 See lines 1011–12 and von Grauert's comments on pp. 8 and 106 of his edition. On glosses suggesting irony, see also Hunt, 'Irony', p. 98.
23 Duff's translation of lines 45–66.
24 'Lucan's invocation', *passim*.
25 *PSW*, IV, 1–4. Ménard, *Le Rire*, p. 448, goes so far as to argue that *gaber* means 'ironiser', but there is no evidence for this. On *gaber*, see also Knudson, 'Serments téméraires', and von Kraemer, 'Sémantique'.
26 On these lines, see *PSW*, IV, 3, and Chabaneau, 'Une nouvelle édition', p. 16, who attributes the meaning 'louer avec exaggération' to *gabar* here.
27 *Irony*, p. 9.
28 As Campbell, 'Irony', p. 300, points out, 'for at least the early part of the Middle Ages, allegory was the supremely ironic mode'.
29 Isidore, *Etymologiae* 1.37.27, Julian, *De vitiis*, p. 94, Hugh, *De grammatica*, lines 2281–3, Gervase, *Ars poetica*, p. 156. Haidu seems to have misunderstood this example (*Aesthetic Distance*, p. 16); it does not mean, as he thinks, 'You are lucky.' Bede discusses *charientismos*, *De schematibus* II.2.12, but he gives no example of the trope.
30 Knox, '*Ironia*', pp. 288–9.
31 *Aesthetic Distance*, p. 19. The vagueness in the definitions of this trope is striking when compared to the precision of definitions of other tropes.
32 That is to say, Donatus, Bede, Isidore, Julian, Hugh and Gervase. It is impossible to say whether later rhetoricians had read the *Institutio* themselves or whether they merely knew of it through Donatus. Given the widespread circulation of the *ad Herennium* in schools, it seems unlikely that these writers did not know of figures like *significatio*; one might conclude that they were omitted deliberately and that different types of figures were discussed in different types of manuals.
33 Green's article passes through seven stages, representing the seven main elements of his definition. The problems he discusses are opposition between literal and intended meaning (pp. 120–3), disparity between real and intended meaning (pp. 124–8), the existence of an initiated and an uninitiated audience (pp. 129–32), the ironist's intentions (pp. 132–8), incongruity (pp. 138–50), signals (pp. 150–6), the presentation of a situation as ironic (pp. 156–9). My discussion mirrors Green's in structure.
34 Marshall, 'Versification', pp. 56–7.
35 The humour and innuendo of this poem have frequently been discussed. See particularly Davis, 'A fuller reading', *passim*; Dronke, *Medieval Lyric*, pp. 110–11; Lejeune, 'L'extraordinaire insolence', p. 136; Nichols, '*Canso→conso*', p. 17; Rieger, 'Guillaume IX', pp. 444–8; Topsfield, *Troubadours*, p. 18. On the identification of Agnes and Arsen, see Goddard, 'The ladies', p. 158.
36 For example, Camproux, '*Faray un vers tot covinen*', *passim*, and Kertesz, 'A full reading', *passim*.
37 Muecke also discusses this song: *Irony and the ironic*, p. 61.
38 *Rhetoric*, p. 35.
39 Adams, *Sexual Vocabulary*, p. 12.
40 *Irony*, p. 2.
41 *L'Ironie*, p. 54; *Rhetoric*, p. 106.
42 See p. 168.

43 *Troubadours*, p. 15.
44 *Troubadours*, p. 15.
45 '*Canso→conso*', p. 18.
46 *L'Ironie*, pp. 59–60.
47 Example from Muecke, *Irony and the Ironic*, pp. 38–9.
48 'Communication', p. 35.
49 Muecke, *Irony*, p. 48.
50 For the best recent account of the conditions of performance and the music of the troubadour lyric, see Page, *Voices*, pp. 12–28.
51 'Communication', p. 37.
52 See Culler, *Structuralist Poetics*, p. 4, and *Signs*, p. ix.
53 *Irony and the ironic*, p. 101.
54 Although I do not regard myself as working rigidly according to a theoretical model, if my approach in this book does coincide with any modern critical theory it is with German reception theory. For a clear exposition in English of the main principles of reception theory, see Jauss, *Aesthetic of Reception*, and particularly p. 22; Meneghetti outlines the importance of reception theory to the study of the troubadours: see *Il pubblico*, pp. 13–37. On the other hand, deconstruction has much to teach the critic interested in irony about the infinitely varied games that can be played in language.
55 In my view Rossman's *Perspectives of Irony in Medieval French Literature* is unsatisfactory precisely because he defines irony linguistically and formally, arguing that it occurs whenever two opposite or incompatible words or terms are present together (p. 31).
56 See, respectively, Jeanroy, *Poésie lyrique*, II, 6; Köhler, 'No sai qui s'es', *passim*; Dronke, 'Guillaume IX', p. 328, and Milone, 'Il *vers*', pp. 138–41; Butturff, 'From cynicism to idealism', pp. 316–17; Lawner, 'Notes', p. 148; Limentani, *L'eccezione narrativa*, pp. 134–53; Mölk, *Trobar clus*, p. 41; Payen, *Le Prince d'Aquitaine*, pp. 87–92; Bezzola, *Les Origines*, II, 296; del Monte, '*En durmen sobre chevau*', p. 140; Topsfield, *Troubadours*, pp. 34–5, and Pasero, '*Devinalh*', p. 116.
57 *L'Ironie*, pp. 19 and 100.
58 *Troubadours*, p. 18.
59 '*Ironia*', pp. 61–2.
60 See 'Recognizing', pp. 14–15, and *Irony*, p. 24; Ménard, *Le Rire*, p. 271, also makes this point.
61 Green, *Irony*, p. 24, and Topsfield, *Troubadours*, p. 36, but see also below pp. 62–5 on this point.
62 *Irony and the Ironic*, p. 52.
63 Muecke, *Irony*, pp. 40–2, and *Compass*, pp. 104–5.
64 Muecke, *Irony*, pp. 27–9, and *Compass*, p. 102.
65 Muecke, *Irony*, p. 20, and *Compass*, pp. 159–81.
66 Muecke, *Irony*, p. 19, and *Compass*, p. 147.
67 'Irony', *passim*, and *The Well-Wrought Urn*, pp. 170–1; for reactions to Brooks's ideas on irony, see Crane, 'Critical monism', *passim*.
68 *Irony*, pp. 97–8. For expositions of the Robertsonian school's ideas, see Robertson himself ('Courtly love') and Benton, 'Clio and Venus'.
69 *Le Rire*, pp. 87–8 and 6.
70 The term 'courtly consensus' is Sarah Kay's.
71 For example, Bezzola, 'Guillaume IX'.
72 For example, Hoepffner, *Les Troubadours*, p. 21.
73 See Topsfield, *Troubadours*, pp. 11–41, for a stimulating exposition of Guilhem's

play on the notions of *sen* and *foudatz*. However, Topsfield only appears to consider this dichotomy important in Guilhem's burlesque poems and, like so many scholars, he considers his burlesque and 'serious' poems separately. On the importance of dialectic in courtly literature, see Hunt, 'Aristotle', *passim*.

74 For example, Rajna, 'Guglielmo, Conte di Poitiers: trovatore bifronte'.

75 On the importance of play in culture, see Huizinga, *Homo Ludens* and on play in poetry, *ibid.* pp. 141–58. It is significant that for Jankélévitch irony is 'une bonne conscience ludique'. On 'gamesmanship' and sincerity in troubadour poetry, see Manning, 'Game and earnest', *passim*.

76 Topsfield, *Troubadours*, p. 112.

77 In her stimulating and influential article 'L'élément théâtral', D. R. Sutherland argues that individual troubadours created for themselves stage personalities which they consciously, but artificially, adopted in their songs; she talks of the love lyric as 'un monologue dramatique' (p. 96) and describes Bernart's '*persona*' (p. 97). Bernart's presentation of himself in his poetry is undoubtedly contrived, but this does not necessarily make the personality that emerges from his songs artificial. On this problem generally, see Kay, 'Rhetoric', pp. 107–10.

78 Raimon Vidal, in his *Razos de trobar*, composed between 1190 and 1213, reproaches Bernart with inconsistency in this song (MS B, 451–60). Lazar, *Bernard*, p. 247, comments 'il semble y avoir une transition trop abrupte entre le contenu des strophes I–IV et V'.

2. MARCABRU

1 *Troubadours*, pp. 8–54, and poems XXV, 23–4, XXXVII, 7–12, XL, 5–7, XLIV, 57–9.

2 Compare John 1:4–9.

3 Compare Guilhem's *Ben vueill* (VI), 57–60. Whereas for Guilhem the gambling image indicates excitement, for Marcabru it evokes immorality.

4 Lewent, 'Beiträge', p. 318.

5 Compare Rieger, 'Dons Costans', p. 448, and Paterson, *Troubadours*, p. 18, note 2, who argue that *costans* means 'inconstant' or a 'vacillating man'. Costans as a proper name is also attested in the poetry of Raimbaut d'Aurenga and Giraut de Borneil: see Chambers, *Proper Names*, p. 101. Raimbaut d'Aurenga's use of the name Costanza to designate an unfaithful wife (XXII, 44) is probably comparable to Marcabru's use of the masculine form as an ironic *senhal*.

6 Harvey, 'Satirical use', pp. 29–33. On the use of *sidons* and *midons* generally, see Cropp, *Vocabulaire*, pp. 27–37, and Hackett, 'Le problème', *passim*; Marcabru's ironic use of *sidons* led both scholars to suggest that he did not use the term with its usual meaning, but if he is using it satirically the problem posed by its meaning is resolved. On the significance of the white shirt in *Bel m'es*, see Gaunt, 'Did Marcabru . . .?', *passim*.

7 On *joven* generally, see Cropp, *Vocabulaire*, pp. 413–21, and Köhler, 'Sens et fonction', *passim*.

8 Nelson, 'Animal imagery', p. 53.

9 Compare V, 1–6, VII, 25–40, IX, 21–3, XI, 55–6, and so on.

10 Nelson, 'Animal imagery', p. 52.

11 Roncaglia, 'I due sirventesi', p. 183. On poem XXIII, see also Mölk, *Trobar clus*, p. 92, who comments that Marcabru's praise of Alfonso is 'hardly convincing'.

12 Compare Morawski, *Proverbes*, 1774, 'que sires done et sers ploure, ce sont lermes perdues'. The proverb in stanza VI is unattested in the Middle Ages, but see Dejeanne, *Poésies complètes*, p. 230, 'ce proberbe existe encore en Bigorre: en

gourgo bantado, yames nat péch, "en étang vanté, jamais aucun poisson"'. On Marcabru's use of proverbs in general, see Goddard, 'Marcabru', *passim.*

13 See the Appendix on the possible ambiguities here.

14 This poem makes Roncaglia's hypothesis ('Due schede', p. 130) that Marcabru stayed continuously in Spain from 1134 until at least 1143 highly unlikely. For other objections to Roncaglia, see Gaunt and Harvey, 'Text and context', pp. 86–95.

15 *Ad Herennium* IV.34.45; Quintilian, *Institutio* VI.3.29, VIII.3.38–9, VIII.3.47; see also Adams, *Sexual Vocabulary,* p. 214.

16 Adams, *Sexual Vocabulary,* p. 3, and for these problems discussed in relation to medieval literature, see Pearcy, 'Modes of signification', pp. 173–4 and 181; Stempel, 'Mittelalterliche Obszönität', pp. 204–5, and Gaunt, 'Pour une esthétique', forthcoming.

17 *Les Fabliaux,* p. 220. For objections to Nykrog, see Stempel, 'Mittelalterliche Obszönität', p. 190.

18 Paden, '*Utrum copularentur*', p. 73; Stempel, 'Mittelalterliche Obszönität', p. 191.

19 For examples, see Nykrog, *Les Fabliaux,* p. 217, and Stempel, 'Mittelalterliche Obszönität', p. 192.

20 Muscatine, 'Courtly literature', pp. 6–7.

21 *Sexual Vocabulary,* pp. 215–17.

22 On obscene innuendo and eroticism, see Paden, '*Utrum copularentur*', pp. 72–3; on obscenity and pornography, see Cooke, 'Pornography', *passim,* and, for example, poems XXXIV and XXXVI in Bec, *Burlesque*; on obscenity in burlesque or scatological poetry, see Bec, *Burlesque,* pp. 7–22; on obscenity in moralizing texts, see Stempel, 'Mittelalterliche Obszönität', pp. 193–7.

23 *Pel,* 'scrotum' (II, 12), *coa,* 'penis' (V, 24, XVIII, 36, XXXVI, 21, XXXVIII, 32), *bosin,* 'testicles' (XIIbis, 27), *verga,* 'penis' (XVIII, 39), *vieg,* 'penis' (XVIII, stanza XVIII in C), *con,* 'vagina' (IV, 34, XI, 49, XVII, 33, XVIII, stanza XVIII in C, XXIV, 22, XLI, 35, XLII, 17), *penchinill,* 'pubic' (XXXVIII, 27), *conin* (<*con,* XIIbis, 33, XVII, 42, XXXI, 21), *borsa,* 'scrotum' (XXXVII, 17) and *fotre,* 'to fuck' (XXIV, 20).

24 Adams, *Sexual Vocabulary,* pp. 14, 19–22, 157–9.

25 On the homosocial bonding and the exclusion of women implicit in Marcabru's representation of sex, see Gaunt, 'Poetry of exclusion', forthcoming.

26 For door or passage metaphors, see XXIV, 19, and XXV, 60–2; for hole metaphors, XIIbis, 14 and 20; for eating and drinking metaphors, II, 13, XVI, 18, XVIII, 29–30, XXIV, 11–12; for scratching and rubbing metaphors, IV, 46, XI, 49; for holding and squeezing metaphors, XI, 64.

27 Compare also VIII, 8, 11–15, XVIII, 13–18, XXXI, 19–22, XL, 21, 28.

28 Lawner, 'Marcabrun', p. 512, suggests that *alos* (line 43) is a metaphor for the vagina. Thiolier-Méjean, *Poésies satiriques,* p. 472, note 1, misses the point of the metaphor: '*alos* désigne l'alleu, le bien héréditaire, tandis que le fief est un bien concédé, mais cette différence n'apporte rien ici'.

29 'Per un'edizione', p. 49. St Privat is not otherwise alluded to by the troubadours: see Wiacek, *Lexique,* p. 163.

30 On *privat,* see Garin lo Brun, *Ensenhamen a la domna,* lines 207–14. On *abat* as an obscene metaphor, see also pp. 157–8, and Gaunt, 'Pour une esthétique', forthcoming.

31 'Satirical use', pp. 30–1.

32 Pollina, '*Si cum Marcabrus*', p. 96.

33 '*Lo vers comenssa*', pp. 23–5. See also Lewent, 'Beiträge', p. 437, and Appel, 'Zu Marcabru', p. 443, note 2. Ricketts compares the *senhal* Chaut-Morsel to Bernart de Venzac, V, 15–19.

Et adoncs planh e s'esmaia
aisselh qui s'apelha drut,
e selh qui l'a fag cornut
a·l donat morsel querrum,
que l'estrangla ans que·l traia.

He comments that 'on est tenté de voir dans le *morsel* le membre viril que l'amant "donne" plus exactment à la femme de l'autre, et ce mari cornard trouve difficile de l'avaler' (p. 24). Note that for Bernart, as in Marcabru, II, XI and XVI, the object of the cuckolder's sexual act is the woman's husband, not the woman herself.

34 On oral sex, see Adams, *Sexual Vocabulary*, pp. 125–8, and compare Marcabru, XVIII, 25–30, XXIV, 10–12, and XXXII, 73–81; on comparisons with animals, see Adams, *Sexual Vocabulary*, p. 205; Nelson, 'Animal imagery', p. 55, and compare XVIII, 49–51, XXXI, 46–9; on homosexuality, see Ménard, *Le Rire*, p. 695, and compare XXXII, 78–81. Guilhem de Berguedà clearly intends to outrage when he accuses the Archbishop of Tarragona of sodomy (VII, 29–35).

35 Compare Pearcy, 'Pornography', pp. 138–9, who comments on pornographic elements in the *fabliaux* of the kind described here, and see also Gaunt, 'Pour une esthétique', forthcoming.

36 'Ironia', pp. 61–2, and 'Recognizing', pp. 14–15.

37 Roncaglia, 'Al departir', pp. 25–7, says that these towns may have been situated in the Garonne, or near Montpellier, or in the Dordogne. Wiacek, *Lexique*, pp. 104 and 166, shows similar uncertainty as to their identification. The difficulty scholars have had in identifying these towns indicates that they were small and insignificant.

38 Probably Guerau de Cabrieira, the author of the *ensenhamen Cabra juglar*: see Pirot, *Recherches*, pp. 146–7.

39 'Doas cuidas', pp. 27–8; see also Olson, 'Marcabru's psychomachy', p. 19.

40 Marshall, 'Doas cuidas', p. 32, note 4, suggests that the meaning he posits for *cuidar* in Occitan is also frequent for OF *cuidier*, citing the examples given by *TL*, II, 1128–31, and *FEW*, II, 838–42, to support his hypothesis. In fact, it would seem that *cuidier* acts as a signal to irony in many of these French examples. For *cuidier* used affirmatively, see Godefroy, II, 395.

41 For *cuidar* as a signal to irony, see I, 10, V, 25, VI, 15, VIII, 9, XV, 16, XVI, 4, XVIII, 55, XIX, 16, 29, 31, 33, 46, 61, XX, 39, XXII, 33, XXIII, 24, XXV, 4, XXVI, 37, XXIX, 30, XXX, 27, XXXIX, 55, XL, 14, XLIV, 7. For *cuidar* used negatively to deny a proposition, see II, 26, VI, 41, XIIbis, 21, XVII, 3. Only in XXXIII, 16, would Marcabru appear to be affirming a proposition with *cuidar*.

42 See II, 21, and I, 36–37, and Olson, 'Marcabru's psychomachy', p. 19.

43 *Troubadours*, pp. 40–1, though this is not the only interpretation. Compare Roncaglia, 'Trobar clus', pp. 49–55, and 'Riflessi', pp. 16–20, who links Marcabru's ideas on nature to those of other medieval writers, particularly Hugh of St Victor and William of St Thierry, and Köhler, *Sociologia*, pp. 260–1, who offers a sociological interpretation.

44 Compare XXXI, 46–52, and XXX, 78–84. The images in stanza II may have sources in Latin poetry: see Scheludko, 'Zur Geschichte', pp. 269 and 282; Paterson, *Troubadours*, pp. 35–9, and Goddard, 'The early troubadours', pp. 143–56.

45 Scheludko, 'Zur Geschichte', *passim*, and Press, 'La strophe printanière', *passim*.

46 On the importance of creating an individual stage personality, see Sutherland, 'L'élément théâtral', *passim*; on the possibility that a troubadour's stage personality might have coincided with his own, see Kay, 'Rhetoric', p. 110. Compare Pickens, 'Jaufré Rudel', p. 324, who argues that the troubadours intended their

poems to be sung, adapted and rewritten by others. The troubadours' own comments belie Pickens's hypothesis: see, for example, Marcabru, IX, 1–4.

47 'Si cum Marcabrus', p. 72.

48 Marcabru names himself twenty-two times in forty-two poems (counting poem VI only once). A table comparing this with how many times other troubadours name themselves shows how remarkable Marcabru is in this respect:

Troubadour	Occurrences of name	Number of poems
Arnaut Daniel	15	18
Bernart de Ventadorn	4	45
Bernart Marti	1	9
Cercamon	3	9
Guilhem IX	0	11
Jaufre Rudel	0	7
Marcabru	22	42
Peire d'Alvernha	4	19
Peire Rogier	2	9
Raimbaut d'Aurenga	3	39

Marcabru clearly wished to associate his name with his work. Only Arnaut Daniel names himself more frequently than Marcabru; this is probably because of his pride in his work. It is interesting in this respect that Marcabru is probably a 'stage name'. Although he goes to great lengths to distinguish his work from that of other troubadours, Marcabru in fact conceals his identity.

49 Audric del Vilar and Ugo Catola both call Marcabru a joglar (VI, 44, and XX, 42). In poems IV and IX he is clearly searching for a patron. Marcabru's social origins and status are obscure; we only have the indications he himself gives in his texts and his name is assumed. However, recent research indicates that Marcabru may have been a younger son from a family of the minor nobility and that he was very probably some kind of paid courtier or administrator with a clerical education. See Pirot, 'L'idéologie', p. 318; Harvey, Marcabru, pp. 12–18, and Goddard, 'The early troubadours', pp. 66–72. This, of course, does not preclude his also being a joglar.

50 Roncaglia identifies Ugo Catola with a knight to whom a letter by Peter the Venerable was addressed between 1134 and 1135 and he dates the tenso c. 1133: see 'La tenzone', pp. 208–13. Ugo Catola may be the author of the two stanzas of a comjat, preserved in D^a only, edited by Dejeanne, Poésies complètes, pp. 219–20. Following Franz (Marcabru, p. 24), Tortoreto ('Cercamon', pp. 79–84) has recently argued on stylistic grounds that the tenso is not genuine, but the work of Marcabru alone. She does not consider the possibility that Ugo may be deliberately imitating Marcabru. All other scholars accept this as a genuine tenso.

51 Roncaglia, 'La tenzone', p. 289.

52 On Amics Marchabrun, see also Meneghetti, Il pubblico, pp. 149–56. She persuasively argues that the two poets' debating technique is influenced by Abelard's Sic et non (PL, CLXXVIII, 1339–610; see particularly 1341–9), and that the whole poem is characterized by jongleuresque insults.

53 Similar playfulness and complicity underpin Marcabru's exchange with Audric del Vilar (XX/XXbis), though all scholars assume their apparent animosity is genuine: see particularly Appel, 'Zu Marcabru', pp. 423–5; Bertoni, 'Due note', p. 650; Chambers, 'D'aisso lau Dieu', passim; Gruber, Dialektik, p. 174; Lewent, 'Beiträge', p. 427; de Riquer, Los trovadores, I, 179; Spanke, Marcabrustudien, pp. 59–60; Thiolier-Méjean, Poésies satiriques, pp. 430 and 489.

54 On the dating of the poem, see Boissonnade, 'Les personnages', pp. 228–9, and Roncaglia, '*Cortesamen*', p. 960. On Marcabru's style in the poem, see Hoepffner, *Les Troubadours*, p. 33; Pollmann, *Trobar clus*, p. 27; Topsfield, *Troubadours*, pp. 57–8.

55 See Harvey, *Marcabru*, pp. 122–39. On Marcabru and Cercamon, see Kastner, 'Marcabrun', *passim*, and Roncaglia, '*Lo vers comens*', pp. 25–7, who reject the assertion of the *vida* in *A* that Marcabru was Cercamon's pupil and argue that the reverse is more likely to have been true. Compare Tortoreto, 'Cercamon', *passim*, who attempts to show that the *vida* may have been correct; her hypothesis exaggerates the importance of Cercamon both in the tradition in general and in relation to Marcabru. See also Meneghetti, *Il pubblico*, pp. 153–4, note 127.

56 The poem is v in Tortoreto's edition and these are lines 36–42, but I quote from Marshall's edition of the poem and follow his interpretation: see 'Tradition', pp. 102–3 and 106–7. I do not intend to address myself to the notorious problems posed by the third line of the stanza. However, if a reading of the name Tristan is accepted, Cercamon is citing him as an example of someone who entered the triangle he condemns and suffered the consequences; his treatment of the Tristan legend would thus be close to Marcabru's: see Gaunt, 'Did Marcabru...?', *passim*. For a full bibliography of the controversy that raged over the interpretation of the third line of the stanza, see Tortoreto, *Cercamon*, pp. 149–52.

57 Lejeune, 'L'allusion', pp. 177–80, and Marshall, 'Tradition', p. 99.

58 Kelly, *Eleanor of Aquitaine*, pp. 60–3. See also Runciman, *History of the Crusades*, II, 278–89, and Harvey, *Marcabru*, pp. 132–4.

59 Harvey, *Marcabru*, pp. 135–9.

60 'Una *vida* pericolosa', pp. 159–60; see also Harvey's comments, *Marcabru*, p. 139. My interpretation nevertheless differs from Meneghetti's. She argues that Marcabru is attacking Jaufre for ironizing at the expense of *fin'amor* and consequently, for deviating from the true ideal. This rests on the assumption, made also by Topsfield, *Troubadours*, pp. 56–8, that the two poets had the same conception of *fin'amor*. Throughout his corpus Marcabru questions the meaning of words like *amor, joi* and *joven*, intimating through irony that some troubadours, like Jaufre, use them to mask immoral activities, thus debasing their true meaning. Is not Marcabru's point in *Cortesamen* that he and Jaufre do not have the same understanding of the term *fin'amor*? I would also question Meneghetti's use of the word irony to describe Jaufre's presentation of love; whilst I agree with her that it is as paradoxical as Guilhem IX's, the presentation of love would seem to be unequivocal in Jaufre's poetry, even if it is not in critical literature devoted to him. On my view of Jaufre's attitude to love, see pp. 100–2.

61 For *cortes* used positively, see IX, 32, XV, 18, XL, 9. *Cortes* may be used ironically in XXX, 32 and 80, and XXXIV, 43.

62 Bernart's *vida* gives a romanticized version of his relationship with Eleanor, but it is generally accepted that she was his patroness: see Appel, *Bernart von Ventadorn*, pp. xxxiv–viii, and de Riquer, *Los trovadores*, I, 343.

3. BERNART MARTI

1 'Le troubadour', pp. 149–50. Hoepffner ('Le troubadour', p. 130), Köhler (*Sociologia*, p. 271) and Mölk (*Trobar clus*, p. 114) consider Bernart a moralist as severe as Marcabru; Appel (*Bernart von Ventadorn*, p. lxvi), Roncaglia ('*Trobar clus*', p. 43) and di Girolamo ('*Trobar clus*', pp. 21–2) consider him as one of the troubadours Marcabru attacked. Other scholars take a middle line, suggesting that he shared

Marcabru's basic standpoint, but had a more pragmatic view of society: see Jeanroy, *Poésie lyriques* II, 31, and de Riquer, *Los trovadores*, I, 247.

2 The attribution of *Belha m'es la flors d'aguilen* (PC 323.5) to Bernart is disputed. Hoepffner argues that it is by Bernart, but prints it in an appendix; Beggiato, rather cavalierly, does not discuss the problem at all. The poem is attributed to Peire d'Alvernha (an attribution which is universally rejected) in *ABDEIKNN²*, to Marcabru in C and to Bernart in the register of C and in R. The poem bears little resemblance to Bernart's work and I do not consider it to be by him. The text is, however, extremely interesting, as it may well be by a contemporary of Marcabru, if not by Marcabru himself.

3 See, for example, I, 17. Hoepffner's corrections to the MSS are often heavy-handed and although Beggiato's edition has the advantage of a complete and accurate glossary, there are several unfortunate misprints (for example, IV, 41, VI, 11), several omissions from the variants (for example, I, 24, III, 63, IV, 13, 29, and so on) and some surprising lacunae in the critical apparatus and notes which make it difficult to ascertain why he has edited as he has.

4 On *mezura* see Wettstein, *Mezura*, particularly p. 56 on the 'domaine social'.

5 Sutherland, 'The love meditation', p. 165.

6 For Cropp, *Le Vocabulaire*, p. 359, *ben* in line 43 'se constitue d'un rire, d'une conversation, de tout ce qui est bon à mettre fin aux souffrances', but it would seem more appropriate to give the line a less innocent reading.

7 Jankélévitch, *L'Ironie*, p. 100. Beggiato offers a different view. He argues that *Amar dei* is a reply to Peire Rogier's *Al pareyssen* (1) and points to several indicators of intertextuality. Beggiato's contention is quite valid, but, as he himself points out, Bernart's poem is much more sophisticated than Peire's, which is of no interest in itself. For Beggiato, *Amar dei* represents an attempt to adopt an ideological position, which is undermined by irony and cynicism; he does not appear to consider the poem introspective. See *Il trovatore*, pp. 24–6.

8 'Le troubadour', p. 127; 'évidemment, ces sentiments sont discutables et l'on aimerait en connaître le degré de la sincérité'.

9 Paterson, *Troubadours*, pp. 37–40.

10 See, respectively, Köhler, *Sociologia*, pp. 23–4; Sutherland, 'L'élément théâtral', pp. 96–7, and Zumthor, *Essai*, p. 192.

11 'Rhetoric', p. 110. See also 'La notion de personnalité', p. 181.

12 Topsfield, *Troubadours*, p. 61, and Payen, 'Bernart', pp. 39–40, offer different interpretations of this stanza.

13 Paterson, *Troubadours*, pp. 58–74.

14 Aubailly, *Monologue*, II, 393–5.

15 Hoepffner, 'Le troubadour', p. 124; Roncaglia, 'Trobar clus', pp. 39–44, and Payen, 'Bernart', pp. 37–8. See also Beggiato, *Il trovatore*, p. 31, who interprets stanza IV as 'una soluzione paradossale ed ironica'.

16 On Bernart and the triangular nature of *fin'amor*, see Roncaglia, 'Trobar clus', p. 41. Both Marcabru and Bernart condemn liars, money-grabbers, cheating and promiscuity, and clearly believe the poet to have a moral responsibility towards society. Bernart cites Marcabru once by name (IX, 26), makes one direct intertextual reference to Marcabru's *pastorela* (III, 27) and may well intend III, 10–15 to be understood as an intertextual reference to Marcabru's *Cortesamen* (XV), 25–30. Bernart was a contemporary of Peire d'Alvernha, who may well have been active as a poet as early as 1147, so it is certainly possible that he was also a contemporary of Marcabru.

17 *Il trovatore*, p. 40.

1 Paterson, *Troubadours*, pp. 54–5.
2 Topsfield, *Troubadours*, p. 162.
3 Paterson, *Troubadours*, pp. 69–74.
4 See, for example, his *Be m'es plazens* (VIII) and the comments of Paterson, *Troubadours*, p. 82.
5 *Los trovadores*, I, 312.
6 It is not within the scope of this book to analyse Peire's use of metaphor and ambiguity. See Paterson, *Troubadours*, pp. 77–85; Topsfield, *Troubadours*, pp. 174–8, and Köhler, *Sociologia*, p. 176.
7 See V, 9, 11, 57, VII, 3, VIII, 56, X, 13, XI, 2, XIV, 1, 10. According to Schutz, 'Some Provençal words', p. 514, '*sen* is good sense, judgement, *saber* wisdom of a higher kind, in which learning should be a component'.
8 See Zenker, *Peire*, p. 698, and Pollmann, *Trobar clus*, p. 28.
9 *Troubadours*, pp. 168–9.
10 *Troubadours*, p. 58. See also '*Jois*', p. 292.
11 'Quelques strophes', pp. 81–2. Beltrami, 'La canzone', p. 99 also interprets the stanza in this way.
12 Skårup, 'Quelques strophes', p. 80. Chiarini also understands lines 31–2 in this way, but he does not see the syntactic link between lines 29 and 31, nor does he understand line 30 as an interjection. See *Il canzoniere*, p. 102.
13 See Runciman, *Crusades*, II, 247–63, on the Second Crusade; on Jaufre's participation, see de Riquer, *Los trovadores*, I, 149.
14 By the end of 1150 the Second Crusade had disintegrated: see Runciman, *Crusades*, II, 286–8. Peire's *rossinhol* poem was composed by 1149: see Lejeune, 'Thèmes communs', pp. 292–8; Pirot, *Recherches*, pp. 148–9, and de Riquer, *Los trovadores*, I, 316. My dating of *Al dessebrar* undermines the theory that there is a progression in Peire's work from worldly to spiritual concerns; it is not, however, the only stumbling block, as poem III, one of Peire's most courtly compositions, dates from after 1168: see Lecoy, '*Peire*', p. 387, and de Riquer, *Los trovadores*, I, 312.
15 For this view of Jaufre's poetry, see Frank, 'Distant love', and Lefèvre, 'Jaufre'; it is taken up in a somewhat different form by Topsfield, *Troubadours*, p. 68.
16 As Topsfield, *Troubadours*, pp. 56–7, contends, Marcabru, VII, 9–24 echo both *Al dessebrar* and Jaufre Rudel and may well represent an intervention in the debate between Peire and Jaufre. He believes that the three poets share the same conception of *fin'amor*, but I argue elsewhere that both Peire and Marcabru are criticizing Jaufre: see my '*Peire*', pp. 101–3, which also contains a shorter exposition (in French) of my view of *Al dessebrar*.
17 Köhler, *Sociologia*, p. 174; Mölk, *Trobar clus*, p. 102; de Riquer, *Los trovadores*, I, 321; Topsfield, *Troubadours*, p. 178.
18 *Peire*, pp. 676–7; see also de Riquer, *Los trovadores*, I, 311.
19 Compare Topsfield, *Troubadours*, p. 180.
20 Roncaglia, '*Trobar clus*', pp. 21–6; Marcabru also refers to Alfonso in poems IX and XI.
21 *Los trovadores*, I, 321.
22 See Harvey, 'Spanish *Lavador*', *passim*.
23 Marcabru plays on *faillir* in a similar way in poem XXIII: see above, pp. 49–50.

24 Compare also O F: 'la septime color est apelee demonstrance por ce que li parleres dit et demonstre ses proprietez et les enseignes d'une chose ou d'un home, por achoison de prover aucune chose qui aparteigne a sa matiere' (*TL*, ii, 1389, *Brun. Lat.*, 488).

25 Topsfield, *Troubadours*, pp. 119–20, and 'Natural fool', *passim*, argues that lines 36–42 are a riposte to Bernart de Ventadorn, xv, 29–35, which he thinks are an attack on Marcabru. This hypothesis is somewhat tenuous.

26 *Peire*, p. 147.

27 De Riquer, *Los trovadores*, i, 311–12.

28 *Peire*, p. 147.

29 On Peire's knowledge of rhetoric, see Paterson, *Troubadours*, pp. 85–6.

30 *Bernart*, p. lxix, and *Peire*, p. 48.

31 See Lejeune, 'Thèmes communs', pp. 289–92 (p. 291 for quotation); Mölk, *Trobar clus*, p. 103, and Gruber, *Dialektik*, pp. 196–8.

32 'Thèmes communs', p. 290.

33 'Thèmes communs', p. 291.

34 The attribution of the *tenso* to Peire d'Alvernha is a tradition of modern criticism, but has no basis in the manuscripts; it is questioned by Marshall, 'Dialogues', p. 40.

35 Poems ix, x, xxiii, xxix, xxxiii, xxxix, xl, xlv. In poem xlv the motif is slightly different: hearing the bird's rejoicing makes the poet's suffering unbearable.

36 For example, stanza ii, where Bernart says he would rather sleep than listen to the nightingale.

37 'The background', p. 19.

38 Roncaglia, 'Due postille', pp. 72–5, argues that the Bernart de Saissac of stanza ix is Bernart Marti. If this identification is correct, there is ironic intertextual play in this stanza; compare Bernart Marti, vii, 7–14, and on this point, see Beggiato, *Il trovatore*, pp. 18–19.

39 I have not been able to consult Roncaglia's edition of the text; his interpretation is reported by de Riquer, *Los trovadores*, i, 335, and Beggiato, 'Per un' edizione', p. 68.

5. RAIMBAUT D'AURENGA

1 Guilhem and Jaufre Rudel, both amateur poets, left eleven and seven poems respectively; compare Marcabru's forty-two poems and Bernart de Ventadorn's forty-four.

2 De Riquer, *Los trovadores*, i, 418.

3 *Troubadours*, pp. 147 and 185.

4 Paterson, *Troubadours*, pp. 145–7. Compare Köhler, *Trobadorlyrik*, pp. 142–3; Milone, 'Il *vers*', p. 124, and Mölk, *Trobar clus*, pp. 116–20. On the identification of the *senhal* Linhaure with Raimbaut in the *tenso* Era·m platz, see Delbouille, 'Les senhals', pp. 59–64.

5 'Rhetoric', pp. 123–9.

6 *Trobadorlyrik*, p. 143.

7 Gruber, *Dialektik*, pp. 218–19, and Paterson, *Troubadours*, p. 168. Compare Jeanroy, *Poésie lyrique*, ii, 43; Mölk, *Trobar clus*, p. 129; Pollmann, *Trobar clus*, p. 35.

8 On *Cars, douz*, see Paterson, *Troubadours*, pp. 147–56, and on the ribald *Ar vei, ibid.*, pp. 156–62.

9 See Paterson, *Troubadours*, pp. 213–20, on the rarity of the rhymes, and p. 227 on the rhyme scheme.

10 On derivative rhymes as a *clus* technique, see Shapiro, '*Entrebescar*', p. 362.
11 *Trobar clus*, p. 127, and *Troubadours*, p. 164. On *laner*, see Evans, *Lanier*, particularly p. 48.
12 On Raimbaut and Giraut, see Delbouille, 'Les *senhals*', pp. 59–64. Peire Rogier addresses a poem to Raimbaut (VIII), whose reply survives (VI). On Raimbaut and Bernart de Ventadorn, see Delbouille, 'Les *senhals*', pp. 64–72; di Girolamo, 'Tristano', *passim*, and Roncaglia, 'Carestia', *passim*. If Raimbaut is the En Raembautz of Peire d'Alvernha's satire, he clearly knew Peire. Gaucelm Faidit composed a cycle of songs addressed to one Linhaure, who may be identifiable with Raimbaut: see de Riquer, *Los trovadores*, II, 756. On Raimbaut and Chrétien, see Roncaglia, 'Carestia', *passim*.
13 See the previous note and Gruber, *Dialektik*, pp. 210–19.
14 *Troubadours*, p. 177, note 1.
15 The *envoi* is missing in *D E I K M N R Sa*; it is preserved in *A C Lf*.
16 'Raimbaut', p. 400, and *Jongleurs*, p. iv.
17 On the dating of *Bel m'es*, see Frank, 'La plus ancienne allusion', *passim*; on the relationship between *Bel m'es* and Alegret's *Ara pareisson*, see Mölk, *Trobar clus*, p. 92, and de Riquer, *Los trovadores*, I, 236; on the criticism of Alegret in *Bel m'es*, see Paterson, *Troubadours*, p. 40, and Gaunt, 'Did Marcabru . . .?', p. 110. Although the attribution of *Bel m'es* to Marcabru is uncontroversial amongst modern scholars, the manuscript attributions are far from conclusive: the table of C and Ra attribute the poem to Alegret, C and the table of M to Marcabru, and M attributes it to Raimbaut d'Aurenga. I can see no grounds for attributing *Bel m'es* to either Alegret or Raimbaut, but clearly my interpretation of the poem would need revision if the poem were not by Marcabru.
18 De Riquer, *Los trovadores*, I, 343–4.
19 I do not count the attributions of *Bel m'es* to Alegret in *CRa*. Chambers, *Proper Names*, p. 42, lists the three occurrences as separate people but with no comment. Paden, 'The role of the *joglar*', p. 100, only lists the occurrence in Bernart and so presumably assumes the three occurrences do not designate the same person: in note 6 (p. 107) he implies that he does not list *joglars* also known as troubadours.
20 *Raimbaut*, p. 194.
21 'Raimbaut', p. 400.
22 Alegret's two poems are in *C M*; he is named by Bernart in *A C Lf* and by Marcabru in *C M Ra*; *C Ra* attribute *Bel m'es* to him (C in the table only). Thus, of the manuscripts to transmit *Als durs*, *Aa* knew Alegret's name only through one mention in another troubadour's song (and in the case of *a* through an attribution), C through an attribution, one song by him and Bernart and Marcabru's poems, and *I K N²* did not know his name. It is scarcely a well-known name.
23 'Raimbaut', p. 400. Pattison also notes the possibility of Alegrat/Alegrar being Alegret.
24 Various troubadours are known to have taken the cloth in later life: apart from the obvious examples of Peire d'Alvernha (a canon according to Bernart Marti, V, 31–5) and the Monk of Montaudon, respective *vidas* tell us that Bernart de Ventadorn, Bertran de Born and Raimon de Miraval entered religious orders. Folquet de Marselha became a bishop.
25 Poems I, II, IV, all of which he dates at the beginning of Raimbaut's career (II and IV on stylistic grounds alone): see *Raimbaut*, p. 45.
26 Paterson, *Troubadours*, p. 214, records only two other occurrences of the rhyme (both in Marcabru) in her corpus of six major troubadours.
27 On *cortes ufaniers*, see Topsfield, *Troubadours*, p. 148, 'one who has the veneer of courtliness'.

28 The 'white shirt' in *Bel m'es* may be a reference to an episode of the Tristan legend: see Gaunt, 'Did Marcabru . . .?', *passim*.

29 On *Non chant*, see Roncaglia, 'Carestia', *passim*, and di Girolamo, 'Tristano', *passim*; on *Pos trobars plans*, see Milone, 'Raimbaut', pp. 10–17; on *Escotatz*, see Köhler, 'No sai qui s'es', *passim*.

30 Compare Köhler, *Trobadorlyrik*, p. 112, and Milone, 'Il vers', p. 124.

31 Bernart Marti, III, 10–15, Jaufre Rudel, II, 17–18, and Peire d'Alvernha, IX, 45–48. On this question in general, see Paden, 'The troubadour's lady', and Press, 'The adulterous nature', who query the assumption that the troubadour's lady is always married.

32 There is, however, a *trouvère* lyric, *Douce dame*, by an otherwise unknown poet, Jacques d'Autun, in which the lover's address is clearly to the poet's wife: see Woledge, *French Verse*, pp. 158–60.

33 De Riquer, *Los trovadores*, I, 439, suggests that the poem is imbued with 'una leve y sutil ironía', but he passes no comment on lines 47–8 and refers to the poet's *dama*. Paden, 'The troubadour's lady', p. 43, comments that Raimbaut 'curses himself for taking a haughty wife', but he does not consider the poem ironic for he concludes that it 'also has a certain chivalrous appeal'.

34 De Riquer, *Los trovadores*, II, 632, and Gruber, *Dialektik*, pp. 160–2. The second stanza of Arnaut's poem begins 'Non sui marritz', which both scholars take to mean 'I am not unhappy'; however, *marritz* could also mean 'husband'. Perhaps Arnaut is playing on Raimbaut's poem in more ways than have been realized.

35 For example, for Pattison, *Raimbaut*, p. 45, XX, XXI, XXIV, XXVII, XXXII, XXXVI are *gaps*.

36 Fechner, 'Zum *gap*', particularly p. 22; Köhler, '*Gabar e rire*', *passim*; Milone, 'Raimbaut', *passim*, 'L'"amors enversa"', *passim*, and 'Retorica', *passim*; the quotation is from 'Raimbaut', p. 25.

37 Milone, 'L'"amors enversa"', pp. 60–1; Topsfield, *Troubadours*, pp. 146–7. Rivers, 'Raimbaut', p. 17, makes the same point, but misses much of the humour in the poem; de Riquer, *Los trovadores*, I, 424, considers the poem an example of *foudatz*.

38 'Raimbaut', p. 25.

39 Poems IX, XI, XIII, XXVII.

40 For Topsfield, *Troubadours*, p. 286, note 6, Raimbaut's *gaug entier* may represent a parody of Peire d'Alvernha's notion of *jois entiers*. The poem is also interesting in relation to the *senhal* Linhaure, used by Giraut de Borneil to designate Raimbaut, for the fictional figure Linhaure was castrated by jealous husbands: see de Riquer, *Los trovadores*, I, 420.

41 *Troubadours*, p. 157. Compare Milone, 'L'"amors enversa"', pp. 46–7, who finds more indications in the poem that Raimbaut suffered from a castration complex. For a stimulating commentary on *Ar resplan*, see Shapiro, '*Entrebescar*', pp. 366–7.

6. GIRAUT DE BORNEIL

1 Giraut's most recent editor, Ruth Sharman, retains the term *canso-sirventes* for poems XL–LI.

2 See *De vulgari eloquentia*, II, ii, and *Purgatorio*, XXVI, 115–20; Paterson, *Troubadours*, p. 144, and de Riquer, *Los trovadores*, I, 473, offer typical modern reactions to Giraut's work.

3 Jeanroy, *Poésie lyrique*, II, 55; Panvini, *Giraldo*, pp. 100–2; Salverda de Grave, *Observations*, p. 16. Paterson gives the most comprehensive account of Giraut's

knowledge of rhetoric (*Troubadours*, pp. 88–144). Even Giraut depicts himself as 'bookish': see XXXIX, 61–70.

4 Sharman, 'Giraut', p. 74.

5 *Cansos*, p. 191.

6 One notable exception is *Be m'an perdut* (XII), see above, pp. 35–8.

7 Based upon § 5 of his *vida*, the theory that Giraut may have been a teacher of rhetoric is upheld by Kolsen, *Sämtliche Lieder*, II, 78; Panvini, *Giraldo*, pp. 100–2, and de Riquer, *Los trovadores*, I, 467.

8 *Cansos*, p. 75.

9 *Cansos*, p. 220.

10 Compare Folquet de Marselha, I, 51–4, and see Morawski, *Proverbes*, 1039.

11 Levy gives 'besogne', 'affaire', 'presse', 'mêlée', 'fournée' among the possible meanings of *cocha*, or *coita* (*PD*), as it might also be written. Not only are all these senses apt for erotic metaphors, but the word is also clearly related to *coit*.

12 *PSW*, VII, 152–3, and *Cansos*, p. 174.

13 Given the use of the word *essaj* in line 66, it is surprising that Nelli does not mention this poem in his discussion of the ritual called *assag* which he posits. A French version of my commentary on *Razon e luec* will be published in my 'Pour une esthétique'.

14 Marcabru, V, 33, VIII, 26–7, XVI, 54, and so on; Raimbaut, II, 25–6.

15 Marcabru, VII, 21–2; Jaufre, V, 56. See also my 'Peire', p. 102.

16 *Cansos*, p. 135. She translates 'Fortune's Favourite' and links the *senhal* with XIX, 24. Kolsen, *Sämtliche Lieder*, I, p. 89, translates 'Glückspilz'.

17 '*Si cum Marcabrus*', p. 96, and see above, p. 58.

18 PC 111.1 is a (thirteenth-century?) *tenso* between one Cavaire and one Bonafos.

19 See above, pp. 57–8, and for a further example of *abat* with an obscene meaning, Gaunt, 'Esthétique', forthcoming.

20 Giraut's *vida* tells us that he was known as the *maestre dels trobadors*, and this title is repeated by Terramagnino of Pisa and Bernart Amoros.

21 *Cansos*, p. 194.

22 It may be significant that in line 47 Giraut talks of his patron's *entier vejaire*.

23 *Cansos*, p. 239.

24 Poems VII, XVI, LVIII, LX.

25 *Troubadours*, pp. 96–7; *Cansos*, p. 158. Compare Salverda de Grave, 'Giraut', p. 301.

26 *Sämtliche Lieder*, II, 16; Panvini, *Giraldo*, p. 32; Nicholson, *Peire*, pp. 24–5, and *Cansos*, p. 65.

27 Sharman, *Cansos*, p. 65.

28 *Soffrir*, 'to suffer', 'to wait patiently', 'to suffer the misconduct of one's wife' (*PD*).

29 *Cansos*, p. 65.

30 *Cansos*, p. 65.

31 *Sämtliche Lieder*, II, 16–17, and *Peire*, p. 24.

32 *Cansos*, p. 65.

33 *Guiraut*, pp. 41–3; *Poésie lyrique*, II, 51–8; *Giraldo*, pp. 9–18.

34 *Trobar clus*, pp. 118–19.

35 De Riquer, *Los trovadores*, I, 472; Salverda de Grave, *Observations*, p. 83, and Sharman, 'Giraut', p. 73.

36 *Troubadours*, p. 89.

37 Paterson, *Troubadours*, pp. 210–11.

38 *Sociologia*, p. 184, and 'Giraut', p. 305; for objections to their hypothesis see Paterson, *Troubadours*, p. 90.

39 *Troubadours*, pp. 98–101; quotation from pp. 208–9.
40 'Giraut', pp. 72–4.
41 Köhler, *Trobadorlyrik*, pp. 142–3; Milone, 'Raimbaut', pp. 6–8; Mölk, *Trobar clus*, pp. 116–20; Paterson, *Troubadours*, pp. 145–57; Pollmann, *Trobar clus*, p. 36; de Riquer, *Los trovadores*, I, 455–8; Salverda de Grave, 'Giraut', pp. 298–9.
42 Sharman, *Cansos*, p. 397; Kay, 'Rhetoric', pp. 125–9.
43 Paterson, *Troubadours*, pp. 105–6.
44 Paterson, *Troubadours*, p. 105.
45 Paterson, *Troubadours*, p. 109.
46 Compare Marcabru, XXXVII, 7, and Raimbaut d'Aurenga, XVII, 7–9.
47 *Troubadours*, p. 107; *Cansos*, p. 287.
48 Compare Marcabru, V, 4, and *Girart de Roussillon*, 422.
49 Text from Paterson, *Troubadours*, pp. 60–5. She translates 'For I have the experience and the bread and knife with which it pleases me to feed (get the better of) the people who have raised up a model for themselves in this profession.' On the expression *aver lo pan e lo coutel*, 'avoir tout ce qu'il faut pour réussir', see Monfrin, 'Notes lexicographiques', pp. 154–5.
50 Compare Paterson, *Troubadours*, p. 135, and Sharman, *Cansos*, p. 288.
51 Paterson, *Troubadours*, p. 134.
52 See above, pp. 146–7.
53 Compare Raimbaut d'Aurenga, X, 56, and XI, 3.
54 Kolsen, *Sämtliche Lieder*, II, 60; de Riquer, *Los trovadores*, I, 478.
55 Kolsen, *Guiraut*, p. 61; Panvini, *Giraldo*, p. 84.
56 Salverda de Grave, 'Giraut', p. 300.
57 *Cansos*, p. 361.
58 Di Girolamo, '*Trobar clus*', p. 15.
59 March 1188–May 1189: see Sharman, *Cansos*, p. 433, but see Hoepffner, 'Deux notes', p. 206, for a different interpretation.
60 'Giraut', p. 74.
61 Salverda de Grave, 'Giraut', pp. 298–9.
62 See above, p. 152.
63 See above, p. 150.
64 *Cansos*, p. 221.
65 See Peire d'Alvernha, XVII, 88; Cercamon, VIII, 28, and Giraut, XXXI, 33.
66 *Sämtliche Lieder*, II, 57; *Trobar clus*, p. 120.
67 Paterson, *Troubadours*, p. 94.
68 'Giraut', p. 97. Consider also Giraut's delight in the *clus* style in poem XXIV; see Paterson's comments, *Troubadours*, pp. 96–7.
69 *Cansos*, p. 297.
70 Matthew 19: 23–4, and Luke 15: 1–7. Köhler, *Sociologia*, p. 59, thinks these lines suggest that Giraut is attempting to persuade nobles to be more generous.
71 Giraut's sense of humour has probably been obscured by Kolsen's rigorous, but often heavy-handed and insensitive, edition. Ruth Sharman's has gone a long way towards restoring much of the humour Giraut no doubt intended and the writing of this chapter was greatly facilitated by working from her edition.

Bibliography

The bibliography contains full references to all the works cited in the notes except for dictionaries and other reference books, which are listed in the table of abbreviations at the front of the book.

1 MANUSCRIPTS

Only manuscripts actually consulted are listed. They are designated in the first instance by the letter assigned to them by Pillet and Carstens in their *Bibliographie*.

C Paris, Bibliothèque Nationale, fonds français 856, Occitan, fourteenth century
E Paris, Bibliothèque Nationale, fonds français 1749, Occitan, fourteenth century
I Paris, Bibliothèque Nationale, fonds français 15211, Italian, fifteenth century
a Modena, Biblioteca Estense, Càmpori γ. N. 8, 4; 11, 12, 13, Italian, sixteenth century

2 PRIMARY SOURCES

Authors are listed alphabetically, anonymous texts under their titles. Only complete critical editions are listed in this section. For anthologies and editions of individual poems, see section 3 below. Where more than one edition of a text or author is listed, the edition usually referred to is marked by an asterisk.

Alegret: in *Jongleurs et troubadours gascons*, ed. by A. Jeanroy, pp. 4–11
Arnaut Daniel: *Arnaut Daniel: Canzoni*, ed. by G. Toja (Florence, 1960)
Balzac, Honoré de: *La Comédie humaine*, 10 vols. (Paris, 1966)
Bede: *De schematibus et tropiis*, in *Bedae Venerabilis: opera*, ed. by C. W. Jones, 2 vols. (Turnholt, 1975), I, 142–71
Bernard of Utrecht: *Commentum in Theodolum*, in *Accessus ad auctores: Bernard d'Utrecht, Conrad d'Hirsau: dialogus super auctores*, ed. by R. B. C. Huygens (Leiden, 1970)
Bernart de Ventadorn: *Bernart von Ventadorn: seine Lieder mit Einleitung und Glossar*, ed. by C. Appel (Halle, 1915)*
Bernard de Ventadour: Chansons d'amour, ed. by M. Lazar (Paris, 1966)
Bernart de Venzac: *Lirica moralistica nell'Occitania del XII secolo: Bernart de Venzac*, ed. by M. P. Simonelli (Modena, 1974)
Bernart Marti: *Les Poésies de Bernart Marti*, ed. by E. Hoepffner (Paris, 1929)
Il trovatore Bernart Marti, ed. by F. Beggiato (Modena, 1984)
Bertran de Born: *L'Amour et la guerre: l'œuvre de Bertran de Born*, ed. by G. Gouiran, 2 vols. (Aix-en-Provence, 1985)

Bibliography

Boncompagno of Signa: extract from rhetorical treatise, ed. by J. F. Benton, in *The Meaning of Courtly Love*, ed. by F. X. Newman (Albany, 1968), pp. 37–42

Cassiodorus: *De schematibus et tropiis*, in *PL*, LXX, 1269–80

Cercamon: *Il trovatore Cercamon*, ed. by V. Tortoreto (Modena, 1981)

Chanson de Roland, ed. by F. Whitehead (London, 1942)

Chrétien de Troyes: *Cligés*, ed. by A. Micha (Paris, 1971)

Cicero: *De oratore*, ed. by A. S. Wilkins (Oxford, 1892)

Pro Cluentio, in *Cicero: The Speeches*, ed. by H. Grose Hodge (London, 1927)

De inventione, ed. by H. M. Hubbel (London, 1949)

De officiis, ed. by W. Miller (London, 1947)

Dante Alighieri: *De vulgari eloquentia*, ed. by M. Meozi (Milan, 1978)

The Divine Comedy, second edition, ed. by J. D. Sinclair, 3 vols. (Oxford, 1948)

Donatus: *Ars grammatica: ars maior*, in *Donat et la tradition de l'enseignement grammatical: étude sur l'Ars Donati et sa diffusion (IVᵉ–IXᵉ) et édition critique*, ed. by L. Holtz (Paris, 1981)

Flors del gay saber, ed. by A. F. Gatien-Arnoult, 3 vols. (Toulouse, 1841–3)

Folquet de Marselha: *Le Troubadour Folquet de Marseille*, ed. by S. Stroński (Cracow, 1910)

Garin lo Brun: *Ensenhamen a la domna* in *Testi didattico-cortesi di Provenza*, ed. by G. E. Sansone (Rome, 1977), pp. 41–107

Geoffrey of Vinsauf: *The Poetria Nova and its Sources in Early Rhetorical Doctrine*, ed. by E. Gallo (The Hague, 1971)

Gervase of Melkley: *Ars poetica*, ed. by H.-J. Gräbener (Münster, 1965)

Girart de Roussillon, ed. by W. M. Hackett, 3 vols. (Paris, 1953–5)

Giraut de Borneil: *Sämtliche Lieder des Trobadors Giraut de Bornelh*, ed. by A. Kolsen, 2 vols. (Halle, 1910 and 1935)

The Cansos and Sirventes of the Troubadour Giraut de Borneil, ed. by R. V. Sharman (Cambridge, 1988)*

Guilhem IX: *Les Chansons de Guillaume IX*, ed. by A. Jeanroy, second edition (Paris, 1927)

Guglielmo d'Aquitania: poesie, ed. by N. Pasero (Modena, 1973)*

Guilhem de Berguedà: *Guillem de Berguedà*, ed. by M. de Riquer, 2 vols. (Abadía de Poblet, 1971)

Guillaume de Lorris and Jean de Meun: *Le Roman de la Rose*, ed. by F. Lecoy, 3 vols. (Paris, 1965–70)

Henry of Würzburg: *Magister Heinrich der Poet in Würzburg und die römische Kurie*, ed. by H. von Grauert (Munich, 1912)

Hugh of St Victor: *De grammatica*, in *Hughes de St. Victor: opera propaedeutica*, ed. by R. Baron (Notre Dame, 1966)

Isidore of Seville: *Etymologiae*, ed. by W. M. Lindsay, 2 vols. (Oxford, 1911)

Jaufre Rudel: *Les Chansons de Jaufre Rudel*, ed. by A. Jeanroy, second edition (Paris, 1924)

Il canzoniere di Jaufre Rudel, ed. by G. Chiarini (Rome, 1985)*

Julian of Toledo: *De vitiis et figuris*, ed. by W. M. Lindsay (Oxford, 1922)

Lucan: *De bello civili*, ed. by J. D. Duff (London, 1928)

Marcabru: *Les Poésies complètes du troubadour Marcabru*, ed. by J.-M.-L. Dejeanne (Toulouse, 1909)

Martianus Capella: *De nuptiis et mercurii*, ed. by W. A. Dick (Leipzig, 1925)

Matthew of Vendôme: *Ars versificatoria*, in Faral, *Les Arts*, pp. 106–93

Nicholas of Bibera: *Carmen Satiricum*, ed. by T. Fischer (Halle, 1870)

Paul the Deacon: *Die Gedichte des Paulus Diaconus*, ed. by C. Neff (Munich, 1908)

Bibliography

Peire d'Alvernha: *Die Lieder Peires von Auvergne*, ed. by R. Zenker (Erlangen, 1900)
Peire d'Alvernha: *Liriche*, ed. by A. del Monte (Turin, 1955)*
Peire Rogier: *The Poems of the Troubadour Peire Rogier*, ed. by D. E. T. Nicholson (Manchester, 1976)
Peire Vidal: *Les Poésies de Peire Vidal*, ed. by J. Anglade, second edition (Paris, 1923)
Pompeius: *Commentum artis Donati*, in Keil, *Grammatici Latini*, v, 81–312
Proverbes français antérieurs au XVᵉ siècle, ed. by J. Morawski (Paris, 1925)
Quintilian: *Institutio oratoria*, ed. by H. E. Butler, 4 vols. (London, 1921–2)
Raimbaut d'Aurenga: *The Life and Works of the Troubadour Raimbaut d'Orange*, ed. by W. T. Pattison (Minneapolis, 1952)
Raimon de Miraval: *Les Poésies du troubadour Raimon de Miraval*, ed. by L. T. Topsfield (Paris, 1971)
Raimon Vidal: *Raimon Vidal: Poetry and Prose II: Abrils issia*, ed. by W. H. W. Field (Chapel Hill, 1971)
The Razos de Trobar of Raimon Vidal and Associated Texts, ed. by J. H. Marshall (London, 1972)
Rhetorica ad Herennium, ed. by H. Caplan (London, 1954)
Uc Faidit: *The Donatz Proensals of Uc Faidit*, ed. by J. H. Marshall (London, 1969)
Vidas: Biographies des troubadours: textes provençaux des XIIIᵉ et XIVᵉ siècles, ed. by J. Boutière and A. H. Schutz, second edition by J. Boutière and I.-M. Cluzel (Paris, 1973)

3 SECONDARY MATERIAL

Abbreviations for reviews

CN   *Cultura Neolatina*
FMLS   *Forum for Modern Language Studies*
MLR   *Modern Language Review*
RLR   *Revue des Langues Romanes*
RN   *Romance Notes*
RP   *Romance Philology*
SM   *Studi Medievali*
ZRP   *Zeitschrift für romanische Philologie*

Adams, J. N., *The Latin Sexual Vocabulary* (London, 1982)
Appel, C., 'Zu Marcabru', ZRP, 43 (1923), 403–69
    'Raimbaut d'Aurenga und Bertran de Born', SM, 2 (1929), 391–408
Ashdown, C., *Armour and Weapons in the Middle Ages* (London, 1925)
Aubailly, J.-C., *Le Monologue dramatique, le dialogue et la sottie*, 2 vols. (Paris, 1976)
Batts, M. S., 'Hartmann's *humanitas*: a new look at *Iwein*', in *Germanic Studies in Honor of Edward Henry Sehrt*, ed. by F. A. Raven, W. K. Legner and J. C. King (Coral Gables, 1968), pp. 37–51
Bec, P., *Burlesque et obscénité chez les troubadours* (Paris, 1984)
Beggiato, F., 'Per un'edizione delle liriche di Bernart Marti', CN, 39 (1979), 63–8
Beltrami, P. G., 'La canzone *Belhs m'es l'estius* di Jaufre Rudel', *Studi Mediolatini e Volgari*, 26 (1978–9), 77–105
Benton, J. F., 'Clio and Venus: an historical view of medieval love', in *The Meaning of Courtly Love*, ed. by F. X. Newman (Albany, 1968), pp. 19–42
Bergson, H. L., *Le Rire* (Paris, 1940)
Bertoni, G., 'Due note provenzali', SM, 3 (1911), 638–57

Bibliography

Bezzola, R. R., 'Guillaume IX et les origines de l'amour courtois', *Romania*, 66 (1940–1), 145–237

Les Origines et la formation de la littérature courtoise en occident, 5 vols. (Paris, 1958–63)

Boissonnade, P., 'Les personnages et les événements de l'histoire de l'Allemagne, de la France et de l'Espagne dans l'œuvre de Marcabru', *Romania*, 48 (1922), 207–42

Bond, G. A., 'Some philological comments on a new edition of the first troubadour', *RP*, 30 (1976–7), 343–61

Booth, W. C., *The Rhetoric of Irony* (Chicago, 1974)

Brooks, C., 'Irony and ironic poetry', *College English*, 9 (1948), 231–7

The Well-Wrought Urn, second edition (London, 1968)

Butturff, D. R., 'From cynicism to idealism: psychology and the genesis of courtly love in the lyrics of Guillaume IX', *Kentucky Romance Quarterly*, 24 (1977), 311–34

Campbell, K. S., 'Irony, medieval and modern, and the allegory of rhetoric', *Allegoria*, 4 (1979), 290–300

Camproux, C., '*Faray un vers tot covinen*', in *Mélanges Frappier*, 2 vols. (Geneva, 1969), I, 159–72

Chabaneau, C., 'Une nouvelle édition du *Roman de Flamenca*', *RLR*, 45 (1902), 5–43

Chambers, F. M., *Proper Names in the Lyrics of the Troubadours* (Chapel Hill, 1971)

'*D'aisso lau Dieu* and Aldric del Vilar', *RP*, 35 (1982), 489–500

Cingolani, S. M., '*Chantador*', *CN*, 42 (1982), 169–80

Cooke, T. D., 'Pornography, the comic spirit and the *Fabliaux*', in *The Humor of the Fabliaux*, ed. by T. D. Cooke and B. L. Honeycutt (Columbia, 1974), pp. 137–62

Coulet, J., 'R. Zenker, *Die Lieder Peires von Auvergne*', *Annales du Midi*, 14 (1902), 374–83

Crane, R. S., 'The critical monism of Cleanth Brooks', in *Critics and Criticism*, ed. by R. S. Crane (Chicago, 1952), pp. 83–107

Cropp, G. M., *Le Vocabulaire courtois des troubadours de l'époque classique* (Paris, 1975)

Culler, J., *Structuralist Poetics* (London, 1975)

The Pursuit of Signs (London, 1981)

Curtius, E. R., *European Literature and the Latin Middle Ages*, translated by W. R. Trask (London, 1953)

Davis, J. M., 'A fuller reading of Guillaume IX's *Companho, faray un vers ... covinen*', *RN*, 16 (1974–5), 445–9

Delbouille, M., 'Les *senhals* littéraires désignant Raimbaut d'Orange', *CN*, 17 (1957), 49–73

Dragonetti, R., *La Technique poétique des trouvères* (Bruges, 1960)

Dronke, P., 'Guillaume IX and "courtoisie"', *Romanische Forschungen*, 73 (1961), 327–38

The Medieval Lyric (London, 1968)

Evans, D., *Lanier: histoire d'un mot* (Geneva, 1967)

Faral, E., *Les Arts poétiques du XIIᵉ et du XIIIᵉ siècle* (Paris, 1924)

Fechner, J. U., 'Zum *gap* in der altprovenzalischen Lyrik', *Germanisch-Romanische Monatsschrift*, 14 (1964), 19–34

Frank, G., 'The distant love of Jaufre Rudel', *Modern Language Notes*, 57 (1942), 528–34

Frank, I., 'La plus ancienne allusion à l'Italie dans la poésie des troubadours', *CN*, 6–7 (1946–7), 33–8

Répertoire métrique de la poésie des troubadours, 2 vols. (Paris, 1966)

Franz, A., *Über den Troubadour Marcabru* (Marburg, 1914)

Bibliography

Gaunt, S. B., 'Did Marcabru know the Tristan legend?', *Medium Aevum*, 55 (1986), 108–13

'Peire d'Alvernha affronte Jaufre Rudel: les troubadours et la deuxième croisade', in *Croisades: réalités et fictions*, ed. by D. Buschinger (Amiens, 1988), pp. 95–106

'Pour une esthétique de l'obscène chez les troubadours', in *Actes du Deuxième Congrès International de l'Association Internationale d'Etudes Occitanes*, ed. by G. Gasca-Queirazza (Turin, 1989), forthcoming

'Poetry of exclusion: a feminist reading of some troubadour lyrics', forthcoming, *MLR*, 85 (1990)

Gaunt, S. B. and Harvey, R. E., 'Text and context in a poem by Marcabru', in *The Troubadours and the Epic*, ed. by S. B. Gaunt and L. M. Paterson (University of Warwick, 1987), pp. 59–101

Girolamo, C. di, '*Trobar clus* e *trobar leu*', *Medioevo Romanzo*, 8 (1981–3), 11–35

'Tristano, Carestia e Chrétien de Troyes', *Medioevo Romanzo*, 9 (1984), 17–26

Goddard, R. N. B., 'The early troubadours and the Latin tradition' (unpublished D.Phil. thesis, Oxford, 1985)

'Marcabru, *Li proverbe au vilain* and the tradition of rustic proverbs', *Neuphilologische Mitteilungen*, 88 (1987), 55–70

'The ladies Agnes and Arsen and William IX's "Companho, farai un vers [qu'er] covinen"', *FMLS*, 26 (1988), 156–62

Godman, P., *Poetry of the Carolingian Renaissance* (London, 1985)

Green, D. H., 'Irony and medieval romance', *FMLS*, 6 (1970), 49–64

'On recognizing medieval irony', in *The Uses of Criticism*, ed. by A. P. Foulkes (Bern, 1974), pp. 11–52

'On damning with faint praise in medieval literature', *Viator*, 6 (1975), 117–71

'*Alieniloquium*: zur Begriffsbestimmung der mittelalterlichen Ironie', in *Verbum et Signum*, ed. by H. Fromm, W. Harms and U. Ruberg, 2 vols. (Munich, 1975), II, 119–59

Irony in the Medieval Romance (Cambridge, 1979)

Gruber, J., *Die Dialektik des Trobar* (Tübingen, 1983)

Guiette, R., 'D'une poésie formelle en France au moyen âge', *Revue des Sciences Humaines*, 54 (1949), 61–8

Hackett, W. M., 'Le problème de "midons"', in *Mélanges Boutière*, ed. by I.-M. Cluzel and F. Pirot, 2 vols. (Liège, 1971), I, 285–94

Haidu, P., *Aesthetic Distance in Chrétien de Troyes* (Geneva, 1968)

Harvey, R. E., 'The satirical use of the courtly expression "sidons" in the works of the troubadour Marcabru', *MLR*, 78 (1983), 24–33

'Marcabru and the Spanish *Lavador*', *FMLS*, 22 (1986), 123–44

The Troubadour Marcabru and Love (London, 1989)

Hathaway, E. J. and Ricketts, P. T., 'Le *vers del lavador* de Marcabru: édition critique, traduction et commentaire', *RLR*, 77 (1966), 1–11

Hoepffner, E., 'Le troubadour Bernart Marti', *Romania*, 53 (1927), 103–50

'Deux notes sur le troubadour Giraut de Bornelh', *Romania*, 63 (1937), 204–25

Les Troubadours dans leur vie et dans leurs œuvres (Paris, 1955)

Holtz, L., 'Tradition et diffusion de l'œuvre de Pompée, commentateur de Donat', *Revue de Philologie, de Littérature et d'Histoire Anciennes*, 45 (1971), 48–83

Huizinga, J., *Homo Ludens: A Study of the Play Element in Culture* (London, 1970)

Hunt, T., 'Aristotle, dialectic and courtly literature', *Viator*, 10 (1979), 95–129

'Irony and the rise of courtly Romance', *German Life and Letters*, 35 (1981–2), 98–104

Jankélévitch, V., *L'Ironie* (Paris, 1964)

Bibliography

Jauss, H. R., *Towards an Aesthetic of Reception*, translated by T. Bahti (Brighton, 1982)

Jeanroy, A., 'R. Zenker, *Die Lieder Peires von Auvergne*', *Romania*, 32 (1906), 313–16

Jongleurs et troubadours gascons des XIIe et XIIIe siècles (Paris, 1923)

La Poésie lyrique des troubadours, 2 vols. (Toulouse, 1934)

Kastner, L. E., 'Marcabrun and Cercamon', *MLR*, 26 (1931), 91–6

Kay, S., 'La notion de personnalité chez les troubadours: encore sur la question de sincérité', in *Mittelalterbilder aus neuer Perspektive*, ed. by E. Ruhe (Munich, 1986), pp. 166–82

'Rhetoric and subjectivity in troubadour poetry', in *The Troubadours and the Epic*, ed. by S. B. Gaunt and L. M. Paterson (University of Warwick, 1987), pp. 102–42

Keil, H., *Grammatici Latini*, 8 vols. (Leipzig, 1857–80)

Kelly, A., *Eleanor of Aquitaine* (Cambridge Mass., 1950)

Kelly, D., 'The scope and treatment of composition in the twelfth- and thirteenth-century Arts of Poetry', *Speculum*, 41 (1966), 261–78

Medieval Imagination (London, 1978)

Kertesz, C., 'A full reading of Guillaume IX's *Companho, faray un vers ... covinen*', *RN*, 12 (1970–1), 461–5

Knox, J. D., 'The concept of rhetorical and Socratic *ironia* in the Middle Ages and the Renaissance' (unpublished Ph.D. thesis, University College, London, 1983)

Knudson, C., 'Serments téméraires et *gabs*: notes sur un thème littéraire', in *Actes et Mémoires du IVe Congrès International de la Société Rencesvals* (Heidelberg, 1969), pp. 254–9

Köhler, E., *Trobadorlyrik und höfischer Roman* (Berlin, 1962)

'No sai qui s'es – No sai que s'es (Wilhelm von Poitiers und Raimbaut von Orange)', in *Mélanges Delbouille*, 2 vols. (Gembloux, 1964), II, 349–66

'Sens et fonction du terme *jeunesse* dans la poésie des troubadours', in *Mélanges Crozet* (Poitiers, 1966), pp. 569–83

Sociologia della fin'amor, translated by M. Mancini (Padua, 1976)

'Gabar e rire: Bemerkungen zum *gap* in der Dichtung der Trobadors', in *Mélanges Wathelet-Willem* (Liège, 1978), pp. 315–28

Kolsen, A., *Guiraut von Bornelh, der Meister der Trobadors* (Berlin, 1894)

Kraemer, E. von, 'Sémantique de l'ancien français *gab* et *gaber* comparée à celle des correspondants dans d'autres langues romanes', in *Mélanges Tuano Nurmela* (Turku, 1967), pp. 73–90

Krewitt, U., *Metapher und tropische Rede in der Auffassung des Mittelalters* (Ratingen, 1971)

Kristeva, J., *Semiotiké* (Paris, 1969)

La Révolution du langage poétique (Paris, 1974)

Lawner, L., 'Notes towards an interpretation of the *vers de dreyt nien*', *CN*, 28 (1968), 147–64

'Marcabrun and the origins of the "trobar clus"', in *Literature and Western Civilization*, ed. by D. Daiches and A. Thorlby, 6 vols. (London, 1973), II, 485–523

Lecoy, F., '*Peire d'Alvernha: liriche*', *Romania*, 77 (1956), 386–92

Lefèvre, Y., 'Jaufre Rudel, professeur de morale', *Annales du Midi*, 78 (1966), 415–22

Lejeune, R., 'Thèmes communs de troubadours et vie de société', in *Littérature et société*, pp. 287–98

'L'allusion à Tristan chez le troubadour Cercamon', in *Littérature et société*, pp. 165–83

Bibliography

'L'extraordinaire insolence du troubadour Guillaume IX d'Aquitaine', in *Littérature et société*, pp. 121–39

'Le troubadour lombard de la "galerie littéraire" satirique de Peire d'Alvernhe', in *Littérature et société*, pp. 313–28

Littérature et société occitanes au moyen âge (Liège, 1979)

'La "galerie littéraire" du troubadour Peire d'Alvernhe et ses implications avec la Catalogne', *Estudis Universitaris Catalans*, 24 (1980), 267–76

Lewent, K., 'Beiträge zum Verständis der Lieder Marcabrus', *ZRP*, 37 (1913), 313–37, 427–51

Limentani, A., *L'eccezione narrativa* (Turin, 1977)

Manning, S., 'Game and earnest in Middle English and Provençal love lyrics', *Comparative Literature*, 18 (1966), 225–41

Marshall, J. H., 'Tradition and innovation in editorial practice: Cercamon's *Ab lo pascor*', in *Proceedings of the Second British Conference on Medieval Occitan*, ed. by P. T. Ricketts (Birmingham, 1982), pp. 87–101 (proceedings privately circulated)

'The *Doas cuidas* of Marcabru', in *Chrétien de Troyes and the Troubadours*, ed. by P. S. Noble and L. M. Paterson (Cambridge, 1984), pp. 27–33

'Une versification lyrique popularisante en ancien provençal', in *Actes du Premier Congrès International de l'Association Internationale d'Etudes Occitanes*, ed. by P. T. Ricketts (London, 1987), pp. 35–66

'Dialogues of the dead: two *tensos* by pseudo-Bernart de Ventadorn', in *The Troubadours and the Epic*, ed. by S. B. Gaunt and L. M. Paterson (University of Warwick, 1987), pp. 37–58

Marti, B. M., 'Lucan's invocation to Nero in the light of medieval glosses', *Quadrivium*, 1 (1956), 7–18

Ménard, P., *Le Rire et le sourire dans le roman courtois en France au moyen âge* (Geneva, 1969)

Meneghetti, M. L., 'Una *vida* pericolosa. La "mediazione" biografica e l'interpretazione della poesia di Jaufre Rudel', *CN*, 40 (1980), 145–63

Il pubblico dei trovatori (Modena, 1984)

Milone, L., 'Retorica del potere e poetica dell'oscuro da Guglielmo IX a Raimbaut d'Aurenga', *Quaderni del Circolo Filologico-Linguistico Padovano*, 10 (1979), 149–77

'Il *vers de dreit nien* e il paradosso dell'amore a distanza', *CN*, 40 (1980), 123–44

'L'"amors enversa" de Raimbaut d'Aurenga', *Museum Patavinium*, 1 (1983), 45–66

'Raimbaut d'Aurenga fra "fin'amor" e "no-poder"', *Romanistische Zeitschrift für Literaturgeschichte*, 7 (1983), 1–27

Mölk, U., *Trobar clus: trobar leu* (Munich, 1968)

Mollard, A., 'La diffusion de l'*Institution oratoire* au XIIᶜ siècle', *Le Moyen Age*, 5 (1934), 161–75, 6 (1935), 1–9

Monfrin, J., 'Notes lexicographiques', in *Mélanges Imbs*, ed. by R. Martin and G. Straka (Strasbourg, 1973), pp. 151–68

Monte, A. del, '*En durmen sobre chevau*', *Filologia Romanza*, 2 (1955), 140–7

Monteverdi, A., 'Peire d'Alvernia in un canzoniere del duecento', *SM*, 12 (1939), 133–59

Muecke, D. C., *The Compass of Irony* (London, 1969)

Irony (London, 1970)

'On the communication of verbal irony', *Journal of Literary Semantics*, 2 (1973), 35–42

Irony and the Ironic (London, 1982)

Bibliography

Murphy, J. J., *Rhetoric in the Middle Ages* (London, 1974)

Muscatine, C., 'Courtly literature and vulgar language', in *Court and Poet*, ed. by G. S. Burgess (Liverpool, 1981), pp. 1–19

Nelli, R., *L'Erotique des troubadours* (Toulouse, 1963)

Nelson, D., 'Animal imagery in Marcabru's poetry', *Studies in Medieval Culture*, 11 (1974), 51–5

Nichols, S. G. Jr, '*Canso→conso*: structures of parodic humour in three songs of Guilhem IX', *L'Esprit Créateur*, 16 (1976), 16–29

Nykrog, P., *Les Fabliaux* (Copenhagen, 1957)

Olson, S. M., 'Marcabru's psychomachy: the concept of Vice and Virtue in the twelfth-century troubadour' (unpublished Ph.D. thesis, Yale, 1969)

Paden, W. D. Jr, 'The troubadour's lady: her marital status and social rank', *Studies in Philology*, 72 (1975), 28–50

'*Utrum copularentur*: of *cors*', *L'Esprit Créateur*, 19 (1979), 70–83

'The role of the *joglar* in troubadour lyric poetry', in *Chrétien de Troyes and the Troubadours*, ed. by P. S. Noble and L. M. Paterson (Cambridge, 1984), pp. 90–111

Page, C., *Voices and Instruments of the Middle Ages* (London, 1987)

Panvini, B., *Giraldo di Bornelh, trovatore del secolo XII* (Catania, 1949)

Pasero, N., '*Devinalh*, "non-senso" e "interiorazzazione testuale"', *CN*, 28 (1968), 113–46

Paterson, L. M., *Troubadours and Eloquence* (Oxford, 1975)

Pattison, W. T., 'The background of Peire d'Alvernhe's *Chantarai d'aquest troba-dors*', *Modern Philology*, 31 (1933), 19–34

Payen, J.-Ch., *Le Prince d'Aquitaine* (Paris, 1980)

'Bernart Marti et la légende de Tristan', in *Chrétien de Troyes and the Troubadours*, ed. by P. S. Noble and L. M. Paterson (Cambridge, 1984), pp. 34–43

Pearcy, R. J., 'Modes of signification and the humor of obscene diction in the *fabliaux*', in *The Humor of the Fabliaux*, ed. by T. D. Cooke and B. L. Honeycutt (Columbia, 1974), pp. 163–96

Pickens, R. T., 'Jaufré Rudel et la poétique de la mouvance', *Cahiers de Civilisation Médiévale*, 10 (1977), 323–37

Pirot, F., 'L'idéologie des troubadours', *Le Moyen Age*, 74 (1968), 301–31

Recherches sur les connaissances littéraires des troubadours (Barcelona, 1972)

'*A la fontana del vergier*', in *Mélanges Imbs*, ed. by R. Martin and G. Straka (Strasbourg, 1973), pp. 621–42

'Le troubadour Eble de Saignes', in *Mélanges Le Gentil* (Paris, 1973), pp. 641–59

Pollina, V., '*Si cum Marcabrus declina*: studies in the poetics of the troubadour Marcabru' (unpublished Ph.D. thesis, Yale, 1982)

Pollmann, L., *Trobar clus* (Münster, 1965)

Press, A. R., 'La strophe printanière chez les troubadours et les poètes latins du moyen âge', *Revue de Langue et de Littérature d'Oc*, 12–13 (1962–3), 70–8

'The adulterous nature of *fin'amors*: a re-examination of the theory', *FMLS*, 6 (1970), 327–41

Rajna, P., 'Guglielmo, Conte di Poitiers: trovatore bifronte', in *Mélanges Jeanroy* (Paris, 1928), pp. 349–60

Ricketts, P. T., '*A l'alena del vent doussa* de Marcabru: édition critique, traduction et commentaire', *RLR*, 78 (1968), 109–15

'*Doas cuidas ai, compaigner* de Marcabru: édition critique, traduction et commentaire', in *Mélanges Camproux*, 2 vols. (Montpellier, 1978), I, 179–94

'*Lo vers comenssa* de Marcabru (PC 293.32): édition critique, traduction et com-

226

Bibliography

mentaire', in *Chrétien de Troyes and the Troubadours*, ed. by P. S. Noble and L. M. Paterson (Cambridge, 1984), pp. 7–26

Rieger, D., 'Guillaume IX d'Aquitaine et l'idéologie troubadouresque', *Romania*, 101, (1980), 433–49

'Dons Costans – der Betrüger: zu Marcabrus *Dirai vos en mon lati*', *Romanische Forschungen*, 94 (1982), 433–50

Riquer, M. de, *Los trovadores*, 3 vols. (Barcelona, 1975)

Rivers, J. E., 'Raimbaut d'Orange and the Old Provençal *gap*: a re-examination', *Annuale Medievale*, 12 (1972), 5–20

Robertson, D. W., 'The concept of courtly love as an impediment to the understanding of medieval texts', in *The Meaning of Courtly Love*, ed. by F. X. Newman (Albany, 1968), pp. 1–18

Roncaglia, A., 'I due sirventesi di Marcabruno ad Alfonso VII', *CN*, 10 (1950), 153–83

'Il *gap* di Marcabruno', *SM*, 17 (1951), 46–70

'*Lo vers comens quan vei del fau*', *CN*, 11 (1951), 25–48

'*Al departir del brau tempier*', *CN*, 13 (1953), 5–33

'Per un'edizione e per l'interpretazione dei testi del trovatore Marcabruno', in *Actes et Mémoires du Premier Congrès International de Langue et de Littérature du Midi de la France* (Avignon, 1957), pp. 47–55

'*Aujatz de chan*', *CN*, 17 (1957), 20–48

'*Carestia*', *CN*, 18 (1958), 121–37

'*Cortesamen vuoill comensar*', *Revista de cultura classica e medioevale*, 7 (1965), 948–61

'Due schede provenzali per gli amici ispanisti', *Studi di Letteratura Spagnola*, 3 (1966), 129–34

'La tenzone fra Ugo Catola e Marcabruno', in *Ommagio a Benvenuto Terracini*, ed. by C. Segre (Milan, 1968), pp. 203–54

'*Trobar clus*: discussione aperta', *CN*, 29 (1969), 1–55

'Due postille alla "galleria letteraria" di Peire d'Alvernhe', *Marche Romane*, 19 (1969), 71–8

'Riflessi di posizioni cistercensi nella poesia del XII secolo: discussione sui fondamenti religiosi del "trobar naturau" di Marcabruno', in *Il cistercensi e il lazio* (Rome, 1978), pp. 11–22

Rossman, V. R., *Perspectives of Irony in Medieval French Literature* (The Hague, 1975)

Roth, C., 'Local personnel des trains: quelques réflexions sur l'ambiguité à propos de Raimbaut d'Orange', in *Mélanges Rychner* (Strasbourg, 1968), pp. 453–67

Runciman, S., *A History of the Crusades*, 3 vols. (Cambridge, 1951)

Salverda de Grave, J. J., 'Giraut de Bornelh et la poésie obscure', in *Mélanges Jacques van Ginneken* (Paris, 1937), pp. 297–306

Observations sur l'art lyrique de Giraut de Bornelh (Amsterdam, 1938)

Scheludko, D., 'Zur Geschichte des Natureingangs bei den Trobadors', *Zeitschrift für französische Sprache und Literatur*, 60 (1936), 257–344

Schutz, A. H., 'Some Provençal words indicative of knowledge', *Speculum*, 33 (1958), 508–14

Shapiro, M., '*Entrebescar los motz*: word weaving and divine rhetoric', *ZRP*, 100 (1984), 355–83

Sharman, R. V., 'Giraut de Borneil, *maestre dels trobadors*', *Medium Aevum*, 52 (1983), 63–76

Skårup, P., 'Quelques strophes de Jaufré Rudel dont la syntaxe a été mal interprétée', *Revue Romane*, 19 (1984), 71–84

Bibliography

Spanke, H., *Marcabrustudien* (Göttingen, 1940)

Stempel, W. D., 'Mittelalterliche Obszönität als literarästhetisches Problem', in *Die nicht mehr schönen Künste*, ed. by H. R. Jauss (Munich, 1968), pp. 187–207

Sutherland, D. R., 'The love meditation in courtly literature', in *Studies in Medieval French Presented to Alfred Ewert* (Oxford, 1961), pp. 165–93

'L'élément théâtral dans la *canso* chez les troubadours de l'époque classique', *Revue de Langue et de Littérature d'Oc*, 12–13 (1962–3), 95–101

Tannenhaus, G. H., 'The Venerable Bede, *Concerning Figures and Tropes*', in *Readings in Medieval Rhetoric*, ed. by J. M. Miller, M. H. Prosser and T. W. Benson (Bloomington, 1973), pp. 96–122

Thiolier-Méjean, S., *Les Poésies satiriques et morales des troubadours* (Paris, 1978)

Topsfield, L. T., '*Jois, Amors*, and *Fin'amors* in the poetry of Jaufre Rudel', *Neuphilologische Mitteilungen*, 71 (1970), 277–305

'The "natural fool" in Peire d'Alvernhe, Marcabru and Bernart de Ventadorn', in *Mélanges Rostaing* (Liège, 1974), pp. 1149–58

Troubadours and Love (Cambridge, 1975)

Tortoreto, V., 'Cercamon, maestro di Marcabru?', *CN*, 36 (1976), 61–93

Wettstein, J., *Mezura* (Zurich, 1945)

Wiacek, W. M., *Lexique des noms géographiques et ethniques dans les poésies des troubadours des XIIᵉ et XIIIᵉ siècles* (Paris, 1968)

Woledge, B., *The Penguin Book of French Verse I: To the Fifteenth Century* (Harmondsworth, 1961)

Zumthor, P., *Essai de poétique médiévale* (Paris, 1972)

Index

References in brackets refer to philological notes in the Appendix

Index

Index

Index

For EU product safety concerns, contact us at Calle de José Abascal, 56–1°,
28003 Madrid, Spain or eugpsr@cambridge.org.

 www.ingramcontent.com/pod-product-compliance
Ingram Content Group UK Ltd.
Pitfield, Milton Keynes, MK11 3LW, UK
UKHW010042140625
459647UK00012BA/1543